MOON GIRL AND THE MARVEL UNIVERSE

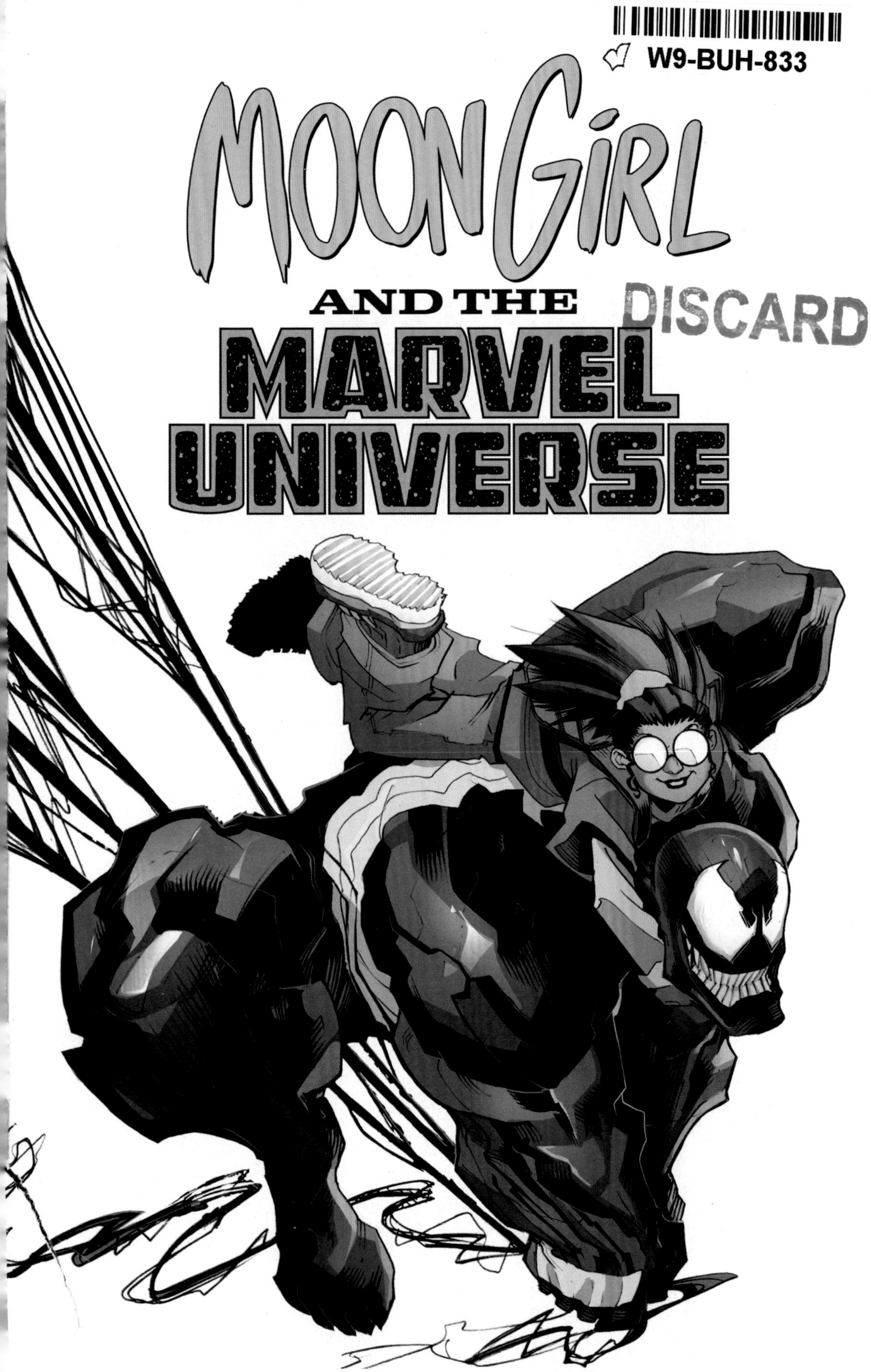

MOON GIRL AND THE MARVEL UNIVERSE

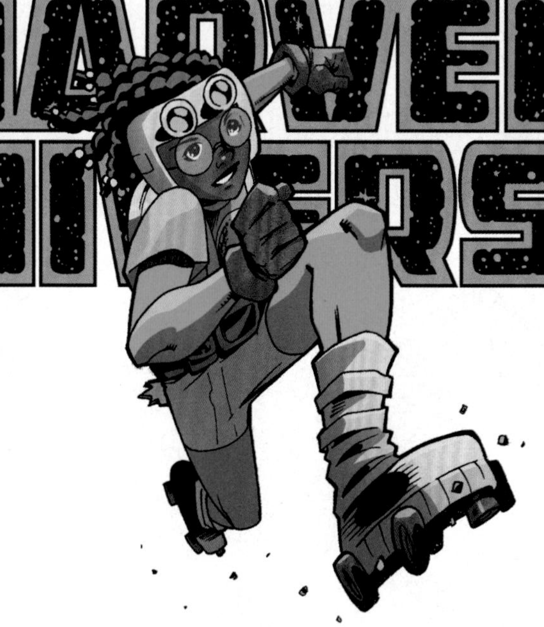

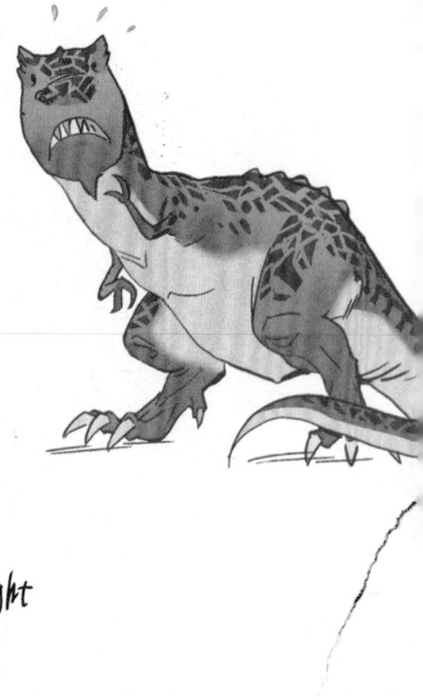

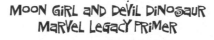

MOON GIRL AND DEVIL DINOSAUR
MARVEL LEGACY PRIMER

WRITER Robbie Thompson
ARTIST Marco Failla
COLORIST Mike Spicer
LETTERER VC's Travis Lanham
ASSISTANT EDITOR Kathleen Wisneski
EDITOR Darren Shan

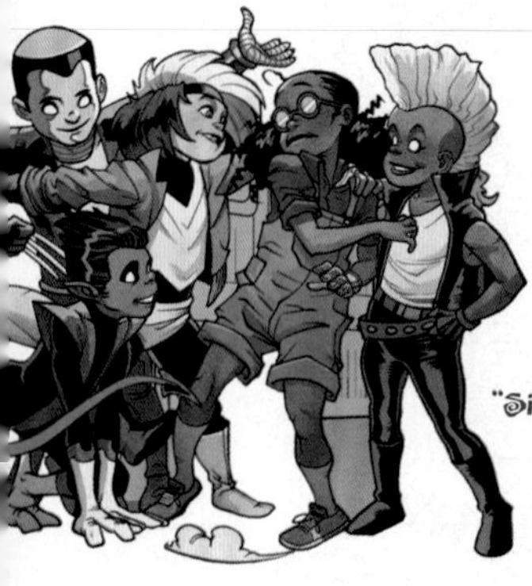

MOON GIRL AND DEVIL DINOSAUR #24

WRITER Brandon Montclare
ARTIST Natacha Bustos
COLOR ARTIST Tamra Bonvillain
"SIGN ON THE DOTTED LINE" ARTIST Ray-Anthony Height
"THINK FAST!" ARTIST Dominike "Domo" Stanton
"BLINDS" ARTIST Michael Shelfer
LETTERER VC's Travis Lanham
COVER ART Natacha Bustos
EDITOR Chris Robinson
SENIOR EDITOR Mark Paniccia

VenoM #153

WRITER Mike Costa
ARTIST Gerardo Sandoval
COLOR ARTIST Dono Sánchez-Almara
LETTERER VC's Clayton Cowles
COVER ART Francisco Herrera
& Fernanda Rizo
ASSISTANT EDITOR Allison Stock
EDITOR Devin Lewis
EXECUTIVE EDITOR Nick Lowe

MONSTERS UNLEASHED #12

WRITER: Justin Jordan
ARTIST: Alberto Alburquerque
COLOR ARTIST: Chris Sotomayor
LETTERER: VC's Travis Lanham
COVER ART: R.B. Silva & Nolan Woodard
EDITOR: Christina Harrington
SENIOR EDITOR: Mark Paniccia

EXTRAORDINARY X-MEN ANNUAL #1
"FORGe. We HaVe a PROBLeM"

WRITER: Brandon Montclare
ARTIST: Rosi Kämpe
COLOR ARTIST: Ian Herring
LETTERER: VC's Joe Caramagna
EDITOR: Chris Robinson
X-MEN GROUP EDITOR: Mark Paniccia

MOON GIRL AND DeVIL DINOSAUR #31

PLOT: Brandon Montclare & Amy Reeder
SCRIPT: Amy Reeder
ARTIST: Ray-Anthony Height
COLORIST: Tamra Bonvillain
COVER ART: Natacha Bustos
EDITOR: Chris Robinson
SUPERVISING EDITOR: Jordan D. White
SPECIAL THANKS TO MARK PANICCIA & SANA AMANAT

DISCARD

COLLECTION EDITOR: Jennifer Grünwald
ASSISTANT EDITOR: Caitlin O'Connell
ASSOCIATE MANAGING EDITOR: Kateri Woody
EDITOR, SPECIAL PROJECTS: Mark D. Beazley
VP, PRODUCTION & SPECIAL PROJECTS: Jeff Youngquist
SVP PRINT, SALES & MARKETING: David Gabriel
BOOK DESIGNER: Jay Bowen

EDITOR IN CHIEF: C.B. Cebulski
CHIEF CREATIVE OFFICER: Joe Quesada
PRESIDENT: Dan Buckley
EXECUTIVE PRODUCER: Alan Fine

MOON GIRL AND THE MARVEL UNIVERSE. Contains material originally published in magazine form as MOON GIRL AND DEVIL DINOSAUR #24 and #31, EXTRAORDINARY X-MEN ANNUAL #1, VENOM #153 and MONSTERS UNLEASHED #12. First printing 2018. ISBN 978-1-302-91370-0. Published by MARVEL WORLDWIDE, INC., a subsidiary of MARVEL ENTERTAINMENT, LLC. OFFICE OF PUBLICATION: 135 West 50th Street, New York, NY 10020. Copyright © 2018 MARVEL No similarity between any of the names, characters, persons, and/or institutions in this magazine with those of any living or dead person or institution is intended, and any such similarity which may exist is purely coincidental. **Printed in Canada.** DAN BUCKLEY, President, Marvel Entertainment; JOHN NEE, Publisher; JOE QUESADA, Chief Creative Officer; TOM BREVOORT, SVP of Publishing; DAVID BOGART, SVP of Business Affairs & Operations, Publishing & Partnership; DAVID GABRIEL, SVP of Sales & Marketing, Publishing; JEFF YOUNGQUIST, VP of Production & Special Projects; DAN CARR, Executive Director of Publishing Technology; ALEX MORALES, Director of Publishing Operations; DAN EDINGTON, Managing Editor; SUSAN CRESPI, Production Manager; STAN LEE, Chairman Emeritus. For information regarding advertising in Marvel Comics or on Marvel.com, please contact Vit DeBellis, Custom Solutions & Integrated Advertising Manager, at vdebellis@marvel.com. For Marvel subscription inquiries, please call 888-511-5480. **Manufactured between 10/5/2018 and 11/6/2018 by SOLISCO PRINTERS, SCOTT, QC, CANADA.**

10 9 8 7 6 5 4 3 2 1

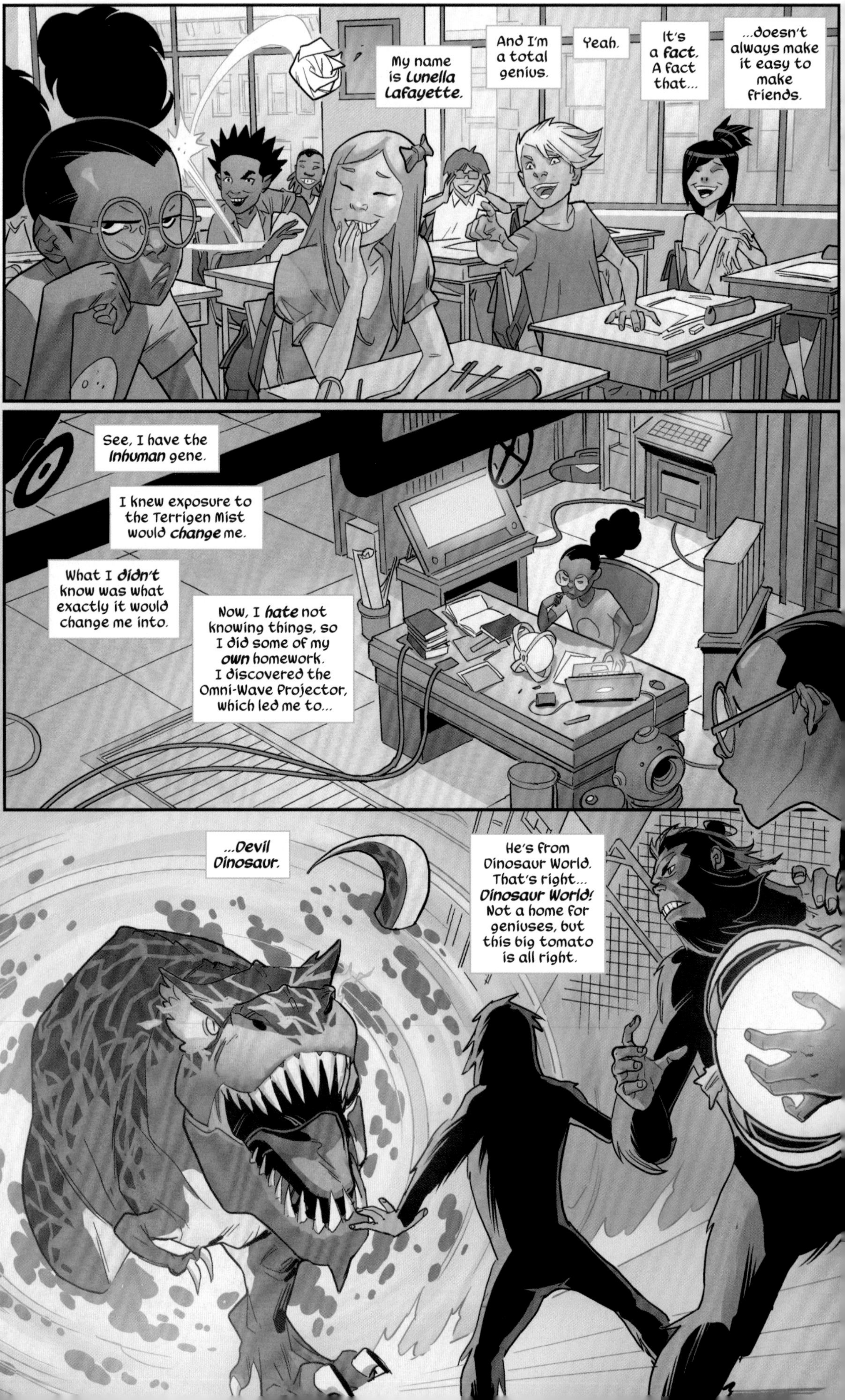
My name is Lunella Lafayette.
And I'm a total genius.
Yeah.
It's a fact. A fact that...
...doesn't always make it easy to make friends.
See, I have the Inhuman gene.
I knew exposure to the Terrigen Mist would change me.
What I didn't know was what exactly it would change me into.
Now, I hate not knowing things, so I did some of my own homework. I discovered the Omni-Wave Projector, which led me to...
...Devil Dinosaur.
He's from Dinosaur World. That's right... Dinosaur World! Not a home for geniuses, but this big tomato is all right.

[redacted]

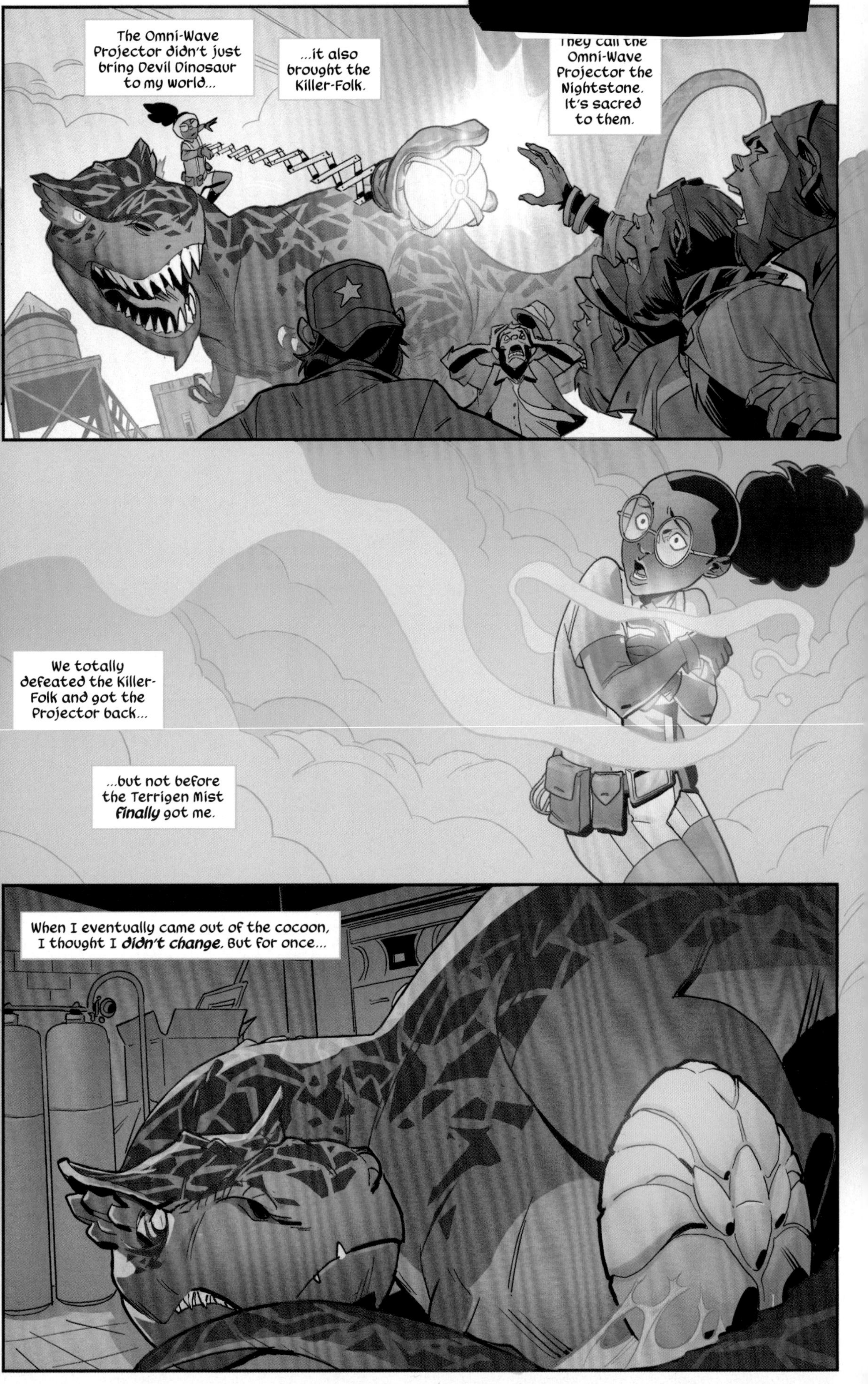

The Omni-Wave Projector didn't just bring Devil Dinosaur to my world...
...it also brought the Killer-Folk.
They call the Omni-Wave Projector the Nightstone. It's sacred to them.
We totally defeated the Killer-Folk and got the Projector back...
...but not before the Terrigen Mist *finally* got me.
When I eventually came out of the cocoon, I thought I *didn't change*. But for once...

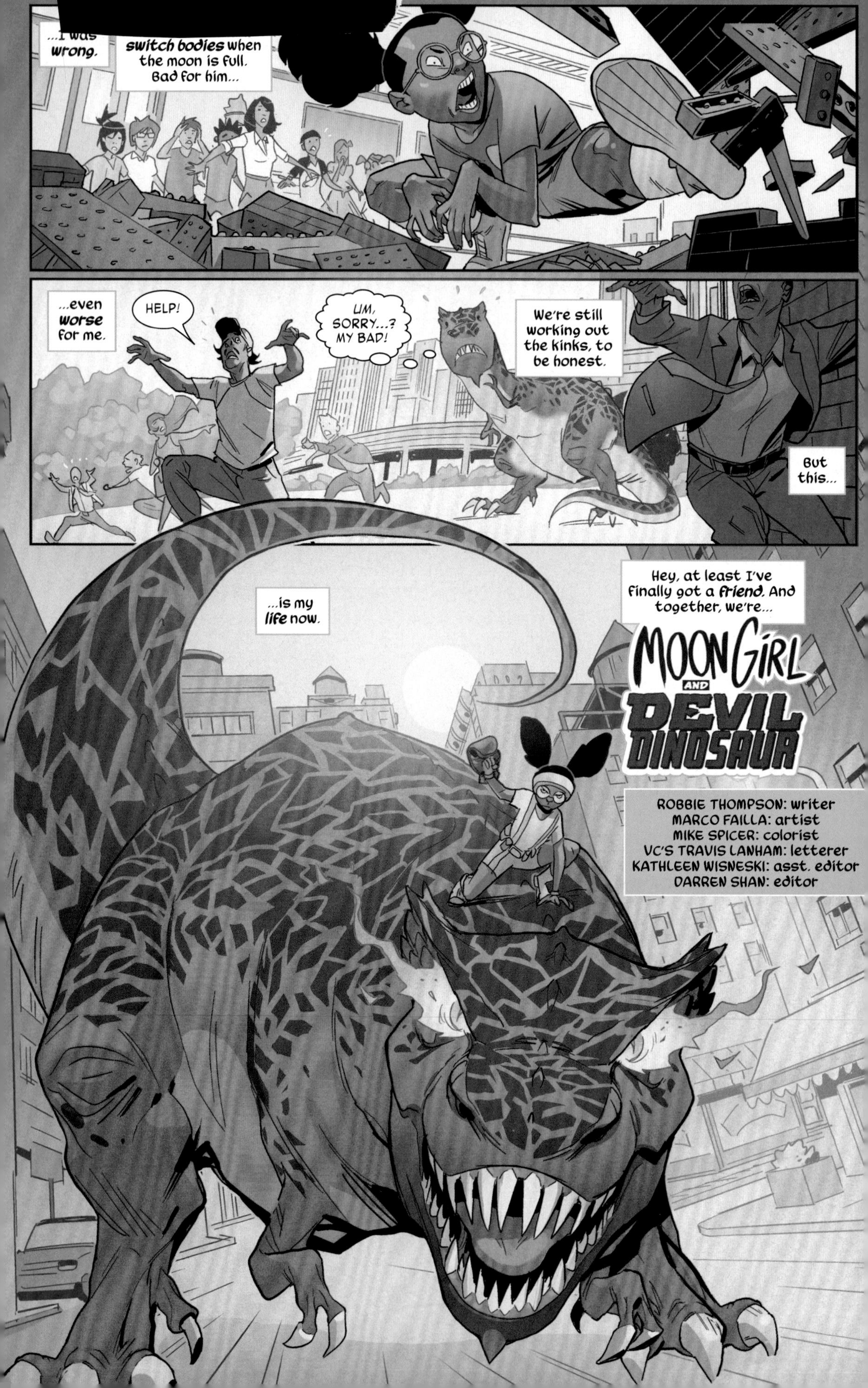

[redacted] wrong.
[redacted] switch bodies when the moon is full. Bad for him...
...even worse for me.
HELP!
UM, SORRY...? MY BAD!
We're still working out the kinks, to be honest.
But this...
...is my life now.
Hey, at least I've finally got a friend. And together, we're...
MOON GIRL AND DEVIL DINOSAUR
ROBBIE THOMPSON: writer
MARCO FAILLA: artist
MIKE SPICER: colorist
VC'S TRAVIS LANHAM: letterer
KATHLEEN WISNESKI: asst. editor
DARREN SHAN: editor

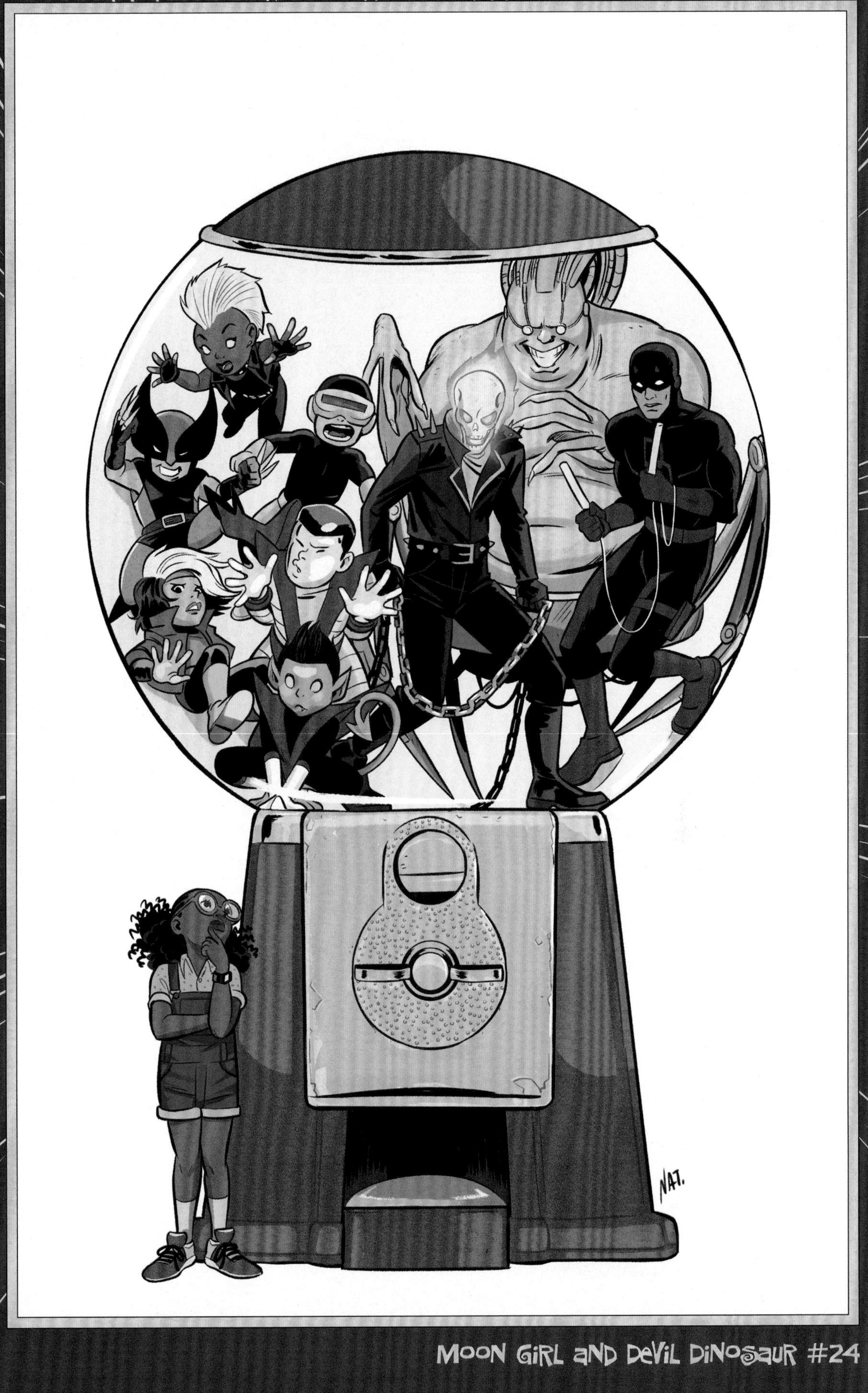
NAT.

MOON GIRL AND DEVIL DINOSAUR #24

MOON GIRL

Lunella Lafayette is a nine-year-old prodigy living with her mom and dad in Manhattan's Lower East Side. Devil Dinosaur is a bright red time-displaced Tyrannosaurus rex. They are shunned and ignored by most, but for better or worse, they have each other! After undergoing Terrigenesis, Lunella discovered that during the full moon lunar phase, she and Devil will intermittently switch brains.

After picking up a distress signal from deep space, Lunella and Devil built a spacecraft powered by the Omni-Wave Projector (the space-time manipulating device that brought D.D. to the present). Following the signal out into the cosmos, they met Illa the Living Moon! To make her happy, Lunella reunited Illa with her father, Ego the Living Planet.

Moon Girl's space travels destroyed the Omni-Wave Projector, but not before she was able to make one more stop: the alternate past Devil came from, the Valley of Flame. Lunella then made the hardest decision of all and left Devil Dinosaur back where he belongs...

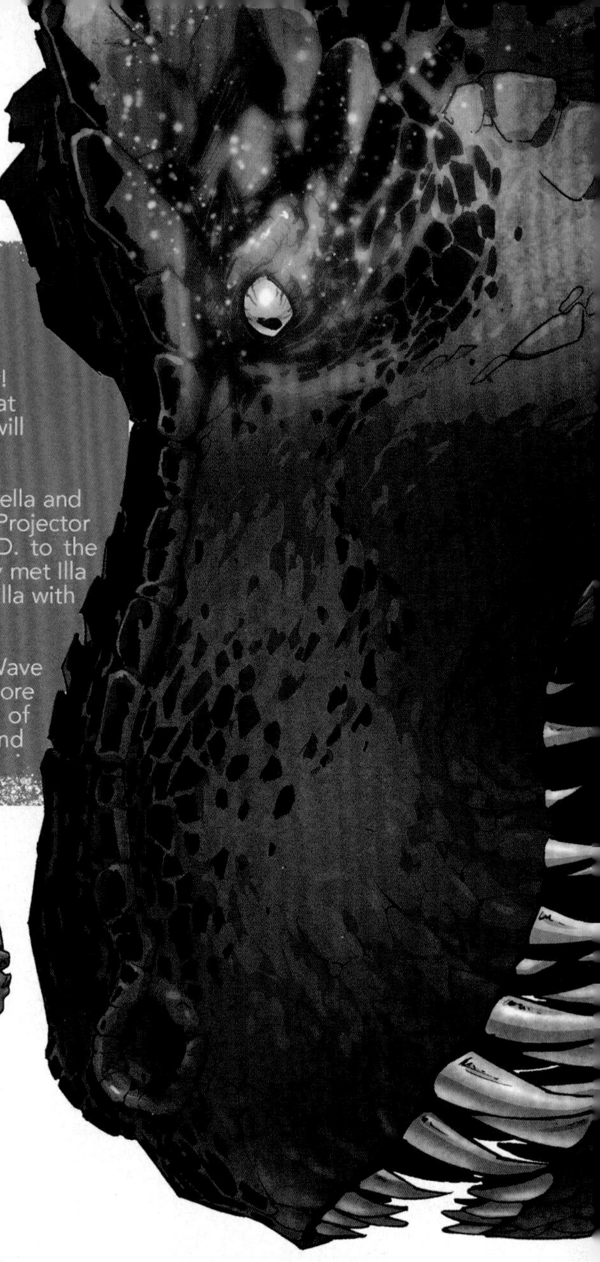

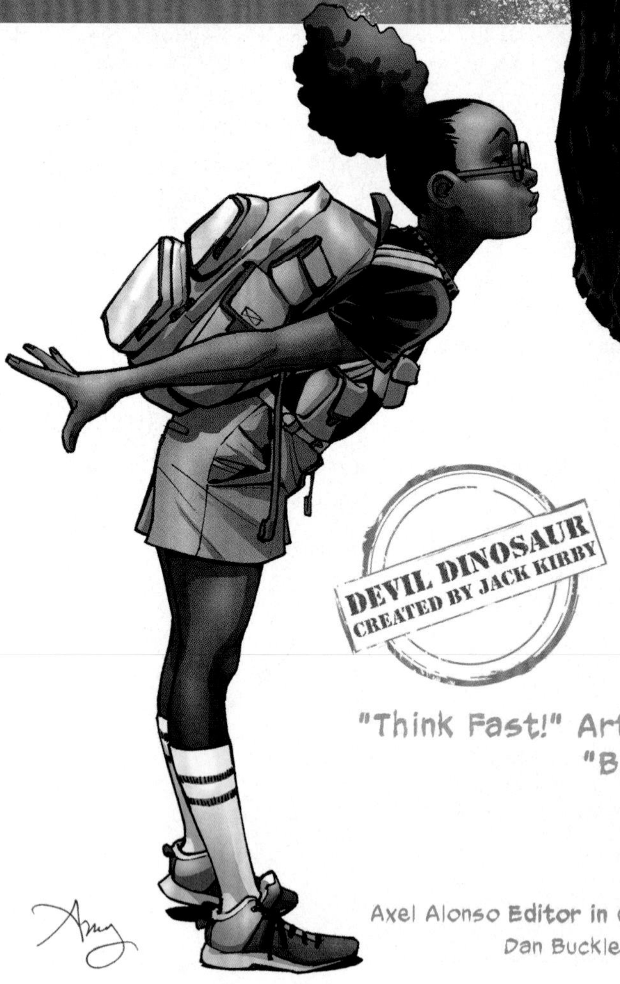

DEVIL DINOSAUR
CREATED BY JACK KIRBY

Writer: Brandon Montclare
Artist: Natacha Bustos
Colorist: Tamra Bonvillain
Letterer: Travis Lanham
"Sign on the Dotted Line..." Artist: Ray-Anthony Height
"Think Fast!" Artist: Dominike "Domo" Stanton
"Blinds" Artist: Michael Shelfer
Cover: Natacha Bustos
Editor: Chris Robinson
Senior Editor: Mark Paniccia
Axel Alonso Editor in Chief Joe Quesada Chief Creative Officer
Dan Buckley President Alan Fine Executive Producer

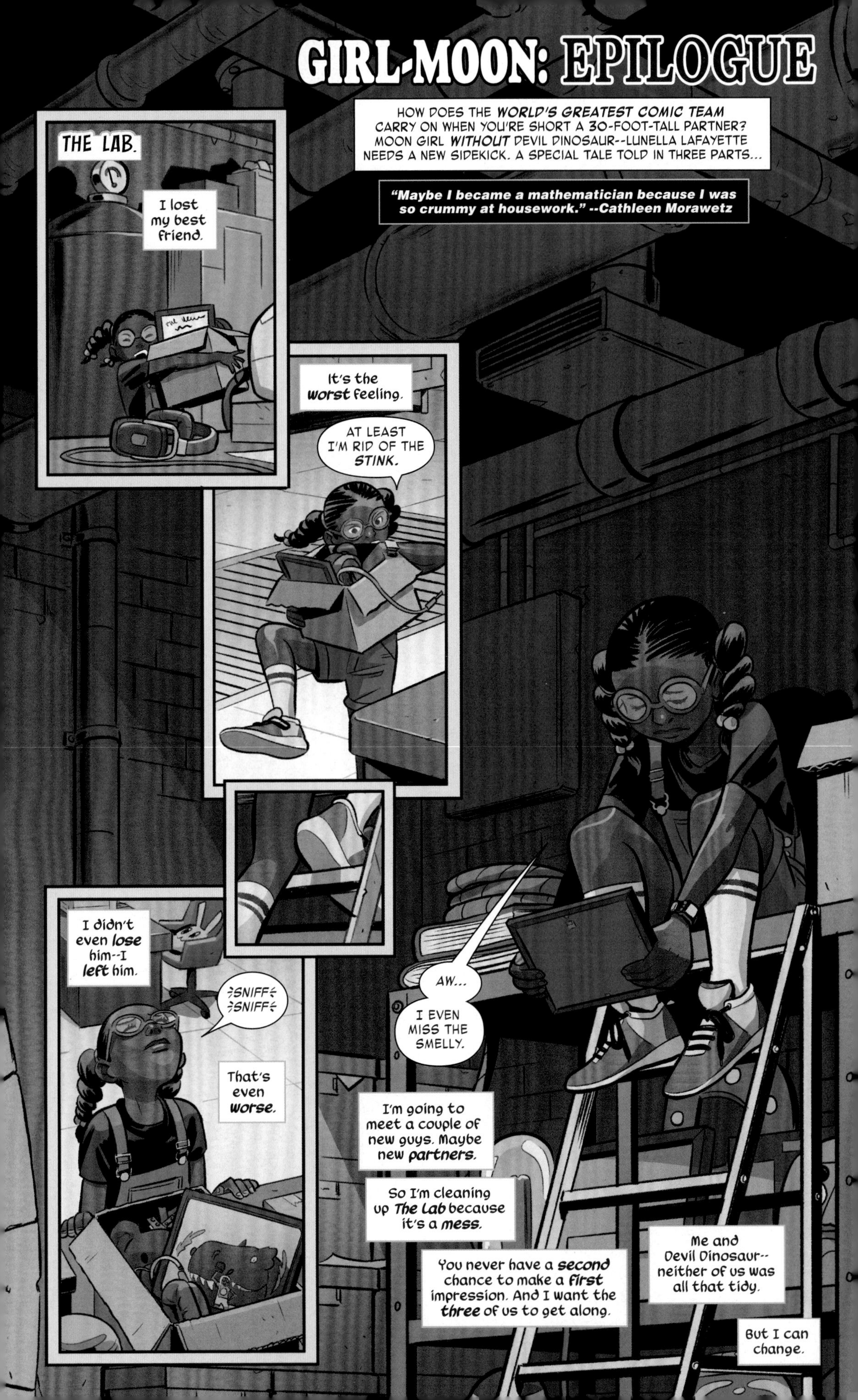
GIRL-MOON: EPILOGUE
HOW DOES THE WORLD'S GREATEST COMIC TEAM CARRY ON WHEN YOU'RE SHORT A 30-FOOT-TALL PARTNER? MOON GIRL WITHOUT DEVIL DINOSAUR--LUNELLA LAFAYETTE NEEDS A NEW SIDEKICK. A SPECIAL TALE TOLD IN THREE PARTS...
"Maybe I became a mathematician because I was so crummy at housework." --Cathleen Morawetz
THE LAB.
I lost my best friend.
It's the worst feeling.
AT LEAST I'M RID OF THE STINK.
I didn't even lose him--I left him.
SNIFF SNIFF
That's even worse.
AW...
I EVEN MISS THE SMELLY.
I'm going to meet a couple of new guys. Maybe new partners.
So I'm cleaning up The Lab because it's a mess.
You never have a second chance to make a first impression. And I want the three of us to get along.
Me and Devil Dinosaur--neither of us was all that tidy.
But I can change.

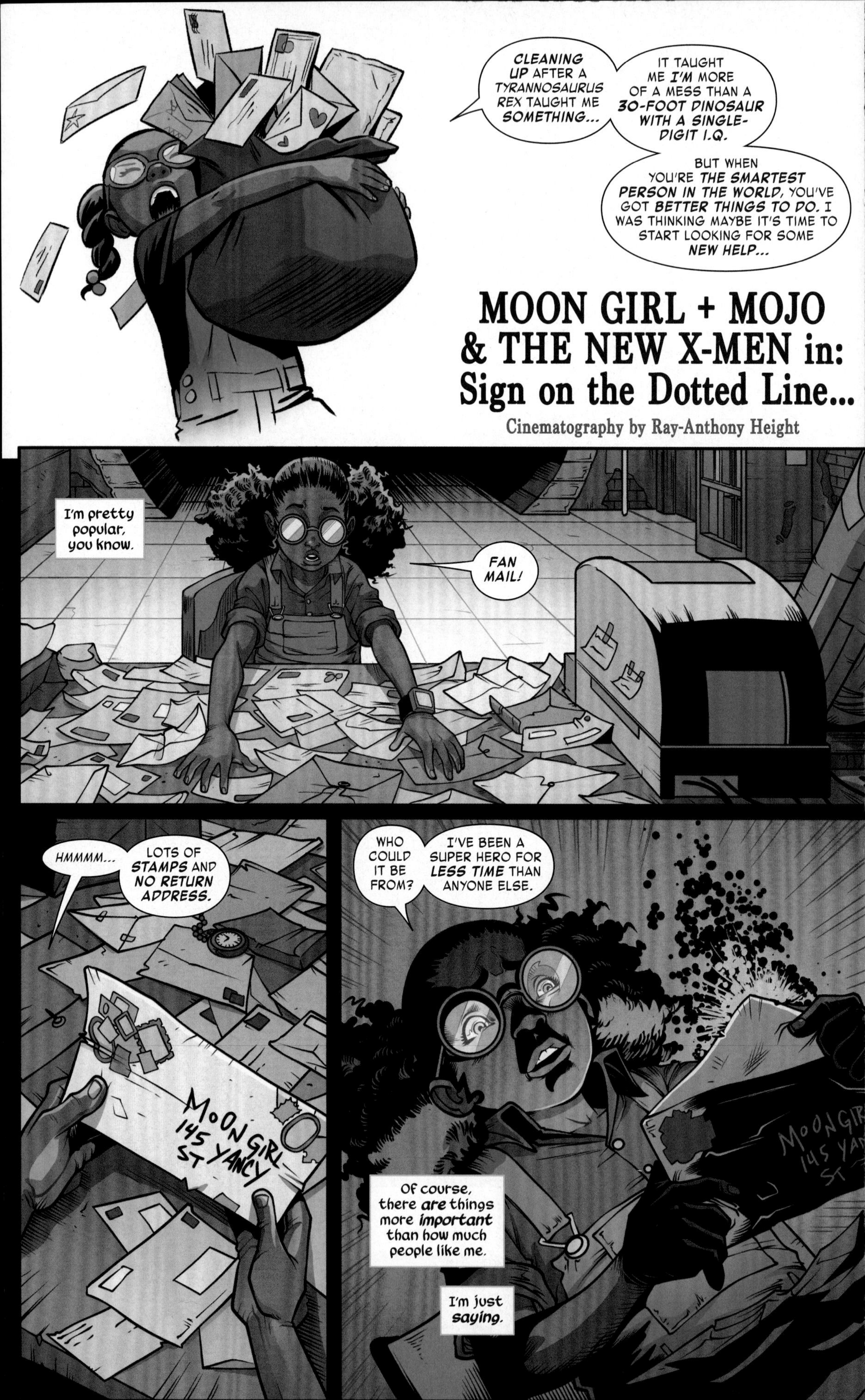

CLEANING UP AFTER A TYRANNOSAURUS REX TAUGHT ME SOMETHING...
IT TAUGHT ME I'M MORE OF A MESS THAN A 30-FOOT DINOSAUR WITH A SINGLE-DIGIT I.Q.
BUT WHEN YOU'RE THE SMARTEST PERSON IN THE WORLD, YOU'VE GOT BETTER THINGS TO DO. I WAS THINKING MAYBE IT'S TIME TO START LOOKING FOR SOME NEW HELP...
MOON GIRL + MOJO
& THE NEW X-MEN in:
Sign on the Dotted Line...
Cinematography by Ray-Anthony Height
I'm pretty popular, you know.
FAN MAIL!
HMMMM...
LOTS OF STAMPS AND NO RETURN ADDRESS.
MOON GIRL
145 YANCY ST
WHO COULD IT BE FROM?
I'VE BEEN A SUPER HERO FOR LESS TIME THAN ANYONE ELSE.
MOON GIRL
145 YA
ST
Of course, there are things more important than how much people like me.
I'm just saying.

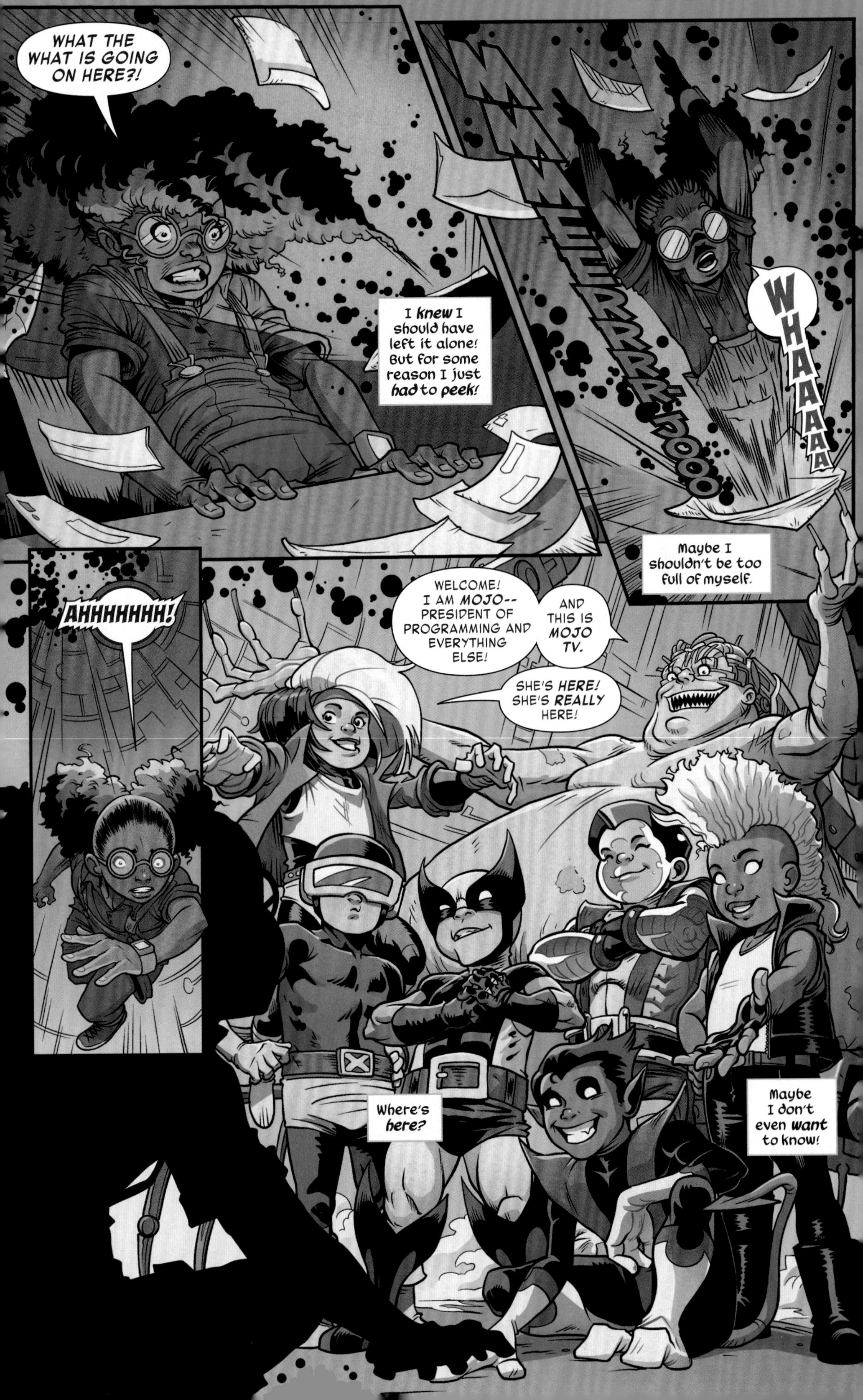
WHAT THE WHAT IS GOING ON HERE?!
I knew I should have left it alone! But for some reason I just had to peek!
MMMMWURRRRR'DOOO
WHAAAAAA
Maybe I shouldn't be too full of myself.
AHHHHHHHH!
WELCOME! I AM MOJO-- PRESIDENT OF PROGRAMMING AND EVERYTHING ELSE!
AND THIS IS MOJO TV.
SHE'S HERE! SHE'S REALLY HERE!
Where's here?
Maybe I don't even want to know!

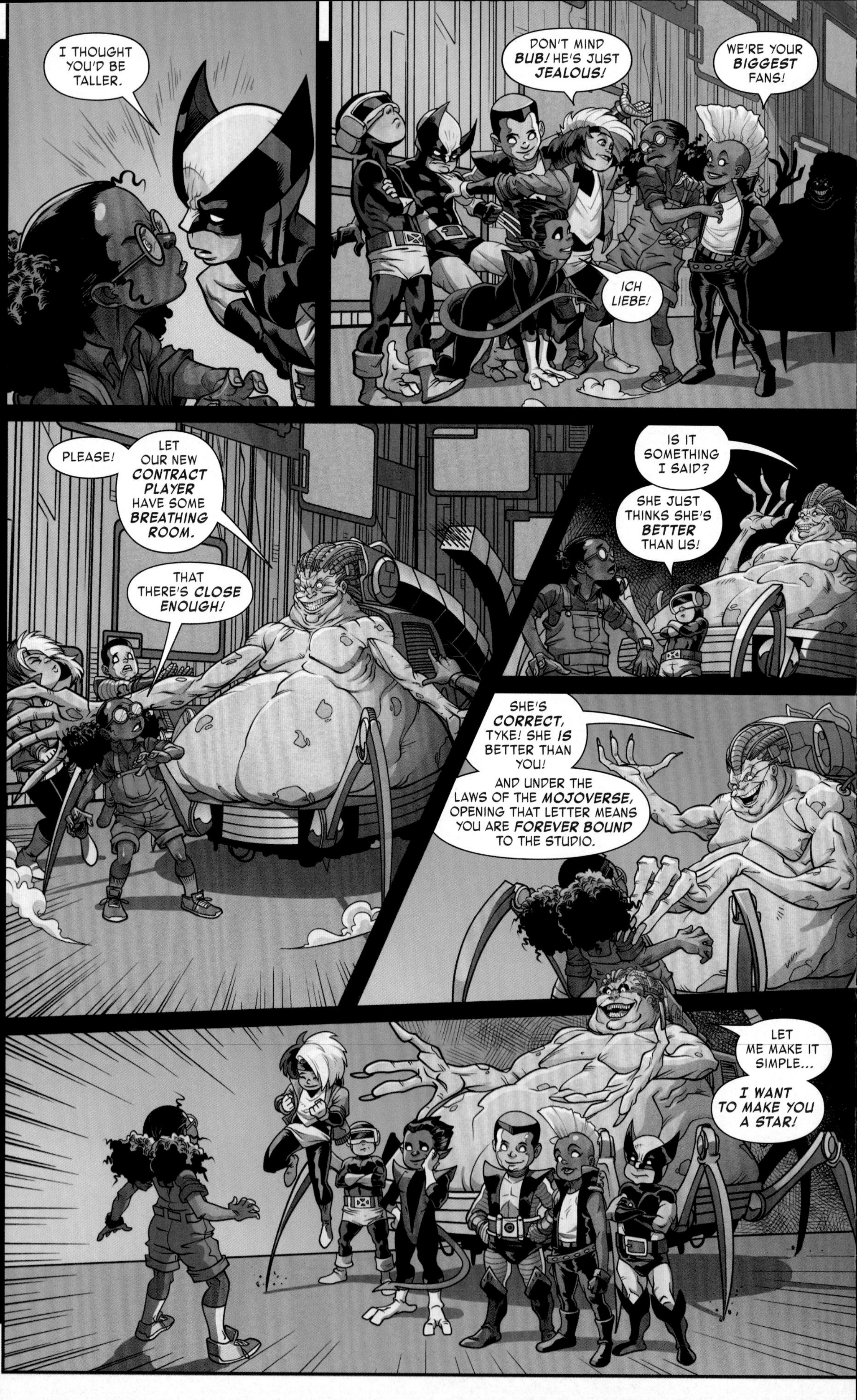
I THOUGHT YOU'D BE TALLER.
DON'T MIND BUB! HE'S JUST JEALOUS!
WE'RE YOUR BIGGEST FANS!
ICH LIEBE!
PLEASE!
LET OUR NEW CONTRACT PLAYER HAVE SOME BREATHING ROOM.
THAT THERE'S CLOSE ENOUGH!
IS IT SOMETHING I SAID?
SHE JUST THINKS SHE'S BETTER THAN US!
SHE'S CORRECT, TYKE! SHE IS BETTER THAN YOU!
AND UNDER THE LAWS OF THE MOJOVERSE, OPENING THAT LETTER MEANS YOU ARE FOREVER BOUND TO THE STUDIO.
LET ME MAKE IT SIMPLE...
I WANT TO MAKE YOU A STAR!

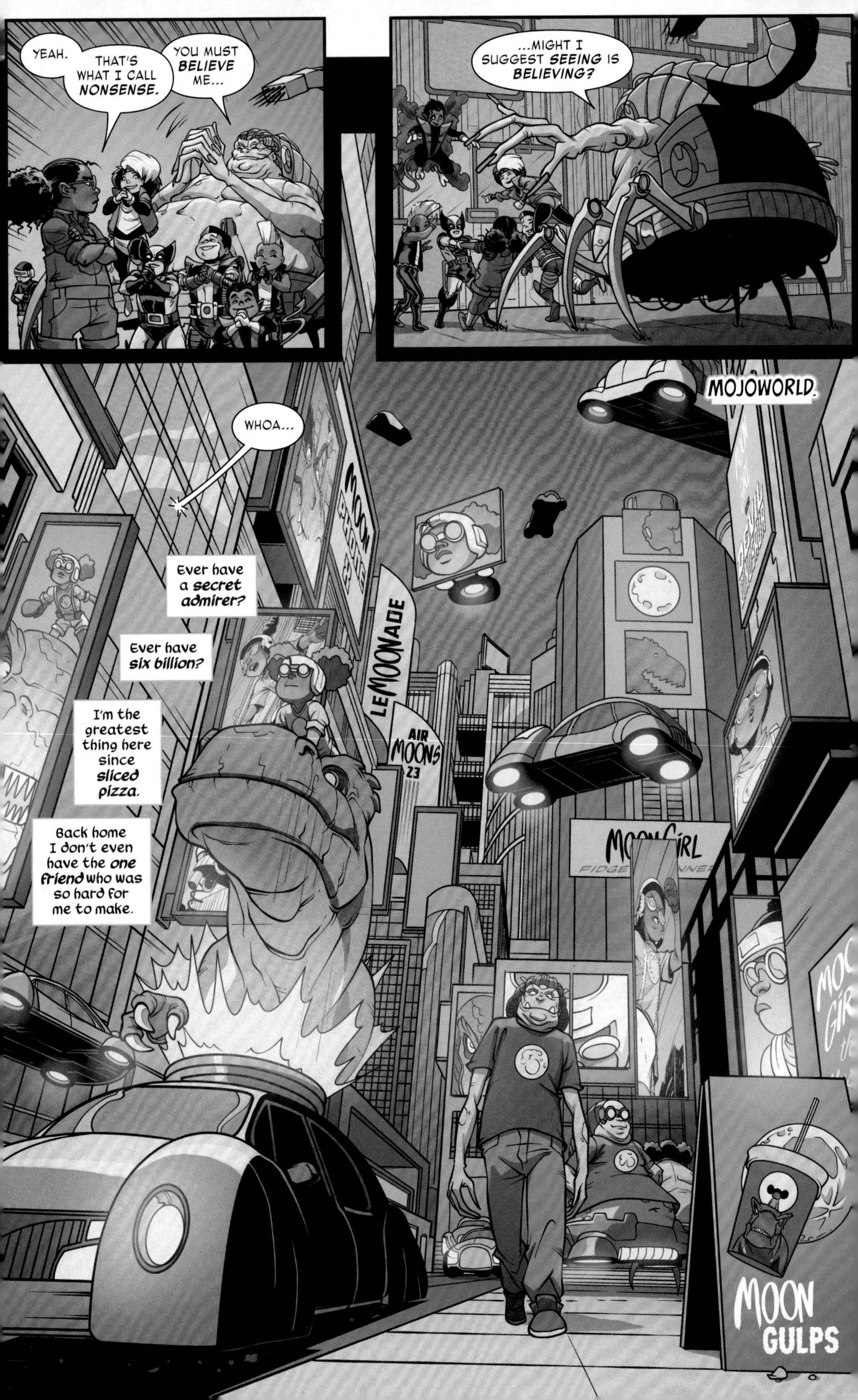
YEAH.
THAT'S WHAT I CALL NONSENSE.
YOU MUST BELIEVE ME...
...MIGHT I SUGGEST SEEING IS BELIEVING?
MOJOWORLD.
WHOA...
Ever have a secret admirer?
Ever have six billion?
I'm the greatest thing here since sliced pizza.
Back home I don't even have the one friend who was so hard for me to make.
LEMOONADE
AIR MOONS 23
MOON GULPS

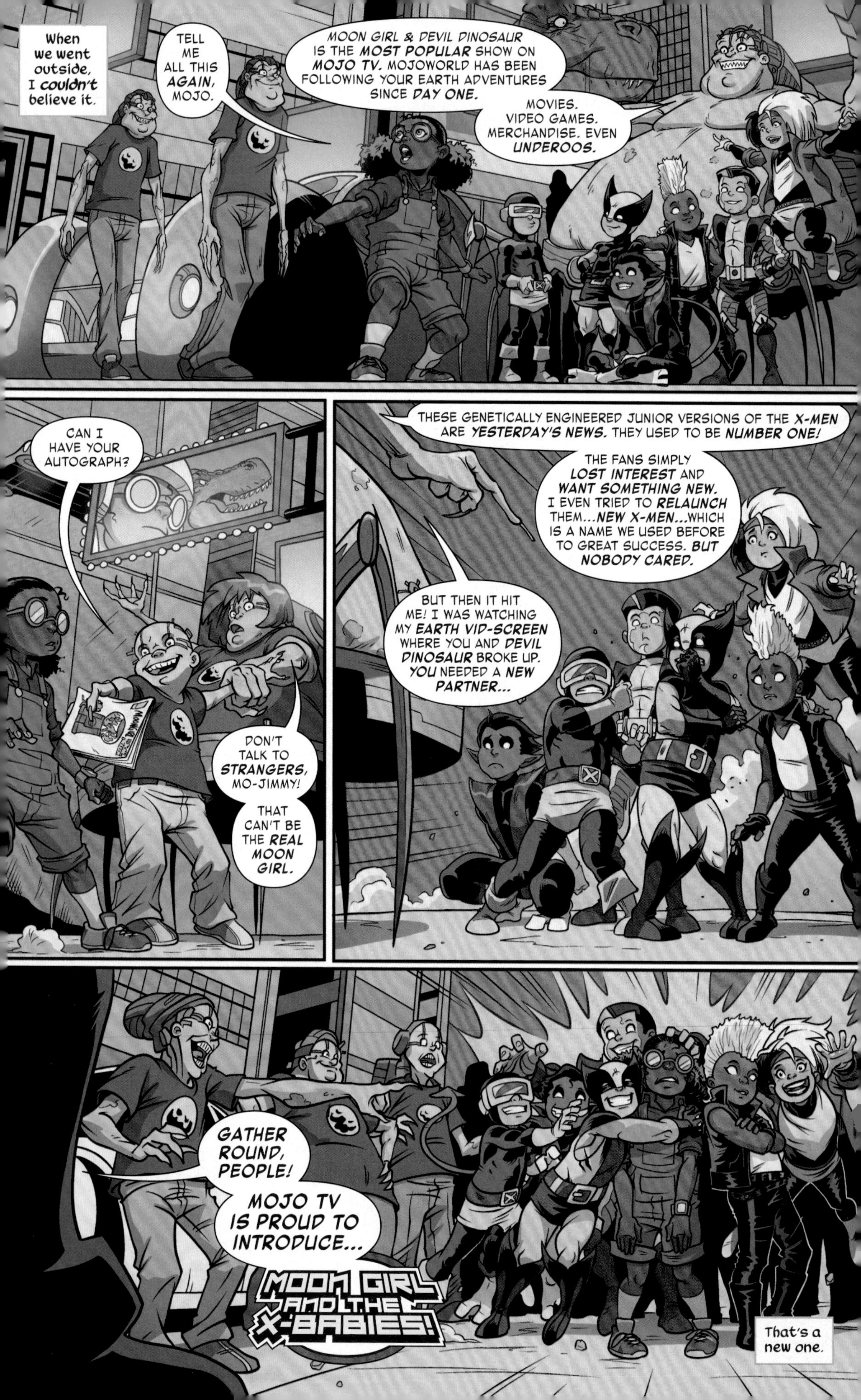
When we went outside, I couldn't believe it.
TELL ME ALL THIS AGAIN, MOJO.
MOON GIRL & DEVIL DINOSAUR IS THE MOST POPULAR SHOW ON MOJO TV. MOJOWORLD HAS BEEN FOLLOWING YOUR EARTH ADVENTURES SINCE DAY ONE.
MOVIES. VIDEO GAMES. MERCHANDISE. EVEN UNDEROOS.
CAN I HAVE YOUR AUTOGRAPH?
DON'T TALK TO STRANGERS, MO-JIMMY!
THAT CAN'T BE THE REAL MOON GIRL.
THESE GENETICALLY ENGINEERED JUNIOR VERSIONS OF THE X-MEN ARE YESTERDAY'S NEWS. THEY USED TO BE NUMBER ONE!
THE FANS SIMPLY LOST INTEREST AND WANT SOMETHING NEW. I EVEN TRIED TO RELAUNCH THEM...NEW X-MEN...WHICH IS A NAME WE USED BEFORE TO GREAT SUCCESS. BUT NOBODY CARED.
BUT THEN IT HIT ME! I WAS WATCHING MY EARTH VID-SCREEN WHERE YOU AND DEVIL DINOSAUR BROKE UP. YOU NEEDED A NEW PARTNER...
GATHER ROUND, PEOPLE!
MOJO TV IS PROUD TO INTRODUCE...
MOON GIRL AND THE X-BABIES!
That's a new one.

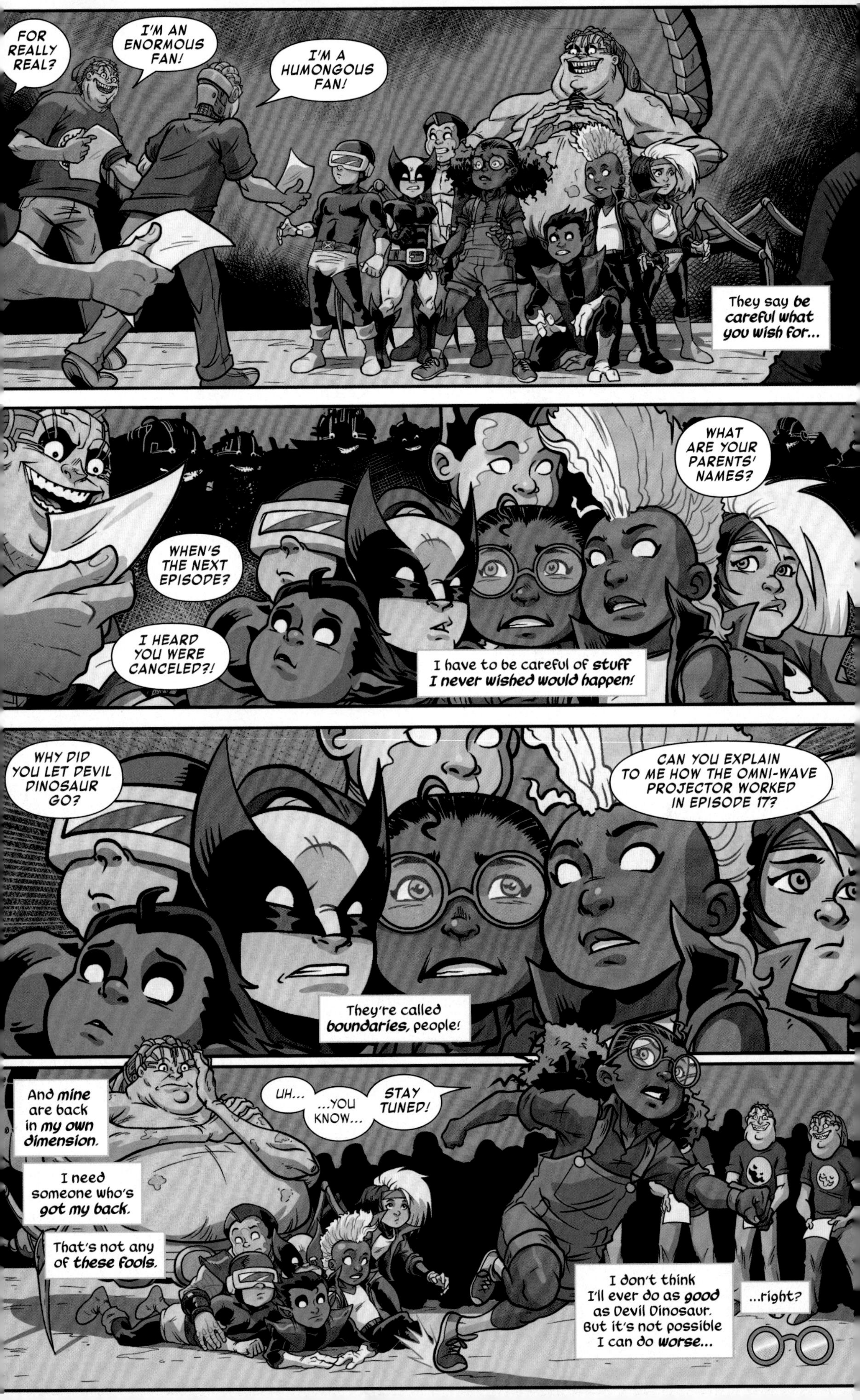
FOR REALLY REAL?
I'M AN ENORMOUS FAN!
I'M A HUMONGOUS FAN!
They say be careful what you wish for...
WHAT ARE YOUR PARENTS' NAMES?
WHEN'S THE NEXT EPISODE?
I HEARD YOU WERE CANCELED?!
I have to be careful of stuff I never wished would happen!
WHY DID YOU LET DEVIL DINOSAUR GO?
CAN YOU EXPLAIN TO ME HOW THE OMNI-WAVE PROJECTOR WORKED IN EPISODE 17?
They're called boundaries, people!
And mine are back in my own dimension.
I need someone who's got my back.
That's not any of these fools.
UH...
...YOU KNOW...
STAY TUNED!
I don't think I'll ever do as good as Devil Dinosaur. But it's not possible I can do worse...
...right?

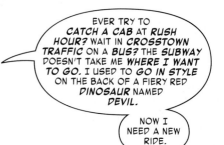

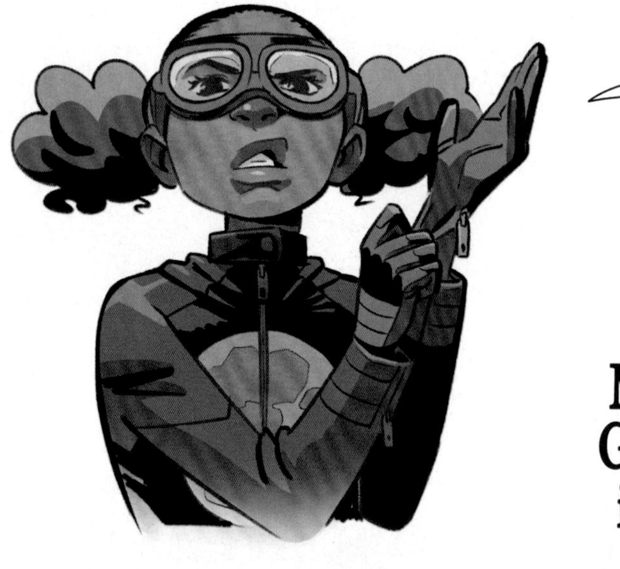
EVER TRY TO CATCH A CAB AT RUSH HOUR? WAIT IN CROSSTOWN TRAFFIC ON A BUS? THE SUBWAY DOESN'T TAKE ME WHERE I WANT TO GO. I USED TO GO IN STYLE ON THE BACK OF A FIERY RED DINOSAUR NAMED DEVIL.
NOW I NEED A NEW RIDE.

MOON GIRL + GHOST RIDER in: Think Fast!

Pit crewed by Domo Stanton

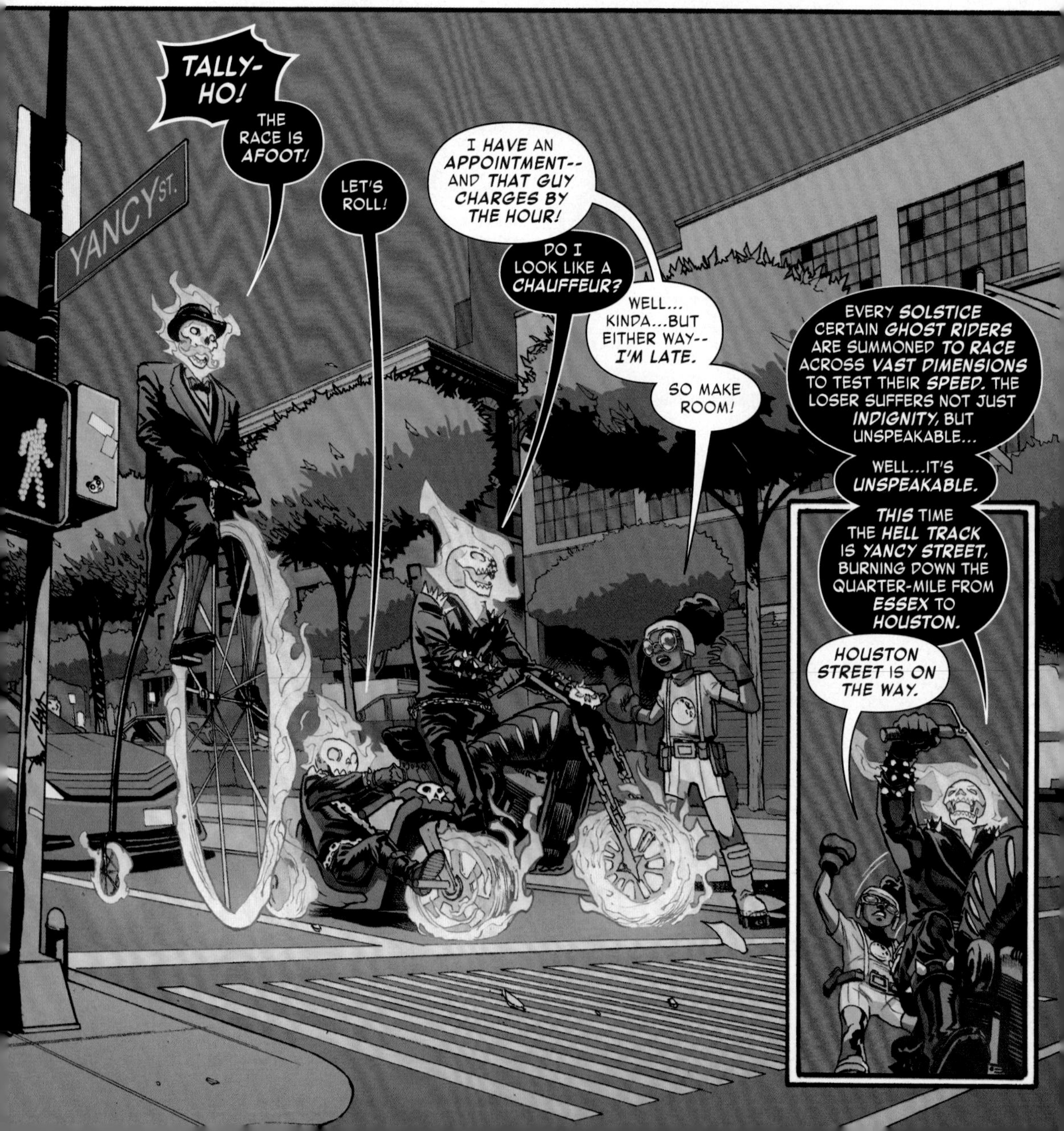
TALLY-HO!
THE RACE IS AFOOT!
LET'S ROLL!
I HAVE AN APPOINTMENT-- AND THAT GUY CHARGES BY THE HOUR!
DO I LOOK LIKE A CHAUFFEUR?
WELL... KINDA...BUT EITHER WAY-- I'M LATE.
SO MAKE ROOM!
YANCY ST.
EVERY SOLSTICE CERTAIN GHOST RIDERS ARE SUMMONED TO RACE ACROSS VAST DIMENSIONS TO TEST THEIR SPEED. THE LOSER SUFFERS NOT JUST INDIGNITY, BUT UNSPEAKABLE...
WELL...IT'S UNSPEAKABLE.
THIS TIME THE HELL TRACK IS YANCY STREET, BURNING DOWN THE QUARTER-MILE FROM ESSEX TO HOUSTON.
HOUSTON STREET IS ON THE WAY.

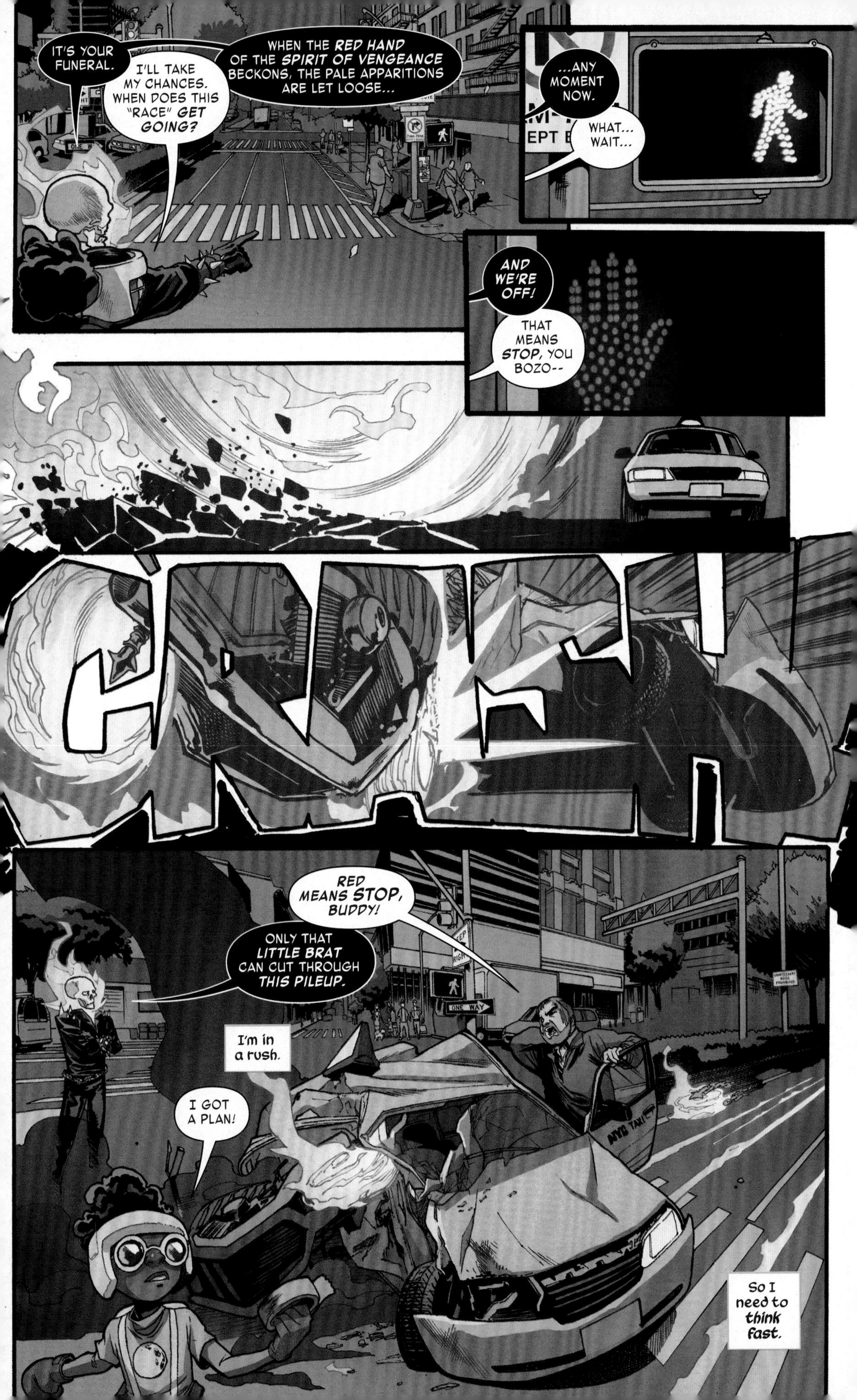

IT'S YOUR FUNERAL.
I'LL TAKE MY CHANCES. WHEN DOES THIS "RACE" GET GOING?
WHEN THE RED HAND OF THE SPIRIT OF VENGEANCE BECKONS, THE PALE APPARITIONS ARE LET LOOSE...
...ANY MOMENT NOW.
WHAT... WAIT...
AND WE'RE OFF!
THAT MEANS STOP, YOU BOZO--
RED MEANS STOP, BUDDY!
ONLY THAT LITTLE BRAT CAN CUT THROUGH THIS PILEUP.
I'm in a rush.
I GOT A PLAN!
So I need to think fast.

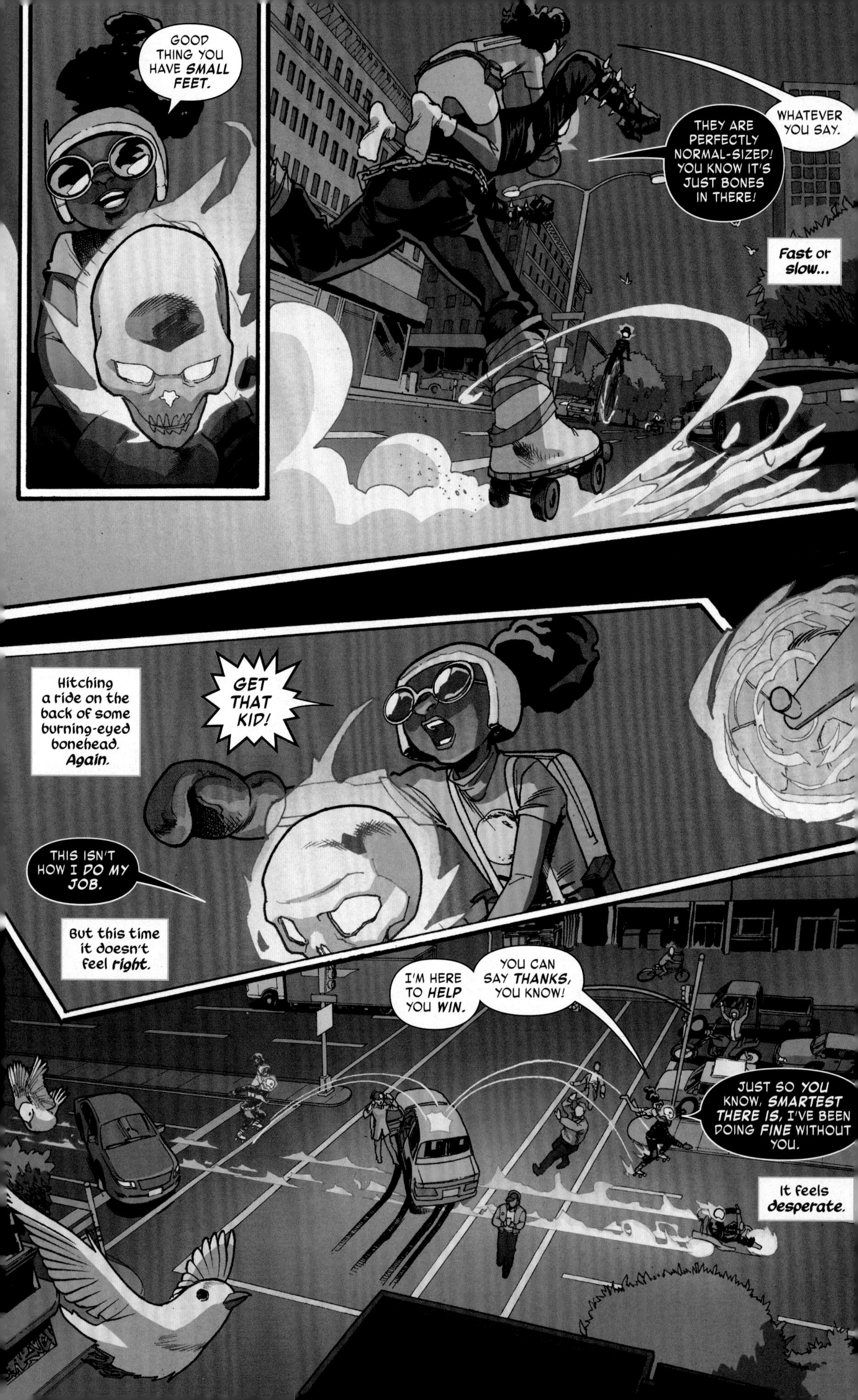
GOOD THING YOU HAVE SMALL FEET.
THEY ARE PERFECTLY NORMAL-SIZED! YOU KNOW IT'S JUST BONES IN THERE!
WHATEVER YOU SAY.
Fast or slow...
Hitching a ride on the back of some burning-eyed bonehead. Again.
GET THAT KID!
THIS ISN'T HOW I DO MY JOB.
But this time it doesn't feel right.
I'M HERE TO HELP YOU WIN.
YOU CAN SAY THANKS, YOU KNOW!
JUST SO YOU KNOW, SMARTEST THERE IS, I'VE BEEN DOING FINE WITHOUT YOU.
It feels desperate.

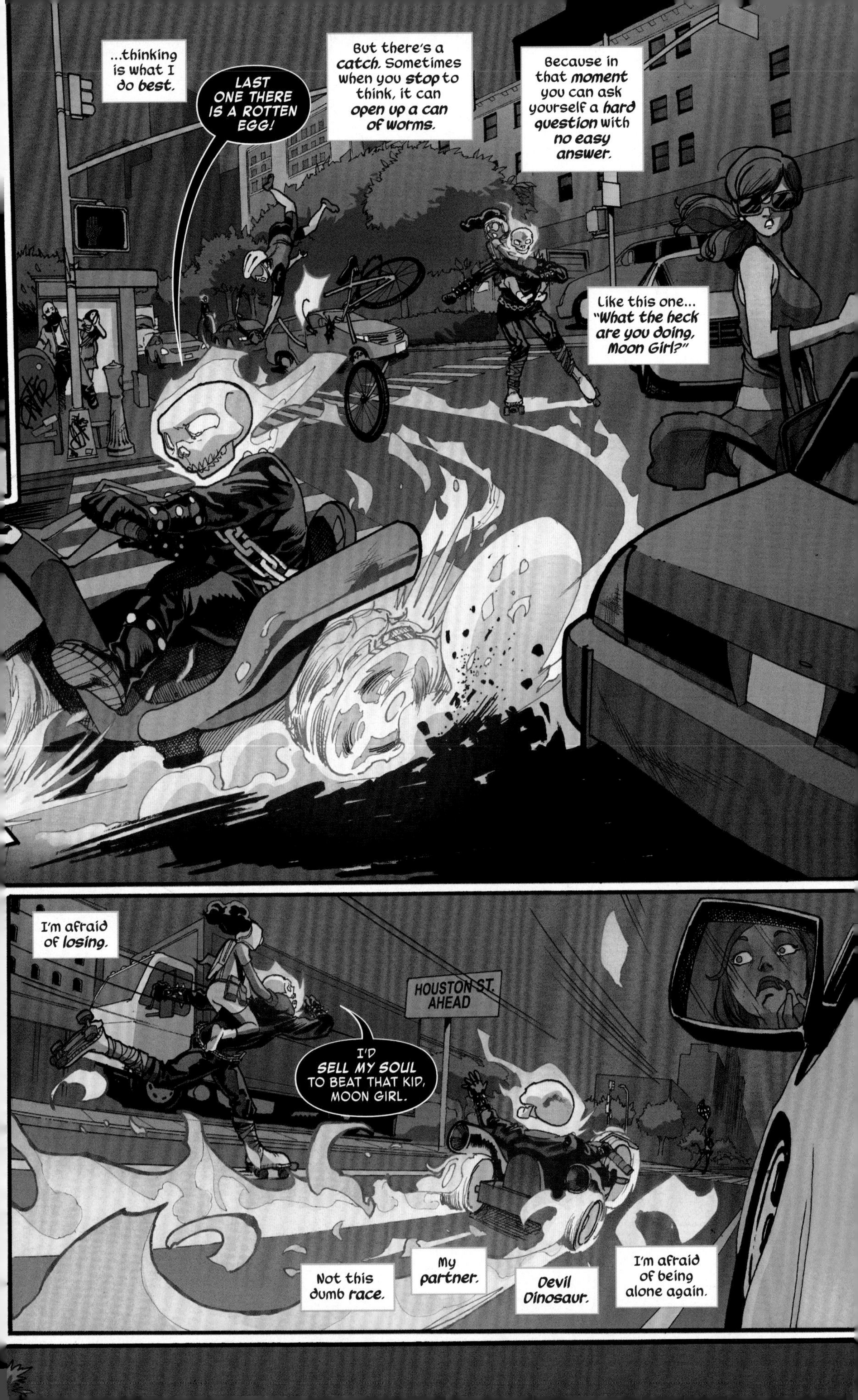
...thinking is what I do best.
LAST ONE THERE IS A ROTTEN EGG!
But there's a catch. Sometimes when you stop to think, it can open up a can of worms.
Because in that moment you can ask yourself a hard question with no easy answer.
Like this one... "What the heck are you doing, Moon Girl?"
I'm afraid of losing.
HOUSTON ST. AHEAD
I'D SELL MY SOUL TO BEAT THAT KID, MOON GIRL.
Not this dumb race.
My partner.
Devil Dinosaur.
I'm afraid of being alone again.

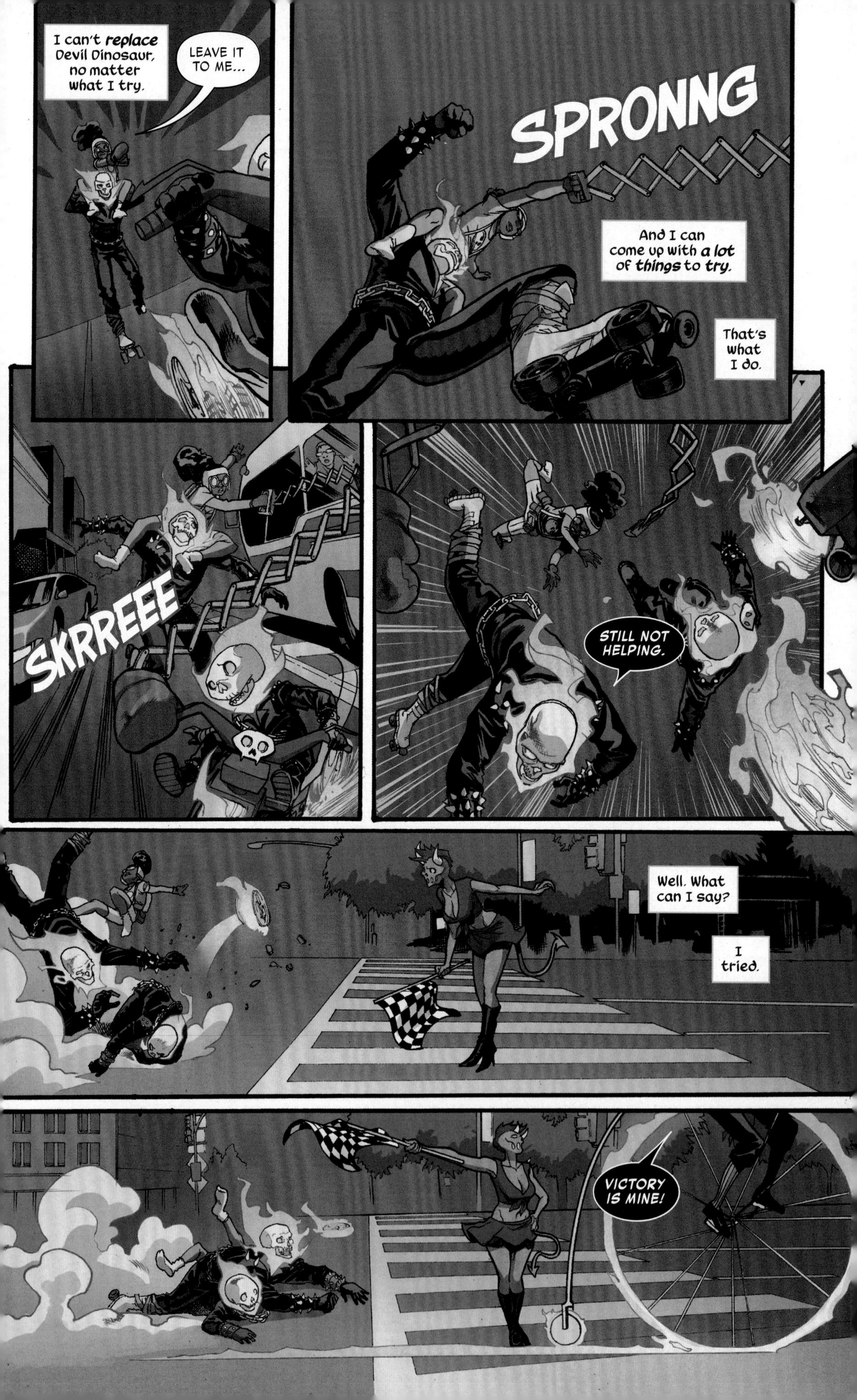
I can't replace Devil Dinosaur, no matter what I try.
LEAVE IT TO ME...
SPRONNG
And I can come up with a lot of things to try.
That's what I do.
SKRREEE
STILL NOT HELPING.
Well. What can I say?
I tried.
VICTORY IS MINE!

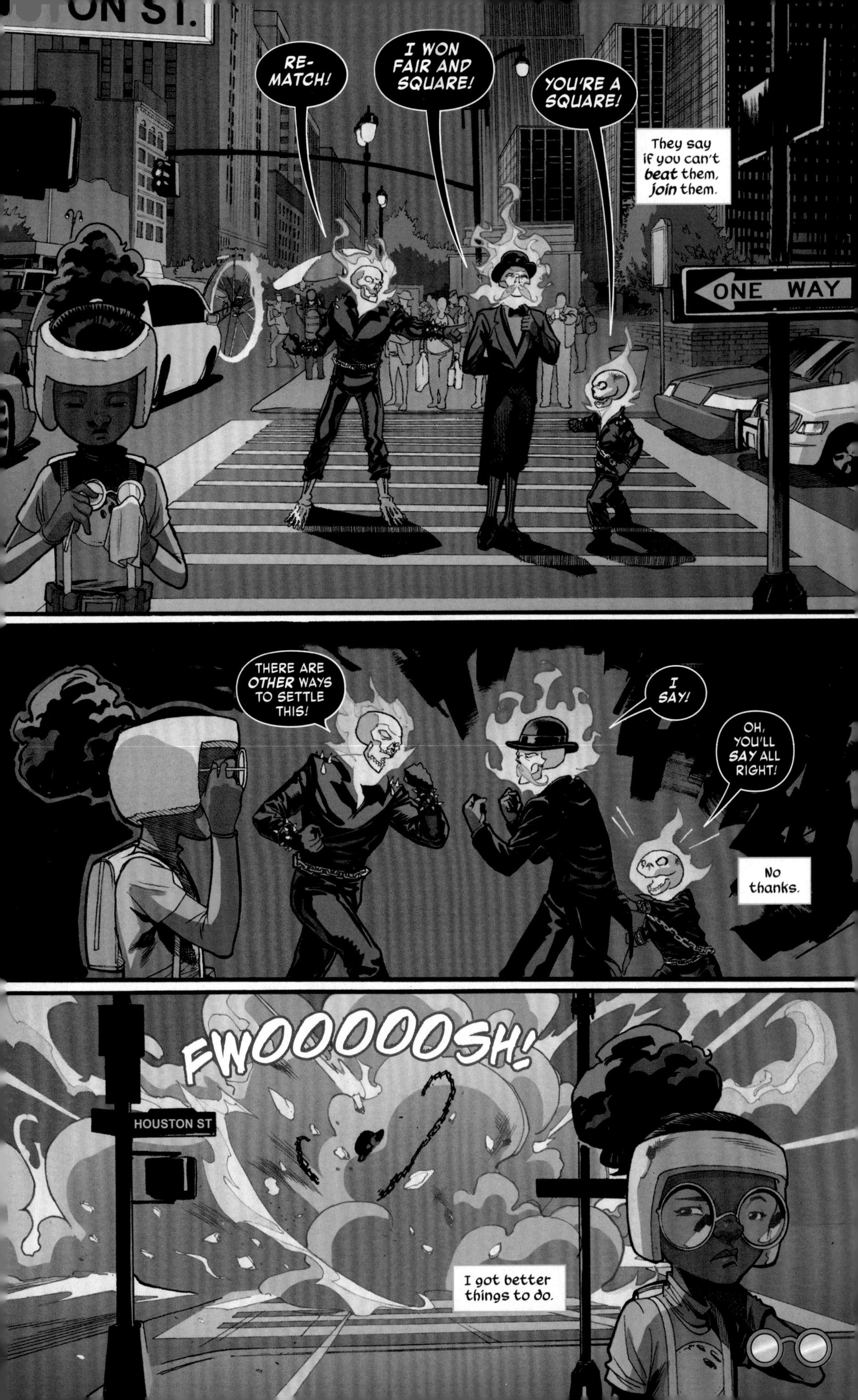
ON ST.
RE-MATCH!
I WON FAIR AND SQUARE!
YOU'RE A SQUARE!
They say if you can't beat them, join them.
ONE WAY
THERE ARE OTHER WAYS TO SETTLE THIS!
I SAY!
OH, YOU'LL SAY ALL RIGHT!
No thanks.
FWOOOOOOSH!
HOUSTON ST
I got better things to do.

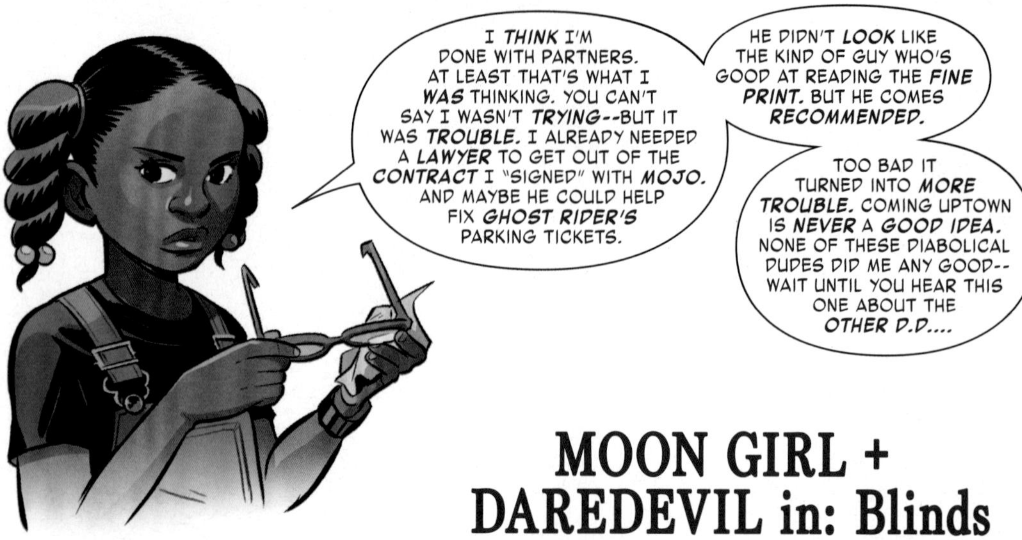
I *THINK* I'M DONE WITH PARTNERS. AT LEAST THAT'S WHAT I *WAS* THINKING. YOU CAN'T SAY I WASN'T *TRYING*--BUT IT WAS *TROUBLE.* I ALREADY NEEDED A *LAWYER* TO GET OUT OF THE *CONTRACT* I "SIGNED" WITH *MOJO.* AND MAYBE HE COULD HELP FIX *GHOST RIDER'S* PARKING TICKETS.
HE DIDN'T *LOOK* LIKE THE KIND OF GUY WHO'S GOOD AT READING THE *FINE PRINT.* BUT HE COMES *RECOMMENDED.*
TOO BAD IT TURNED INTO *MORE TROUBLE.* COMING UPTOWN IS *NEVER* A *GOOD IDEA.* NONE OF THESE DIABOLICAL DUDES DID ME ANY GOOD--WAIT UNTIL YOU HEAR THIS ONE ABOUT THE *OTHER D.D....*

MOON GIRL + DAREDEVIL in: Blinds

Courtroom sketches by Michael Shelfer

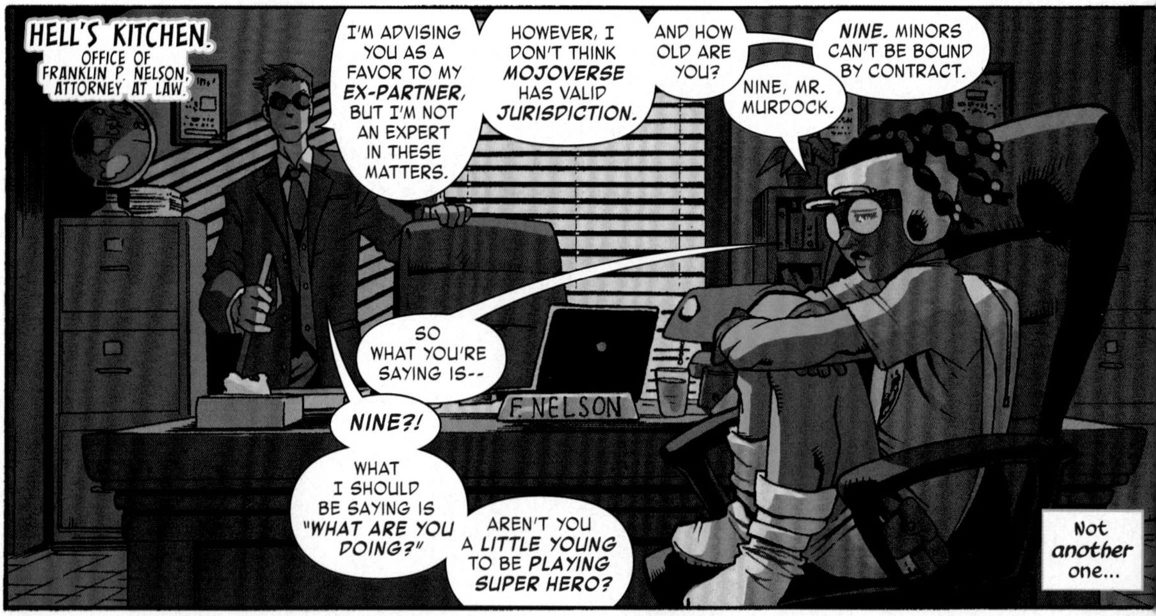
HELL'S KITCHEN. OFFICE OF FRANKLIN P. NELSON, ATTORNEY AT LAW.
I'M ADVISING YOU AS A FAVOR TO MY *EX-PARTNER*, BUT I'M NOT AN EXPERT IN THESE MATTERS.
HOWEVER, I DON'T THINK *MOJOVERSE* HAS VALID *JURISDICTION.*
AND HOW OLD ARE YOU?
NINE. MINORS CAN'T BE BOUND BY CONTRACT.
NINE, MR. MURDOCK.
SO WHAT YOU'RE SAYING IS--
F. NELSON
NINE?!
WHAT I SHOULD BE SAYING IS *"WHAT ARE YOU DOING?"*
AREN'T YOU A *LITTLE YOUNG* TO BE *PLAYING SUPER HERO?*
Not *another* one...

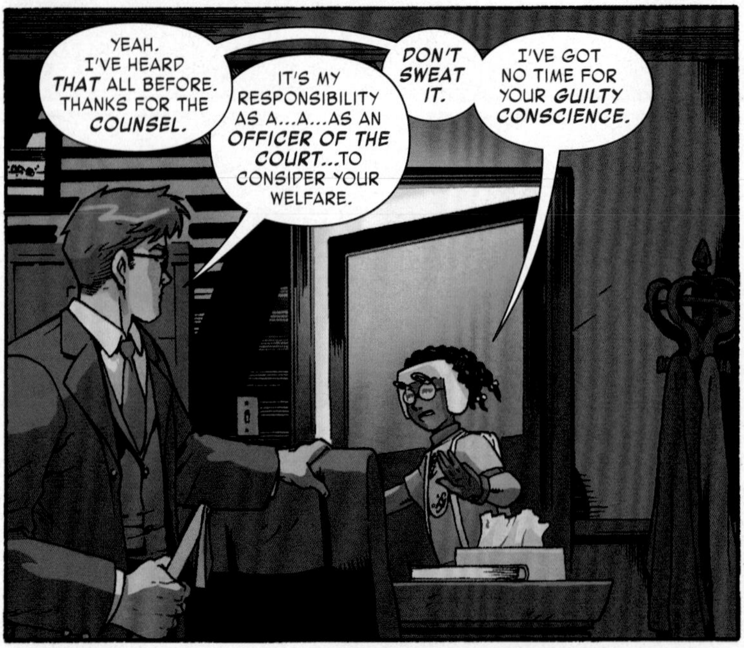
YEAH. I'VE HEARD *THAT* ALL BEFORE. THANKS FOR THE *COUNSEL.*
IT'S MY RESPONSIBILITY AS A...A...AS AN *OFFICER OF THE COURT...*TO CONSIDER YOUR WELFARE.
DON'T SWEAT IT.
I'VE GOT NO TIME FOR YOUR *GUILTY CONSCIENCE.*

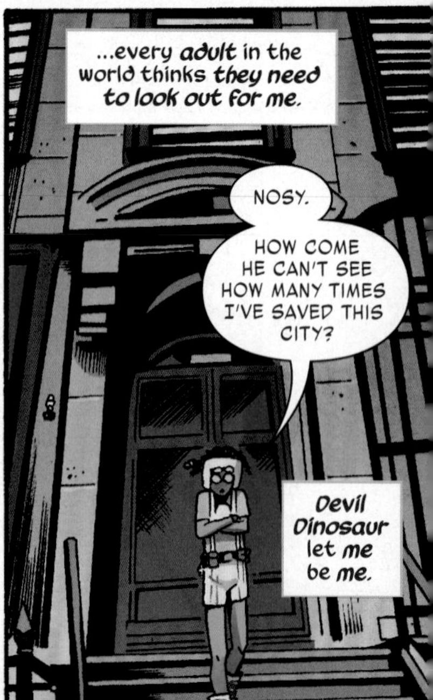
...every *adult* in the world thinks *they need to look out for me.*
NOSY.
HOW COME HE CAN'T SEE HOW MANY TIMES I'VE SAVED THIS CITY?
Devil Dinosaur let *me* be *me.*

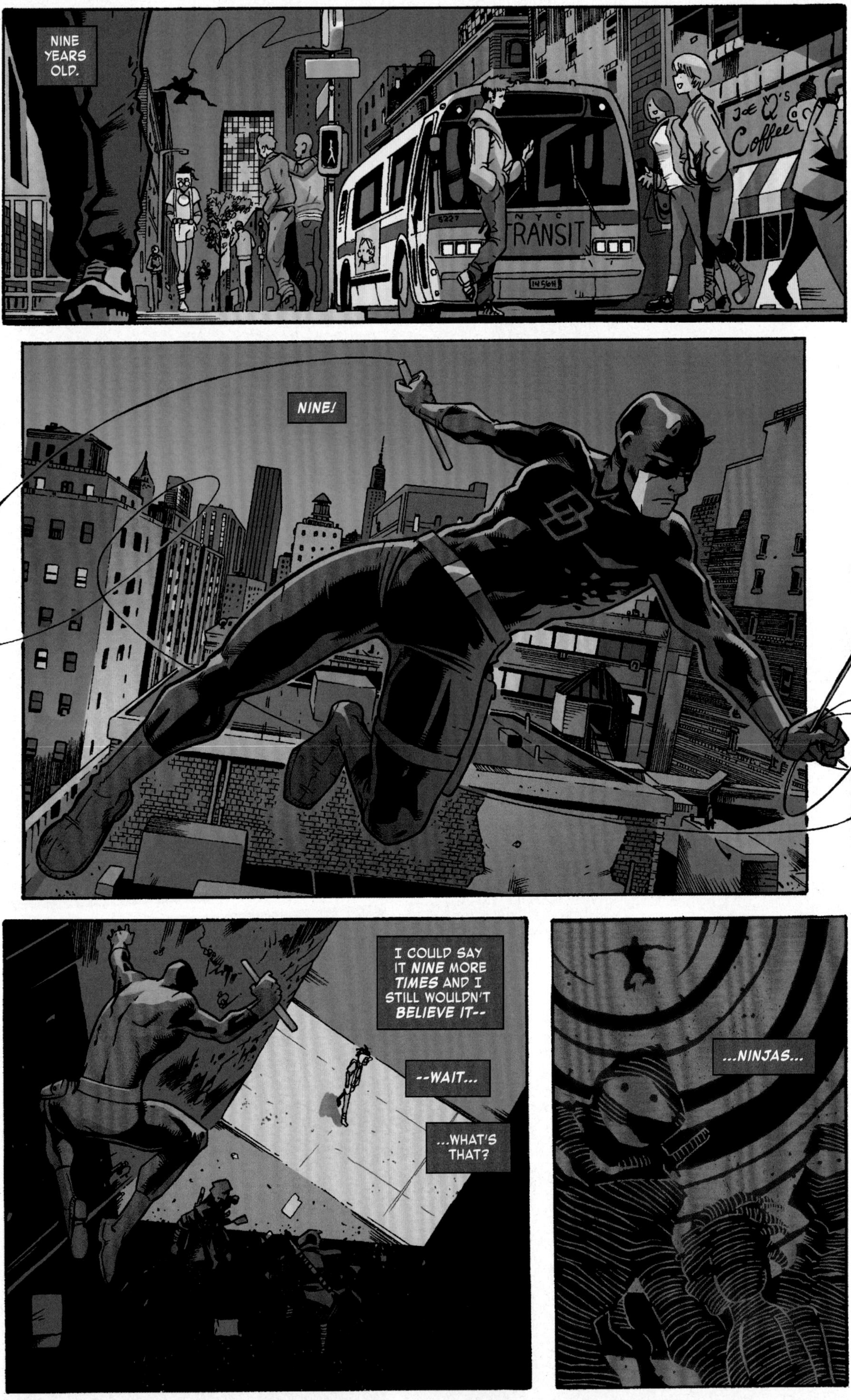
NINE YEARS OLD.
NYC TRANSIT
JOE Q'S Coffee
NINE!
I COULD SAY IT NINE MORE TIMES AND I STILL WOULDN'T BELIEVE IT--
--WAIT...
...WHAT'S THAT?
...NINJAS...

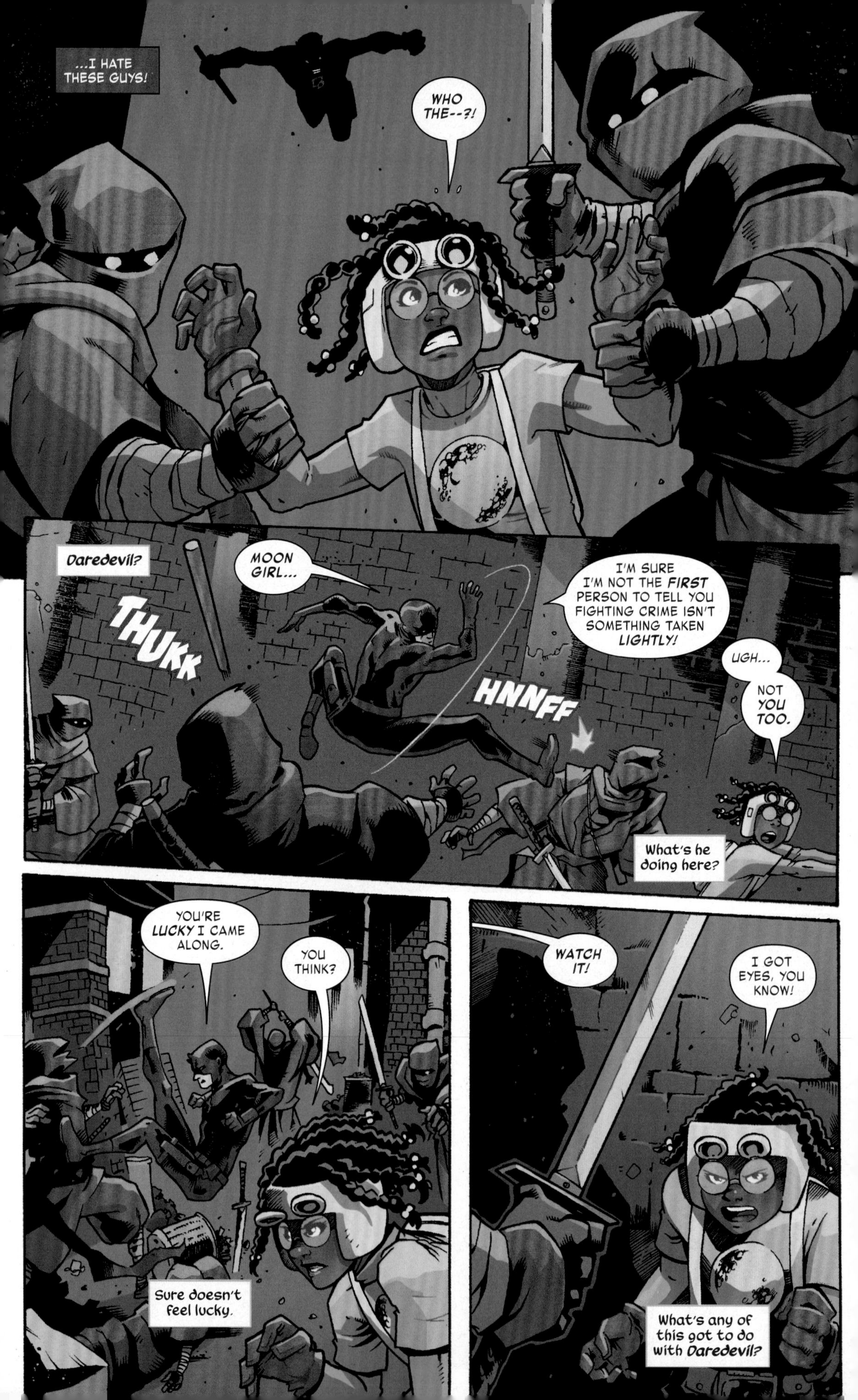
...I HATE THESE GUYS!
WHO THE--?!
Daredevil?
MOON GIRL...
THUKK
I'M SURE I'M NOT THE FIRST PERSON TO TELL YOU FIGHTING CRIME ISN'T SOMETHING TAKEN LIGHTLY!
HNNFF
UGH...
NOT YOU TOO.
What's he doing here?
YOU'RE LUCKY I CAME ALONG.
YOU THINK?
Sure doesn't feel lucky.
WATCH IT!
I GOT EYES, YOU KNOW!
What's any of this got to do with Daredevil?

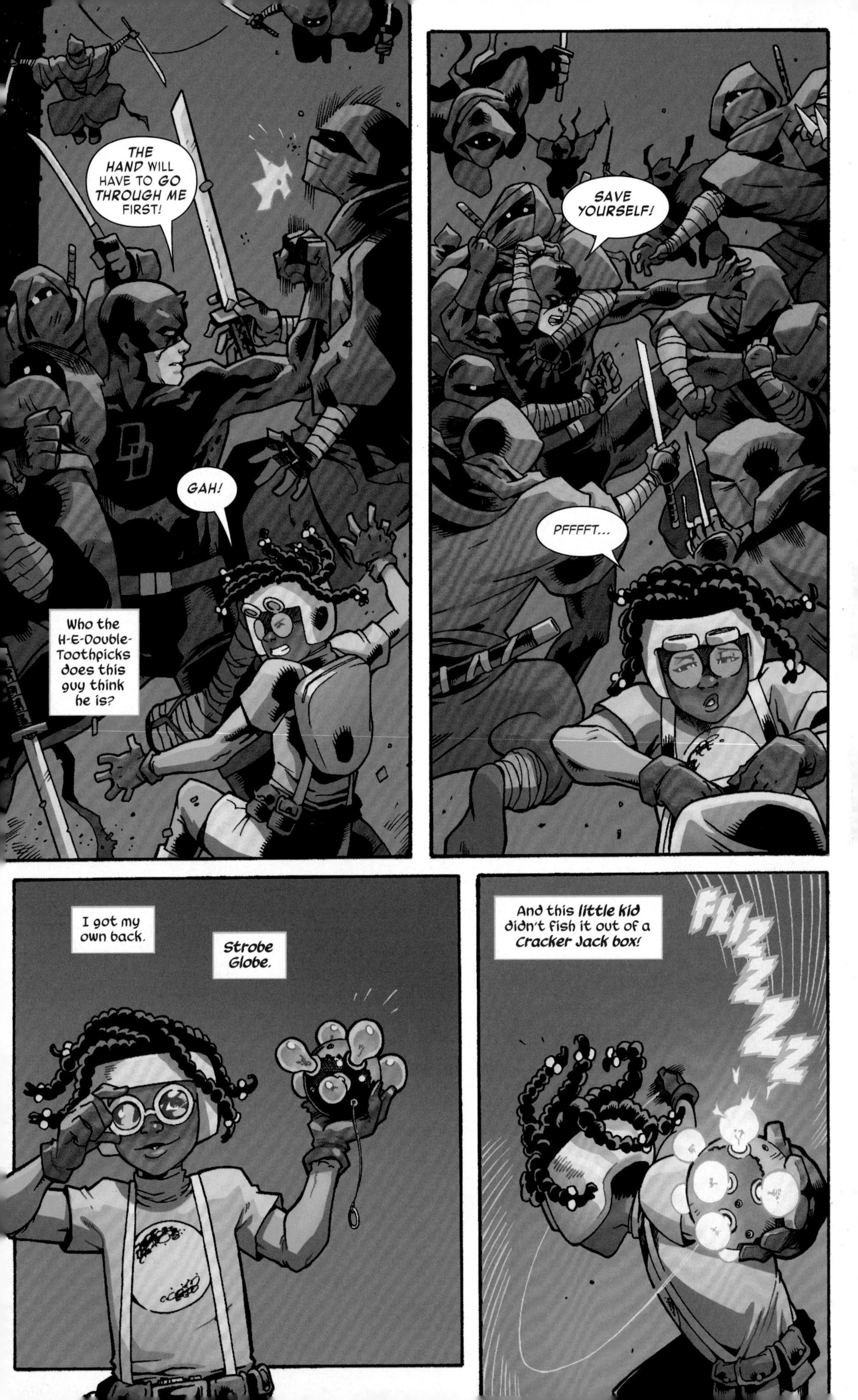
THE HAND WILL HAVE TO GO THROUGH ME FIRST!
GAH!
Who the H-E-Double-Toothpicks does this guy think he is?
SAVE YOURSELF!
PFFFFT...
I got my own back.
Strobe Globe.
And this little kid didn't fish it out of a Cracker Jack box!
FLIZZZZ

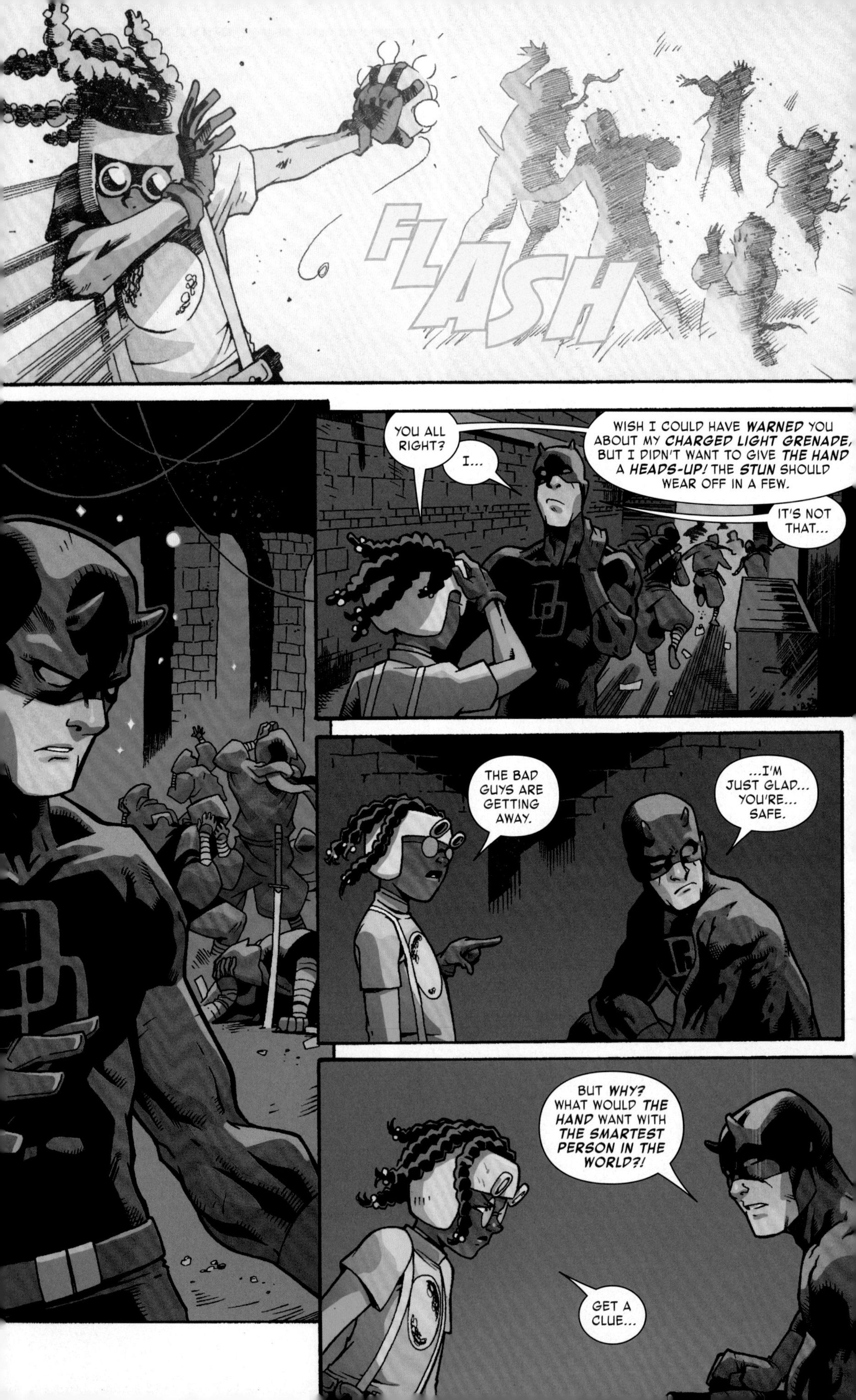
FLASH
YOU ALL RIGHT?
I...
WISH I COULD HAVE WARNED YOU ABOUT MY CHARGED LIGHT GRENADE, BUT I DIDN'T WANT TO GIVE THE HAND A HEADS-UP! THE STUN SHOULD WEAR OFF IN A FEW.
IT'S NOT THAT...
THE BAD GUYS ARE GETTING AWAY.
...I'M JUST GLAD... YOU'RE... SAFE.
BUT WHY? WHAT WOULD THE HAND WANT WITH THE SMARTEST PERSON IN THE WORLD?!
GET A CLUE...

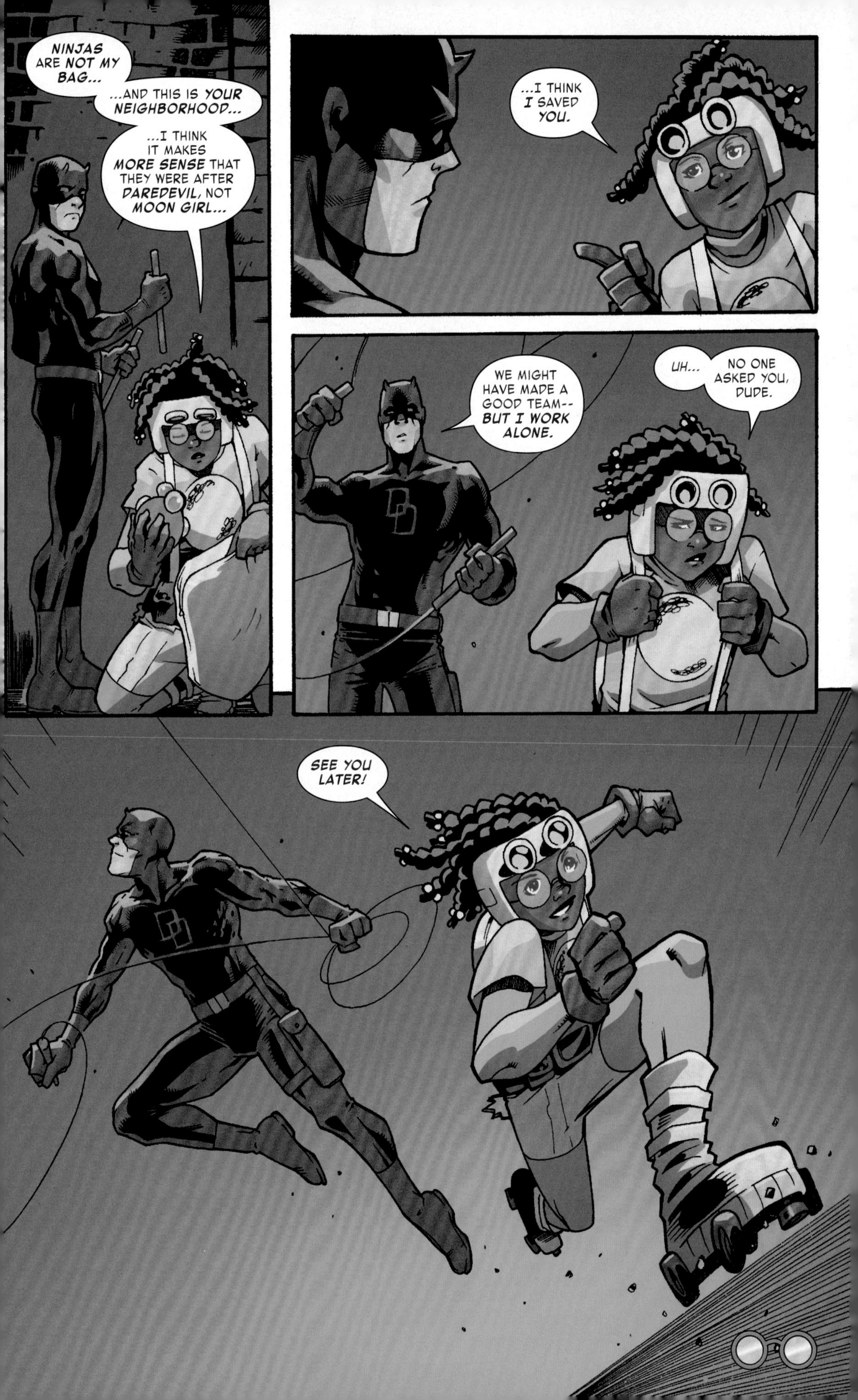
NINJAS ARE NOT MY BAG...
...AND THIS IS YOUR NEIGHBORHOOD...
...I THINK IT MAKES MORE SENSE THAT THEY WERE AFTER DAREDEVIL, NOT MOON GIRL...
...I THINK I SAVED YOU.
WE MIGHT HAVE MADE A GOOD TEAM-- BUT I WORK ALONE.
UH...
NO ONE ASKED YOU, DUDE.
SEE YOU LATER!

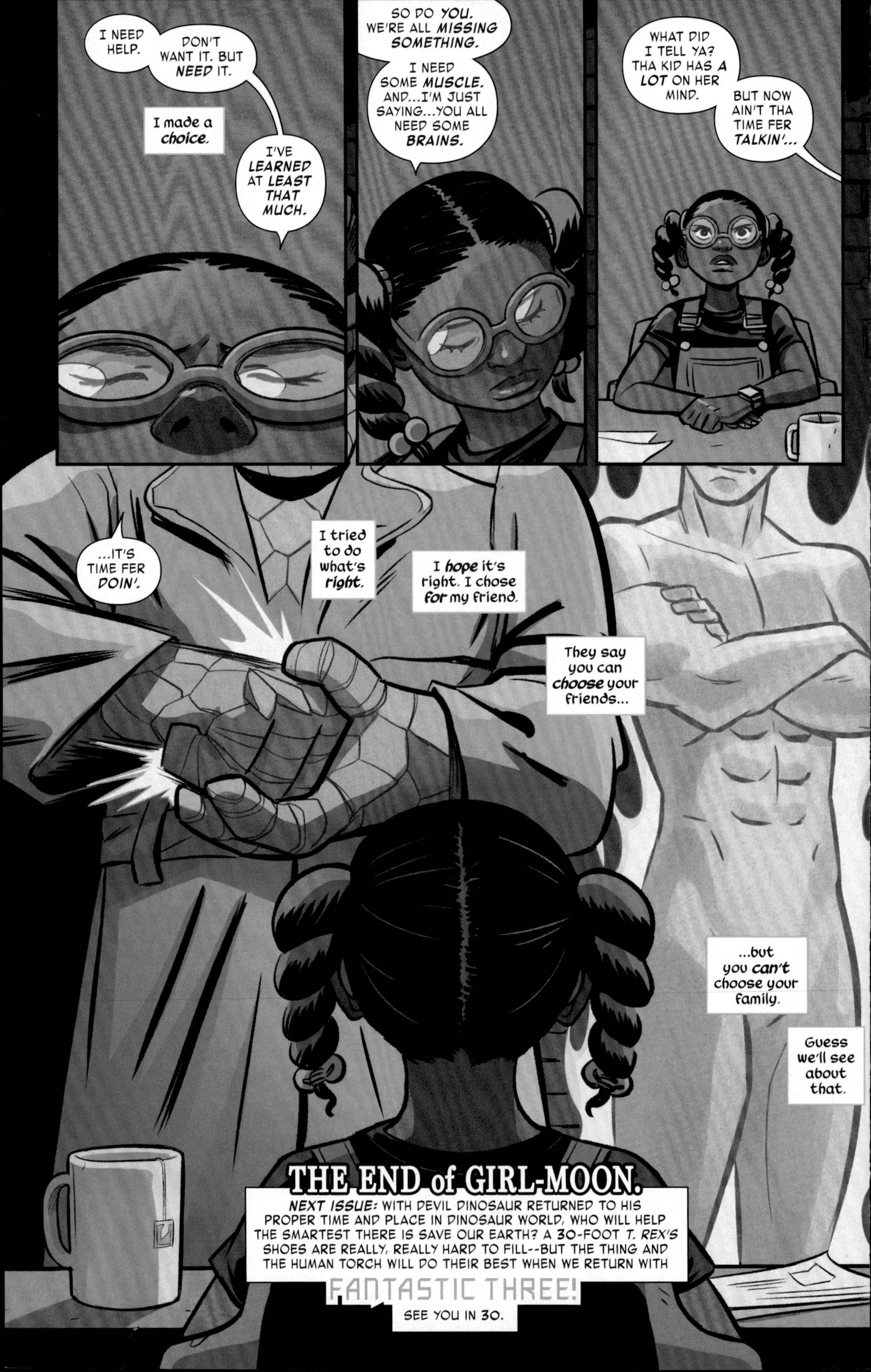

I NEED HELP.
DON'T WANT IT. BUT NEED IT.
I made a choice.
I'VE LEARNED AT LEAST THAT MUCH.
SO DO YOU. WE'RE ALL MISSING SOMETHING.
I NEED SOME MUSCLE. AND...I'M JUST SAYING...YOU ALL NEED SOME BRAINS.
WHAT DID I TELL YA? THA KID HAS A LOT ON HER MIND.
BUT NOW AIN'T THA TIME FER TALKIN'...
...IT'S TIME FER DOIN'.
I tried to do what's right.
I hope it's right. I chose for my friend.
They say you can choose your friends...
...but you can't choose your family.
Guess we'll see about that.
THE END of GIRL-MOON.
NEXT ISSUE: WITH DEVIL DINOSAUR RETURNED TO HIS PROPER TIME AND PLACE IN DINOSAUR WORLD, WHO WILL HELP THE SMARTEST THERE IS SAVE OUR EARTH? A 30-FOOT T. REX'S SHOES ARE REALLY, REALLY HARD TO FILL--BUT THE THING AND THE HUMAN TORCH WILL DO THEIR BEST WHEN WE RETURN WITH
FANTASTIC THREE!
SEE YOU IN 30.

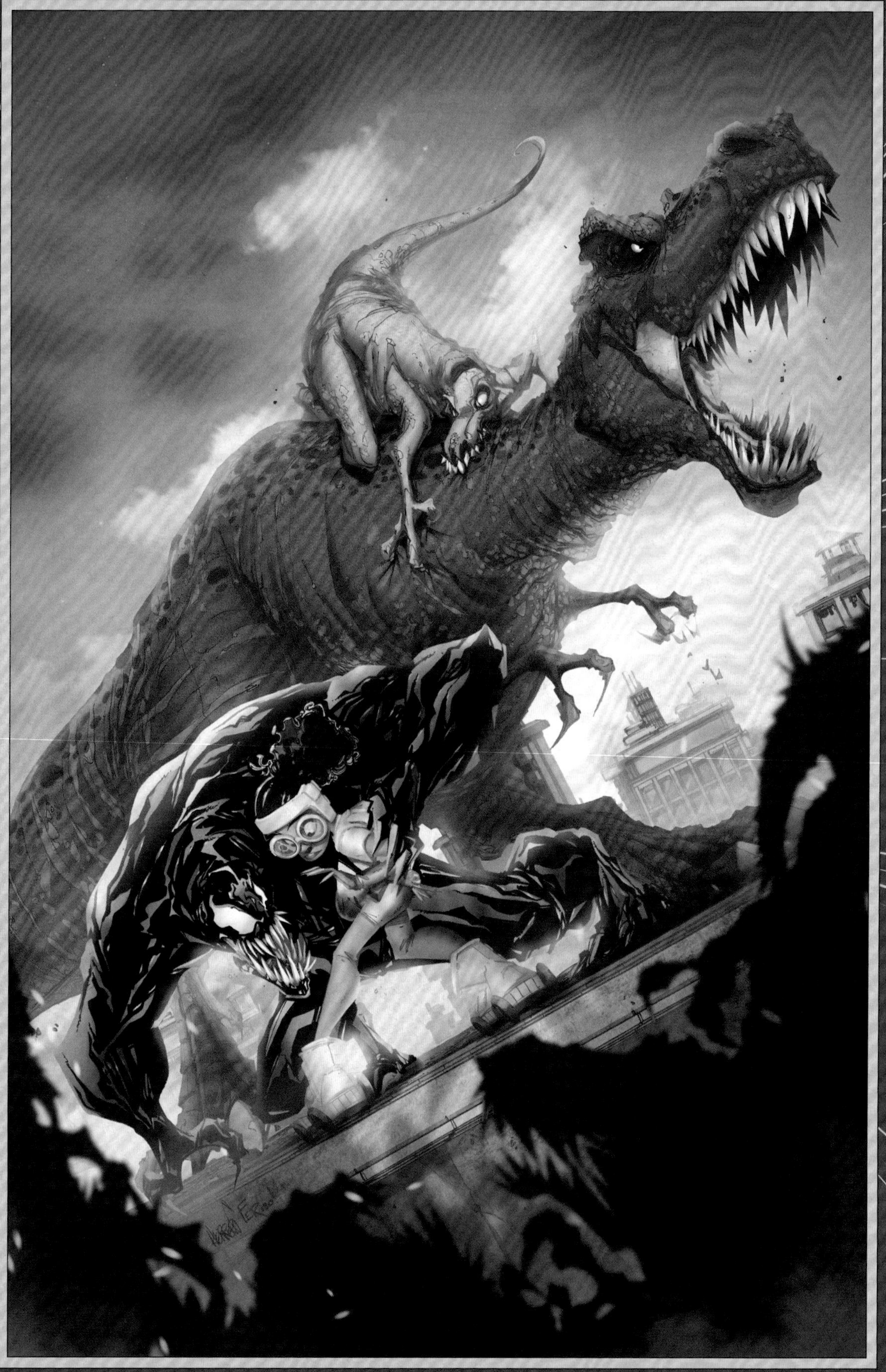

VENOM #153

YEARS AGO, PETER PARKER (A.K.A. THE AMAZING SPIDER-MAN) ACCIDENTALLY BONDED WITH AN ALIEN BEING CALLED A SYMBIOTE. WHEN PETER REALIZED THE COSTUME WAS ACTUALLY AN AGGRESSIVE LIVING ORGANISM, HE REJECTED IT. BUT DURING THEIR TIME TOGETHER, THE SYMBIOTE HAD ACCESS TO SPIDER-MAN'S GENETIC CODE, AND NOW GRANTS WHOMEVER IT BONDS WITH SKILLS SIMILAR TO HIS: WALL-CRAWLING, THE POWER TO GENERATE BIOORGANIC WEBBING, AND UNIQUE ABILITIES TO SHAPE-SHIFT AND BECOME INVISIBLE, TURNING THEM INTO...

VENOM

EDDIE BROCK AND THE VENOM SYMBIOTE HAVE BEEN REUNITED, BUT THE SYMBIOTE IS NOT WELL. AFTER A TIME WITH AN ABUSIVE HOST, IT CANNOT CONTROL ITS VIOLENT IMPULSES AND HAS BEGUN TO HURT INNOCENTS IT PERCEIVES AS A THREAT TO ITS RELATIONSHIP WITH EDDIE.

AFTER A MONSTER ATTACK IN HIS NEIGHBORHOOD, EDDIE FEARED THE SYMBIOTE WAS RESPONSIBLE. AN INVESTIGATION LED HIM TO THE SEWERS, WHERE HE FOUND A HUMANOID DINOSAUR BRANDED WITH THE ALCHEMAX LOGO. EDDIE RETURNED THE CREATURE TO ALCHEMAX'S C.E.O., LIZ ALLAN, WHO REVEALED THAT IT WAS ONCE A HUMAN WHO HAD BEEN SUBJECTED TO EXPERIMENTS BY *STEGRON THE DINOSAUR MAN* WHILE IN THE COMPANY'S CUSTODY.

EDDIE AND LIZ STRUCK A BARGAIN — IN EXCHANGE FOR VENOM'S HELP CAPTURING STEGRON AND THE CREATURES IN THE SEWER, LIZ WILL USE ALCHEMAX'S RESOURCES TO FIND A CURE FOR THE AILING SYMBIOTE.

BUT WHEN HE WENT TO COLLECT STEGRON AND HIS SUBJECTS, VENOM FOUND *MOON GIRL AND DEVIL DINOSAUR* ALREADY ON THE CASE!

THE LAND BEFORE CRIME CONCLUSION

MIKE COSTA
WRITER

GERARDO SANDOVAL
ARTIST

DONO SÁNCHEZ-ALMARA
COLOR ARTIST

VC'S CLAYTON COWLES
LETTERER

FRANCISCO HERRERA & FERNANDA RIZO
COVER ARTISTS

ALLISON STOCK
ASST. EDITOR

DEVIN LEWIS
EDITOR

NICK LOWE
EXECUTIVE EDITOR

AXEL ALONSO
EDITOR IN CHIEF

JOE QUESADA
CHIEF CREATIVE OFFICER

DAN BUCKLEY
PRESIDENT

ALAN FINE
EXEC. PRODUCER

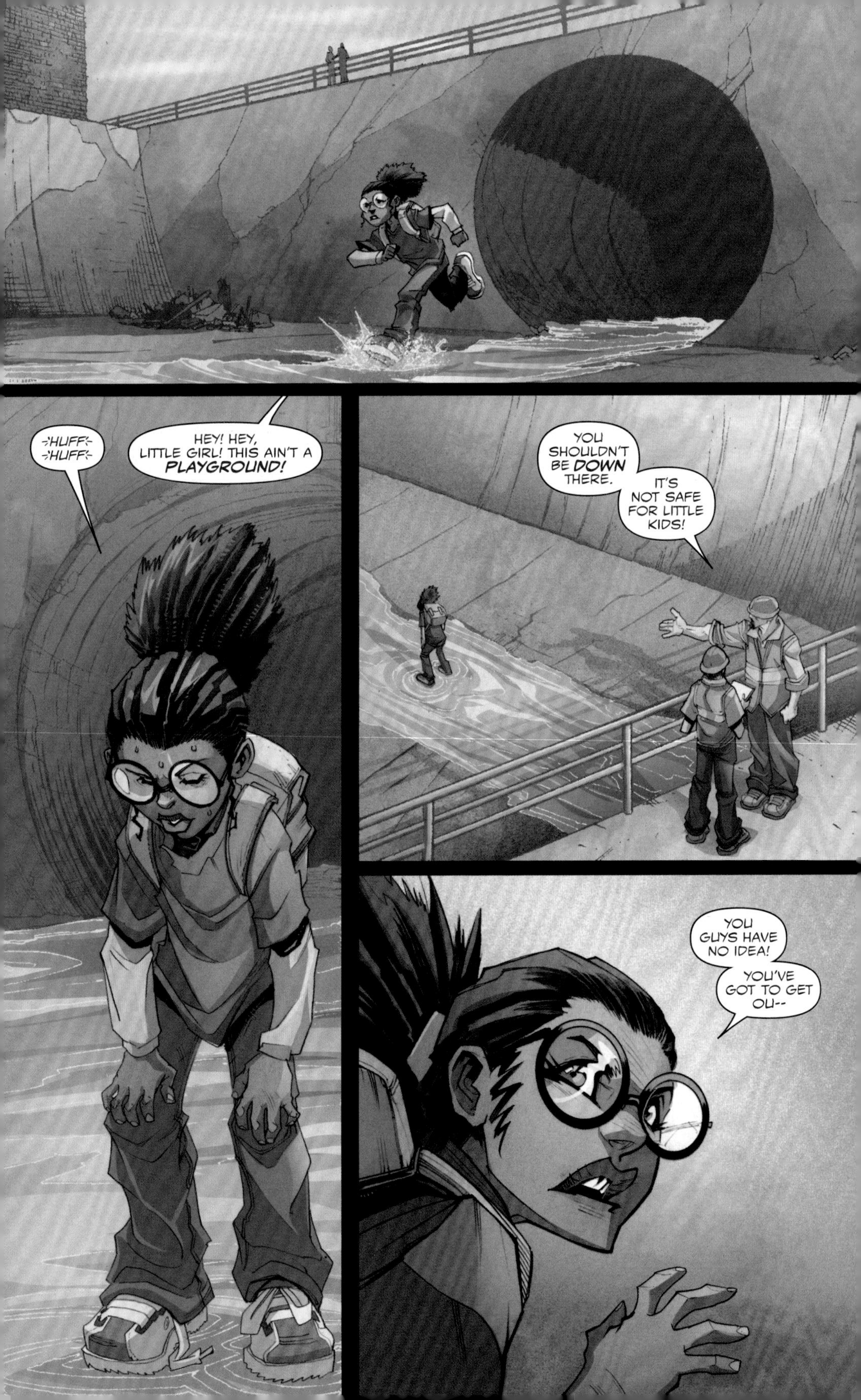

-HUFF-
-HUFF-
HEY! HEY, LITTLE GIRL! THIS AIN'T A PLAYGROUND!
YOU SHOULDN'T BE DOWN THERE.
IT'S NOT SAFE FOR LITTLE KIDS!
YOU GUYS HAVE NO IDEA!
YOU'VE GOT TO GET OU--

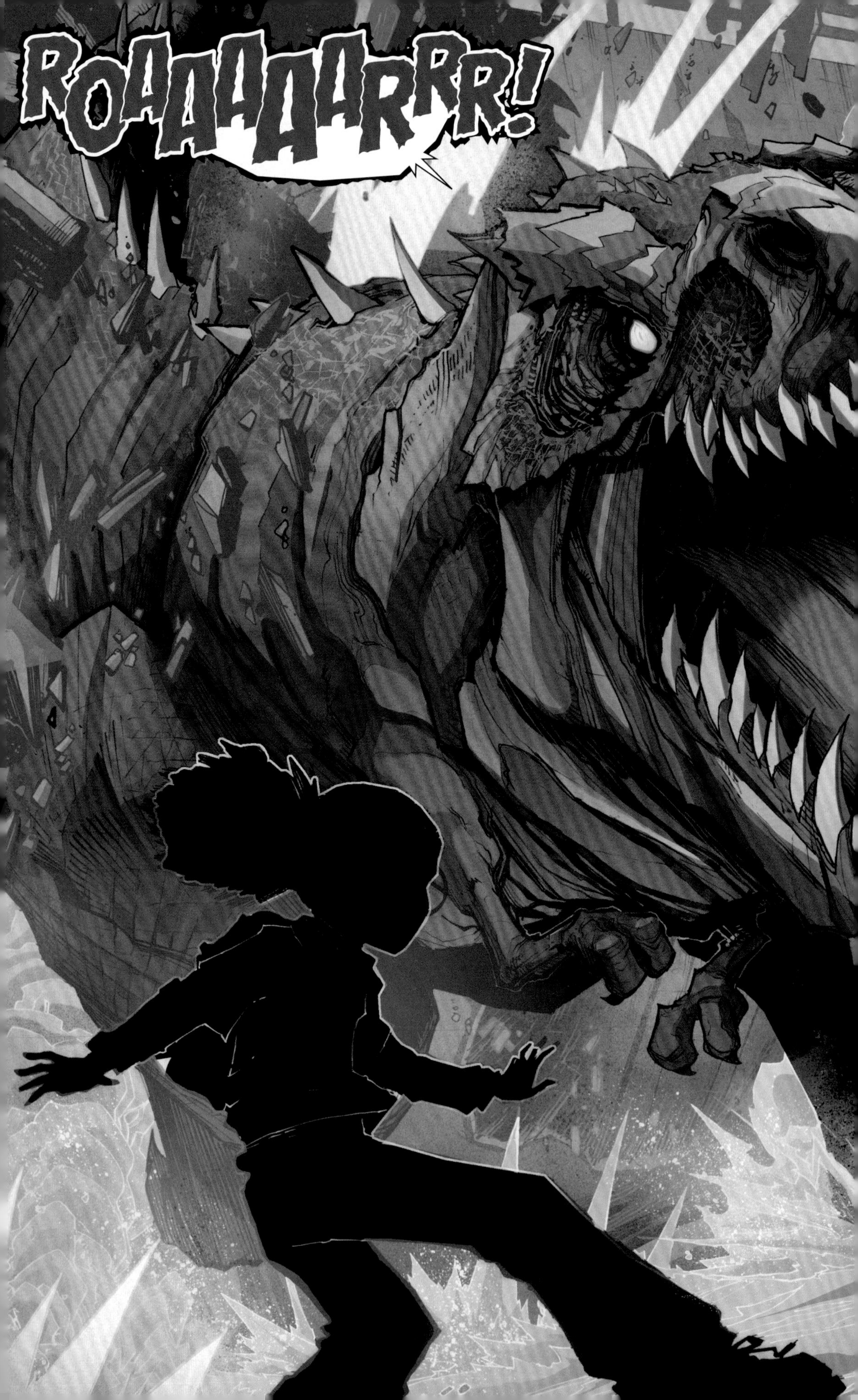
ROAAAAARRR!

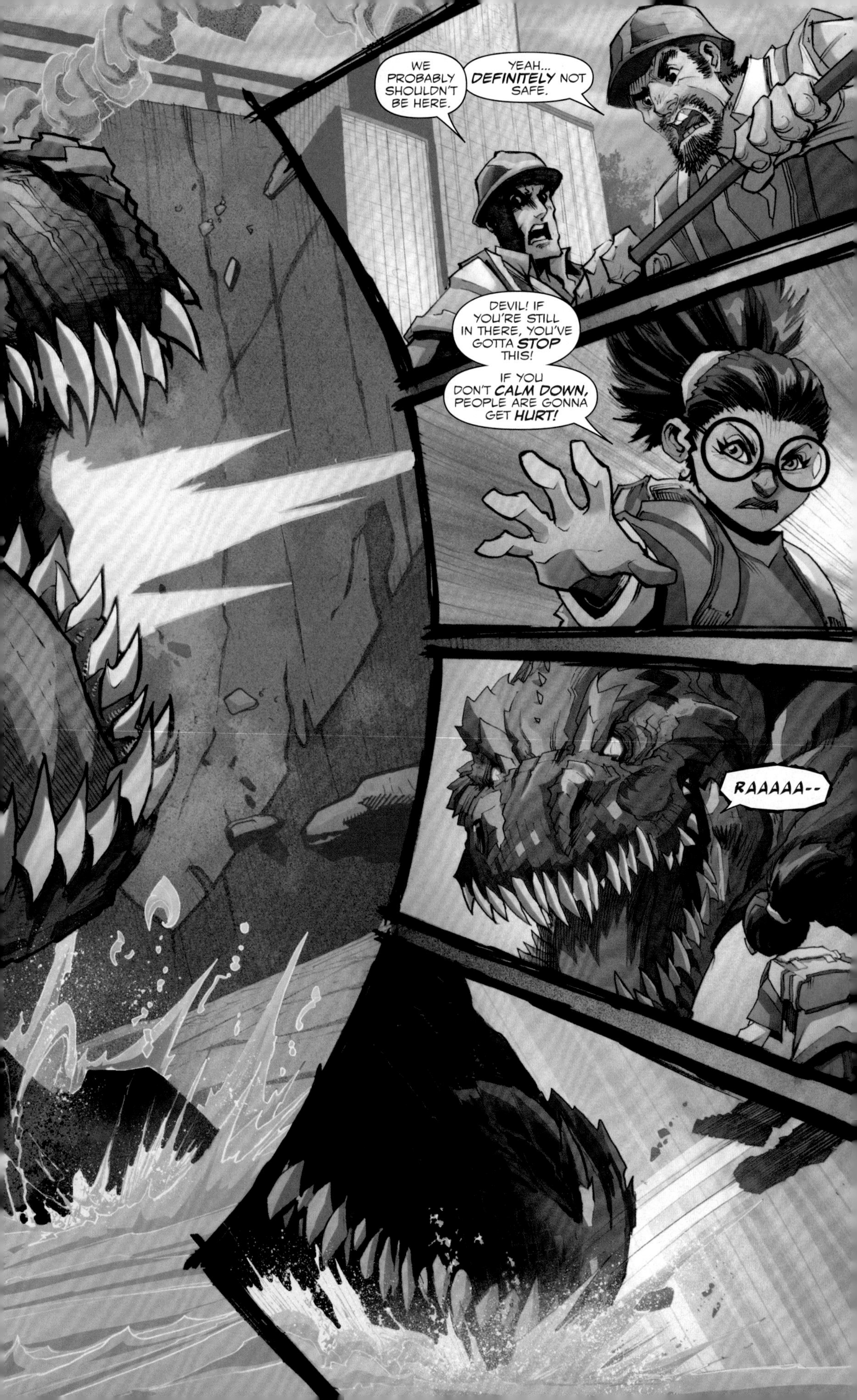

WE PROBABLY SHOULDN'T BE HERE.
YEAH... DEFINITELY NOT SAFE.
DEVIL! IF YOU'RE STILL IN THERE, YOU'VE GOTTA STOP THIS!
IF YOU DON'T CALM DOWN, PEOPLE ARE GONNA GET HURT!
RAAAAA--

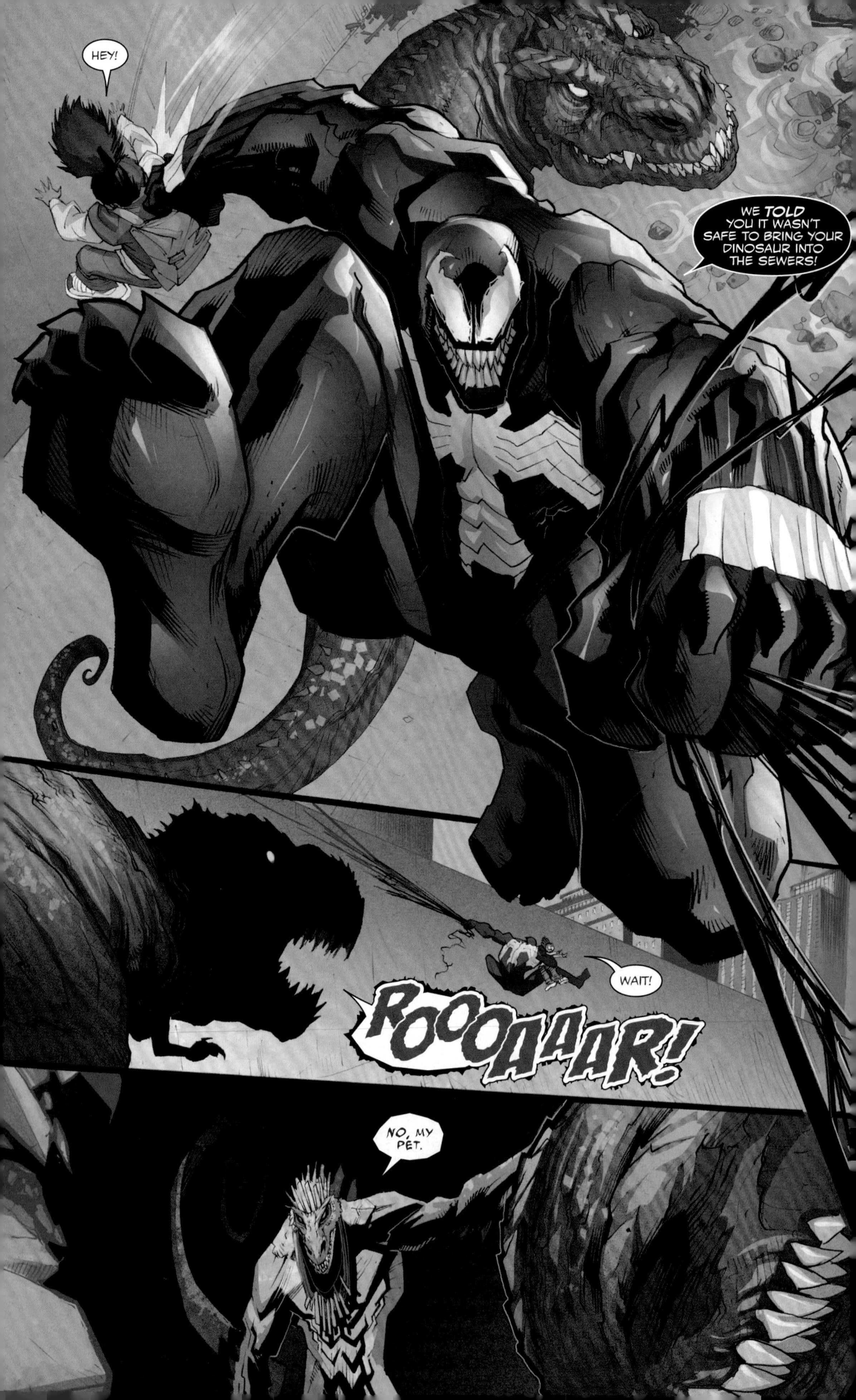
HEY!
WE TOLD YOU IT WASN'T SAFE TO BRING YOUR DINOSAUR INTO THE SEWERS!
WAIT!
ROOOAAAR!
NO, MY PET.

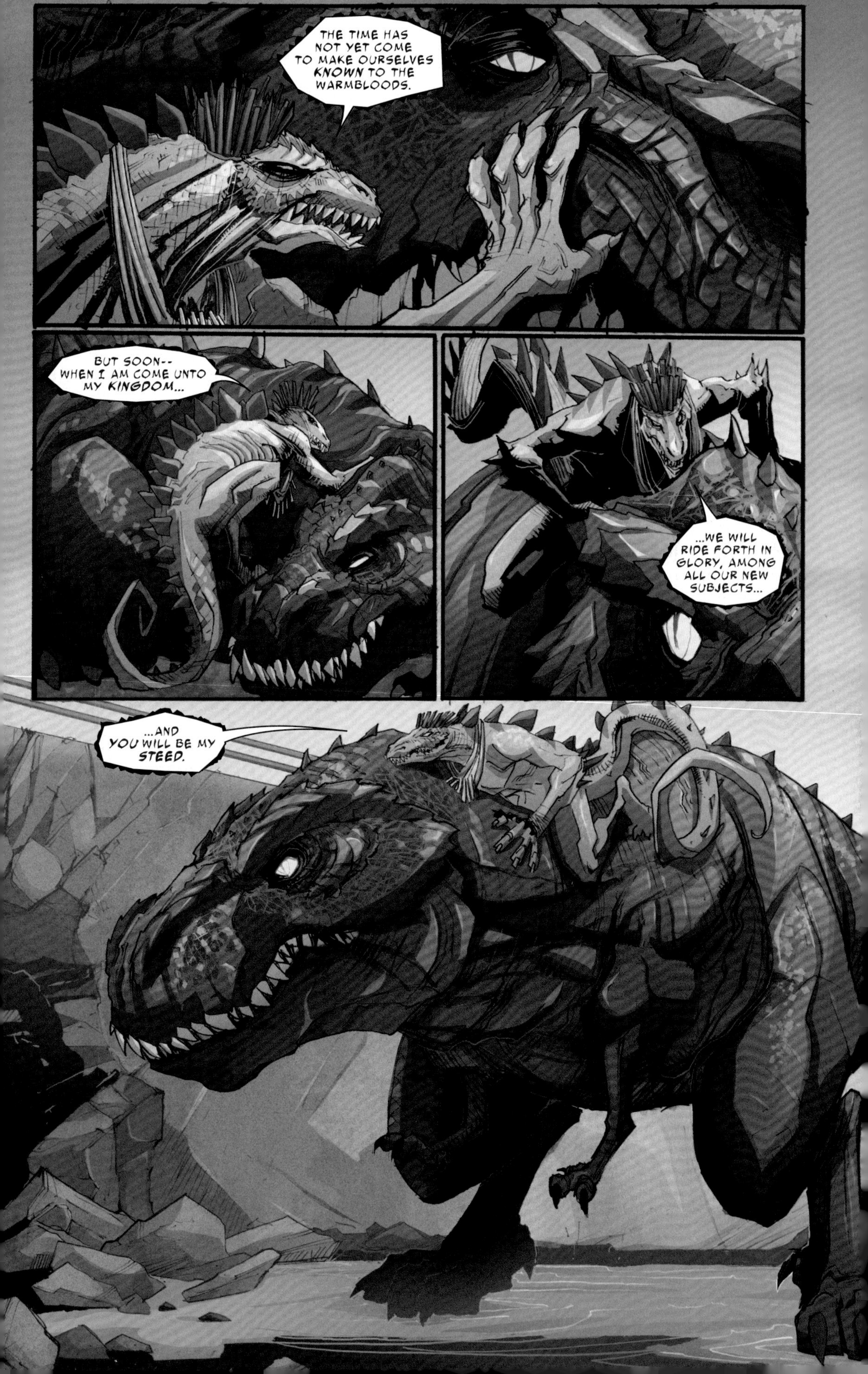
THE TIME HAS NOT YET COME TO MAKE OURSELVES KNOWN TO THE WARMBLOODS.
BUT SOON-- WHEN I AM COME UNTO MY KINGDOM...
...WE WILL RIDE FORTH IN GLORY, AMONG ALL OUR NEW SUBJECTS...
...AND YOU WILL BE MY STEED.

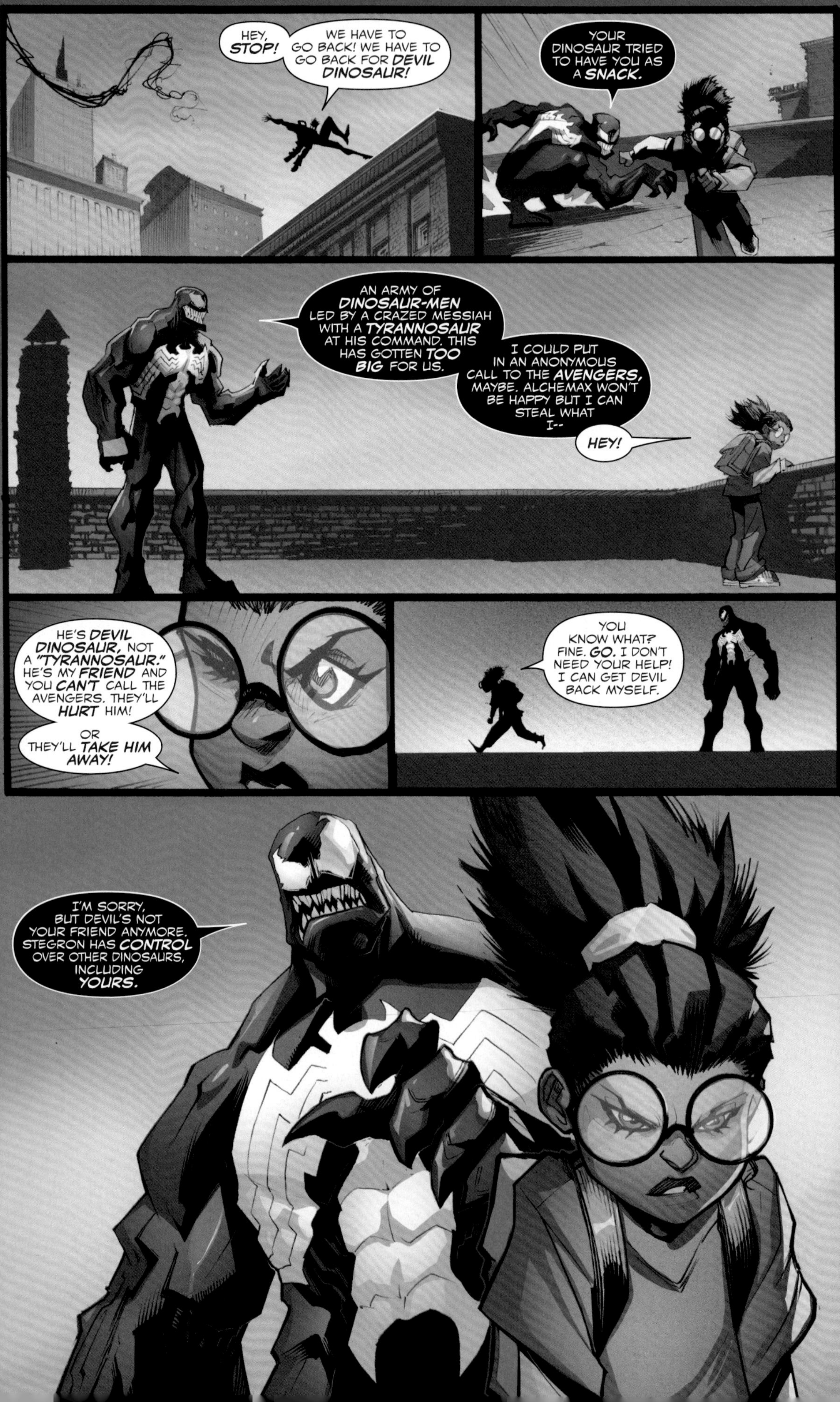

HEY, STOP!
WE HAVE TO GO BACK! WE HAVE TO GO BACK FOR DEVIL DINOSAUR!
YOUR DINOSAUR TRIED TO HAVE YOU AS A SNACK.
AN ARMY OF DINOSAUR-MEN LED BY A CRAZED MESSIAH WITH A TYRANNOSAUR AT HIS COMMAND. THIS HAS GOTTEN TOO BIG FOR US.
I COULD PUT IN AN ANONYMOUS CALL TO THE AVENGERS, MAYBE. ALCHEMAX WON'T BE HAPPY BUT I CAN STEAL WHAT I--
HEY!
HE'S DEVIL DINOSAUR, NOT A "TYRANNOSAUR." HE'S MY FRIEND AND YOU CAN'T CALL THE AVENGERS. THEY'LL HURT HIM!
OR THEY'LL TAKE HIM AWAY!
YOU KNOW WHAT? FINE. GO. I DON'T NEED YOUR HELP! I CAN GET DEVIL BACK MYSELF.
I'M SORRY, BUT DEVIL'S NOT YOUR FRIEND ANYMORE. STEGRON HAS CONTROL OVER OTHER DINOSAURS, INCLUDING YOURS.

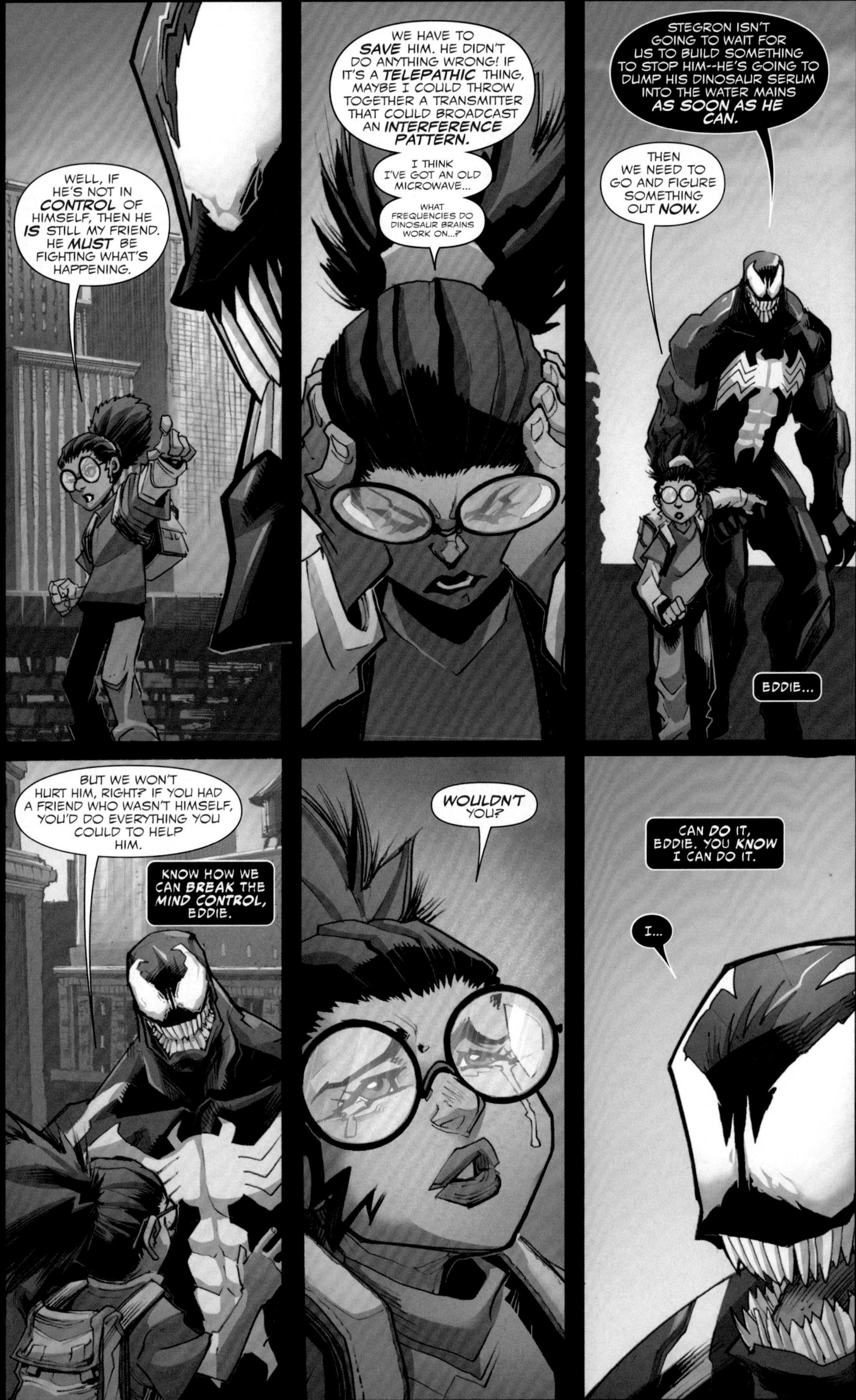
WELL, IF HE'S NOT IN CONTROL OF HIMSELF, THEN HE IS STILL MY FRIEND. HE MUST BE FIGHTING WHAT'S HAPPENING.
WE HAVE TO SAVE HIM. HE DIDN'T DO ANYTHING WRONG! IF IT'S A TELEPATHIC THING, MAYBE I COULD THROW TOGETHER A TRANSMITTER THAT COULD BROADCAST AN INTERFERENCE PATTERN.
I THINK I'VE GOT AN OLD MICROWAVE...
WHAT FREQUENCIES DO DINOSAUR BRAINS WORK ON...?
STEGRON ISN'T GOING TO WAIT FOR US TO BUILD SOMETHING TO STOP HIM--HE'S GOING TO DUMP HIS DINOSAUR SERUM INTO THE WATER MAINS AS SOON AS HE CAN.
THEN WE NEED TO GO AND FIGURE SOMETHING OUT NOW.
EDDIE...
BUT WE WON'T HURT HIM, RIGHT? IF YOU HAD A FRIEND WHO WASN'T HIMSELF, YOU'D DO EVERYTHING YOU COULD TO HELP HIM.
KNOW HOW WE CAN BREAK THE MIND CONTROL, EDDIE.
WOULDN'T YOU?
CAN DO IT, EDDIE. YOU KNOW I CAN DO IT.
I...

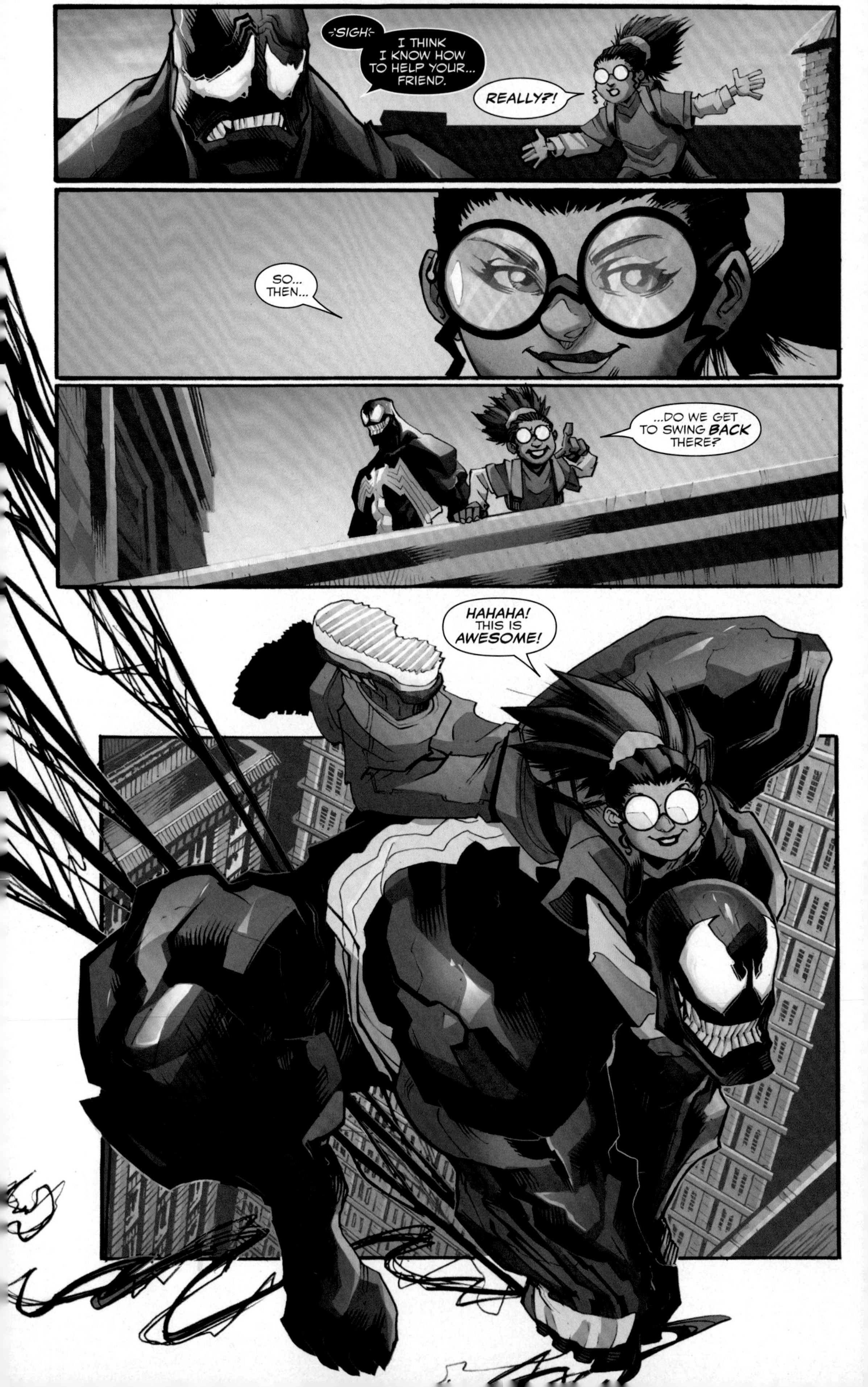
-SIGH-
I THINK I KNOW HOW TO HELP YOUR... FRIEND.
REALLY?!
SO... THEN...
...DO WE GET TO SWING BACK THERE?
HAHAHA! THIS IS AWESOME!

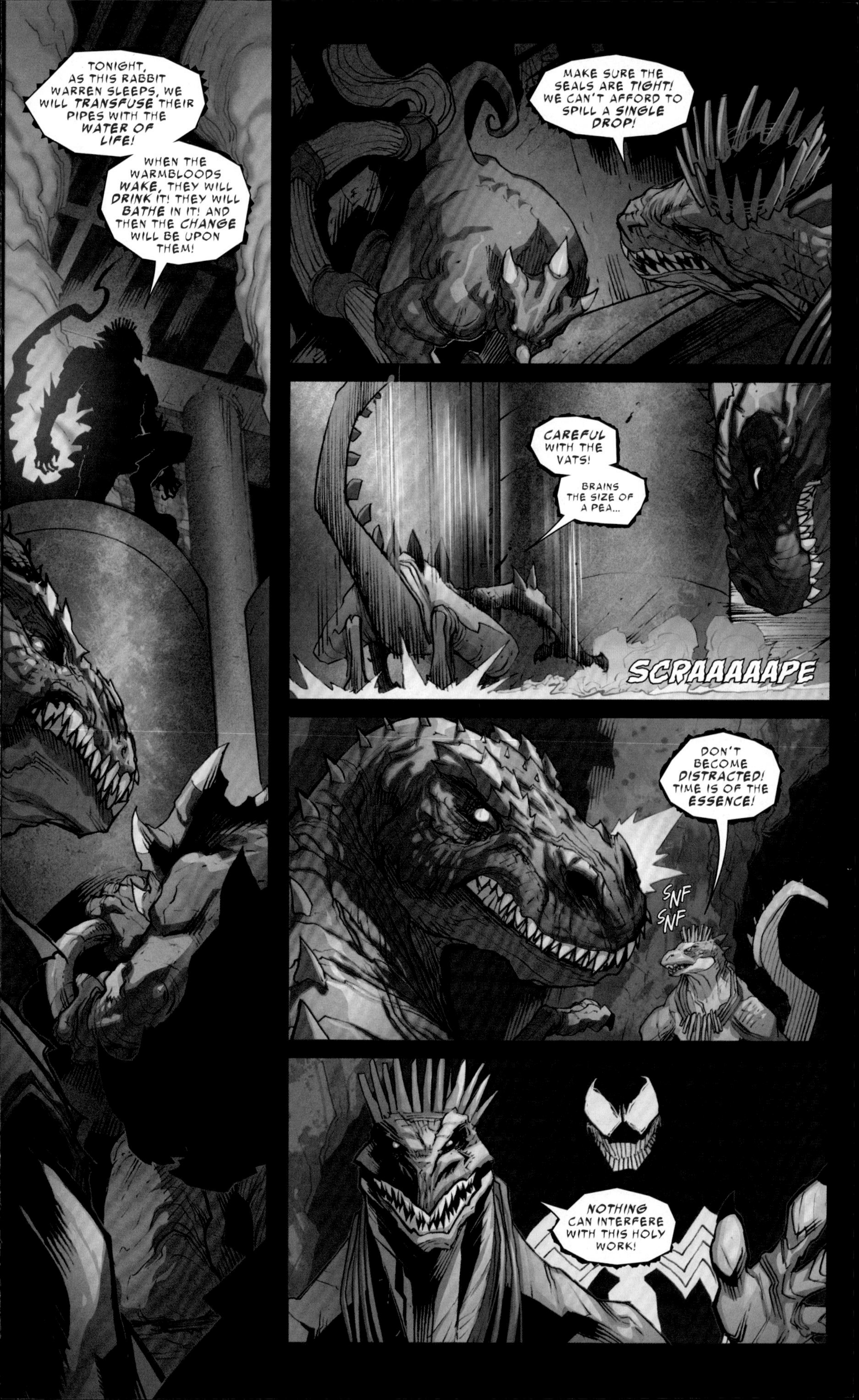

TONIGHT, AS THIS RABBIT WARREN SLEEPS, WE WILL TRANSFUSE THEIR PIPES WITH THE WATER OF LIFE!
WHEN THE WARMBLOODS WAKE, THEY WILL DRINK IT! THEY WILL BATHE IN IT! AND THEN THE CHANGE WILL BE UPON THEM!
MAKE SURE THE SEALS ARE TIGHT! WE CAN'T AFFORD TO SPILL A SINGLE DROP!
CAREFUL WITH THE VATS!
BRAINS THE SIZE OF A PEA...
SCRAAAAAAPE
DON'T BECOME DISTRACTED! TIME IS OF THE ESSENCE!
SNF SNF
NOTHING CAN INTERFERE WITH THIS HOLY WORK!

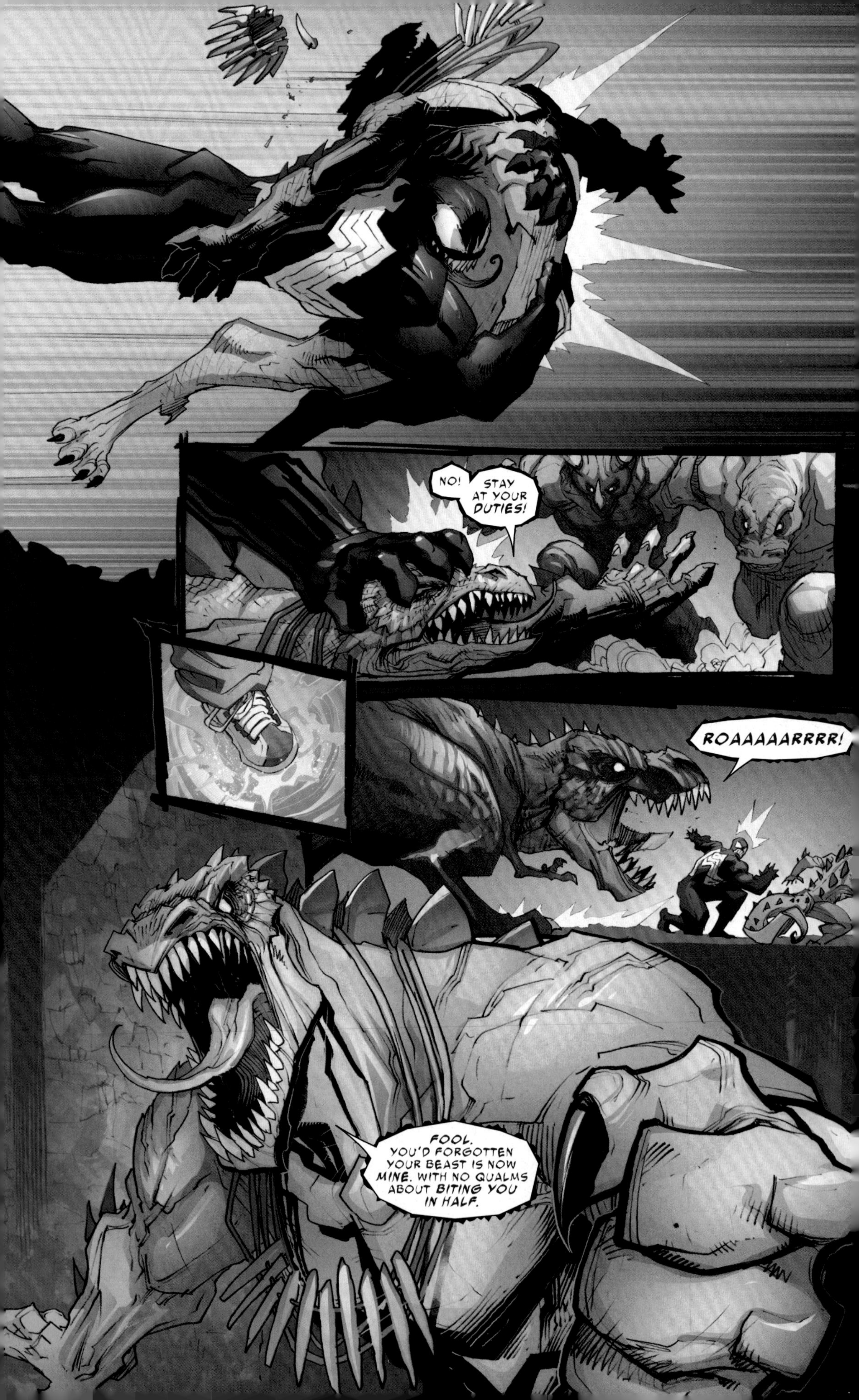
NO!
STAY AT YOUR DUTIES!
ROAAAAARRRR!
FOOL. YOU'D FORGOTTEN YOUR BEAST IS NOW MINE. WITH NO QUALMS ABOUT BITING YOU IN HALF.

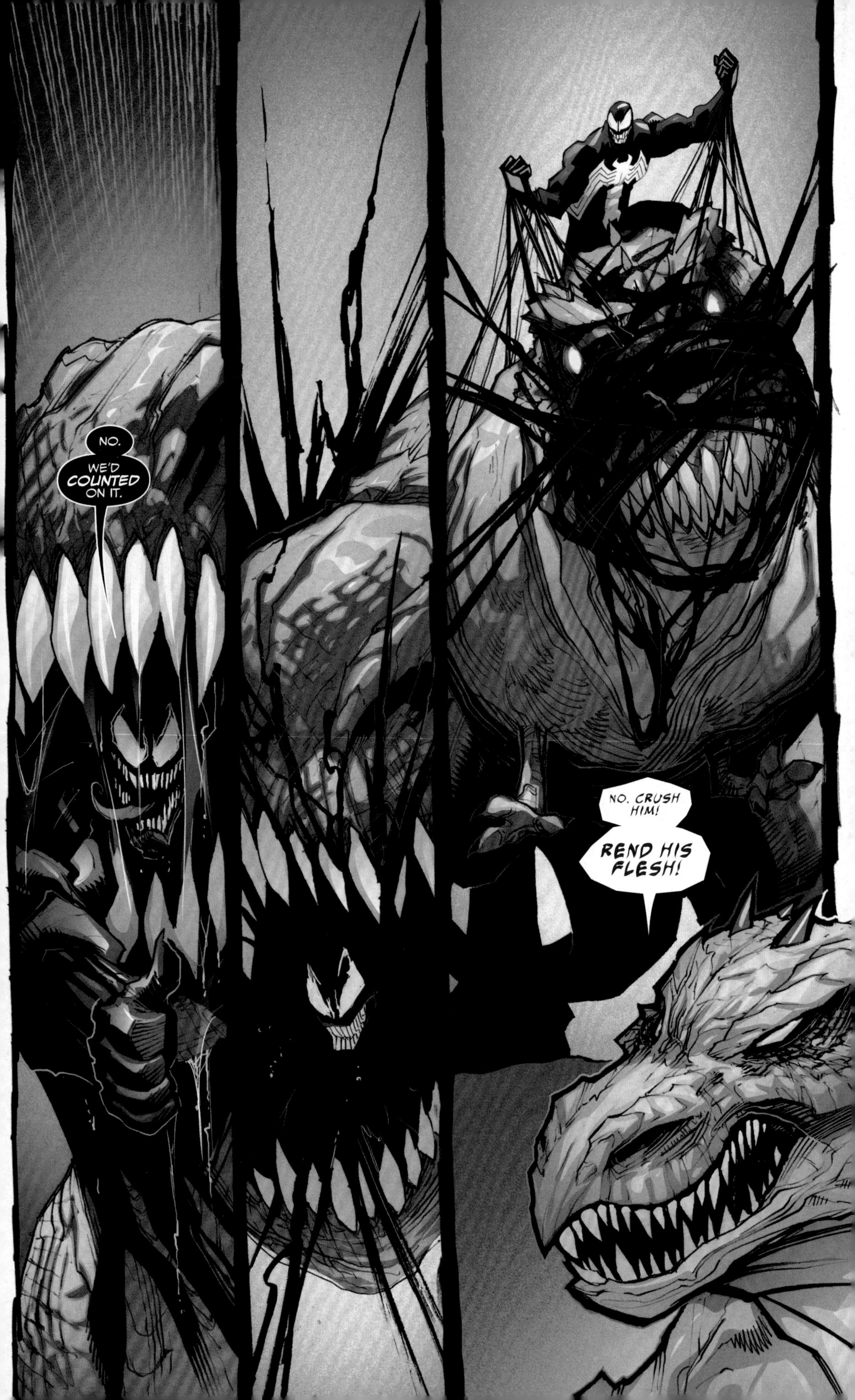
NO.
WE'D COUNTED ON IT.
NO. CRUSH HIM!
REND HIS FLESH!

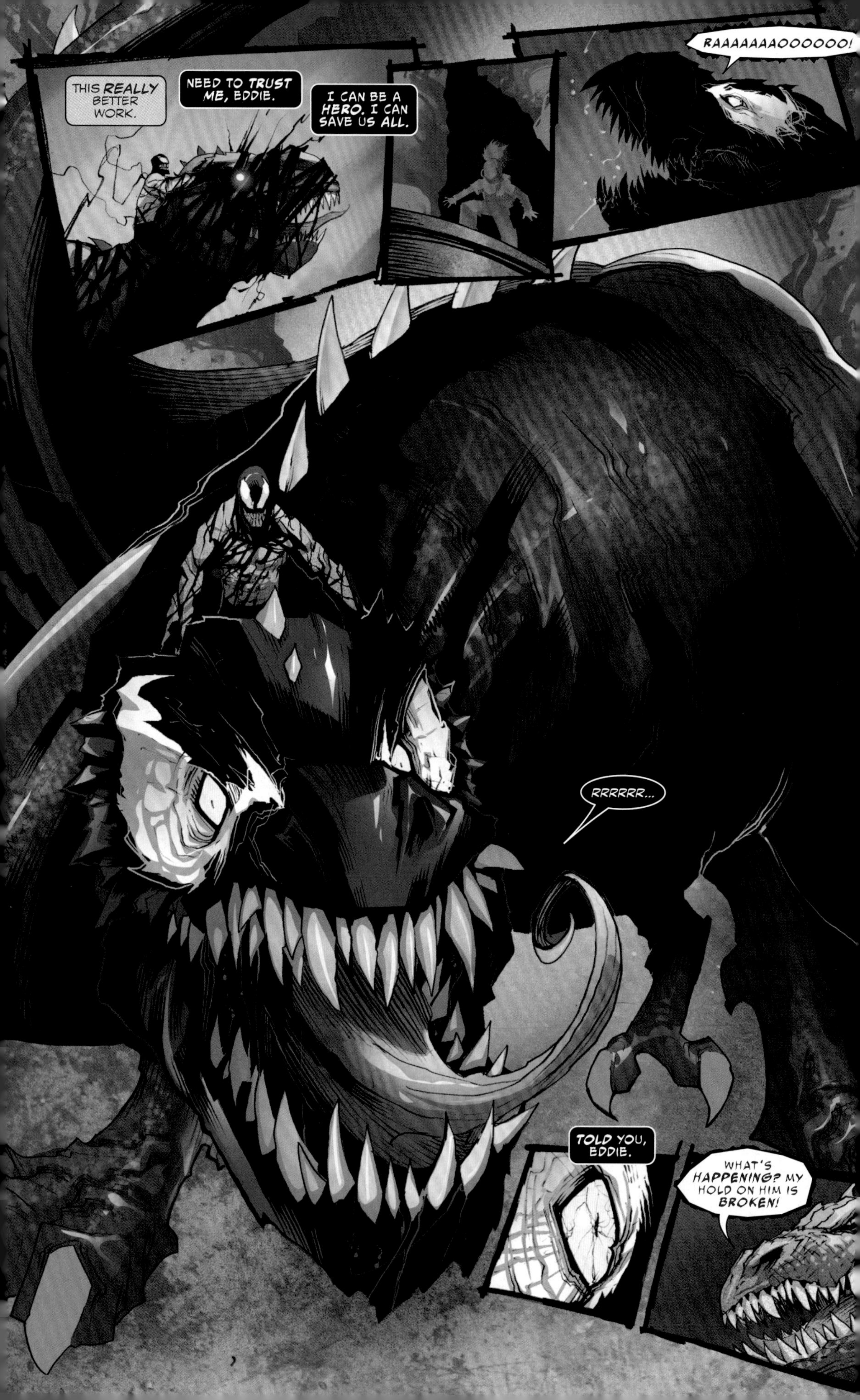
THIS REALLY BETTER WORK.
NEED TO TRUST ME, EDDIE.
I CAN BE A HERO. I CAN SAVE US ALL.
RAAAAAAAOOOOOO!
RRRRRR...
TOLD YOU, EDDIE.
WHAT'S HAPPENING? MY HOLD ON HIM IS BROKEN!

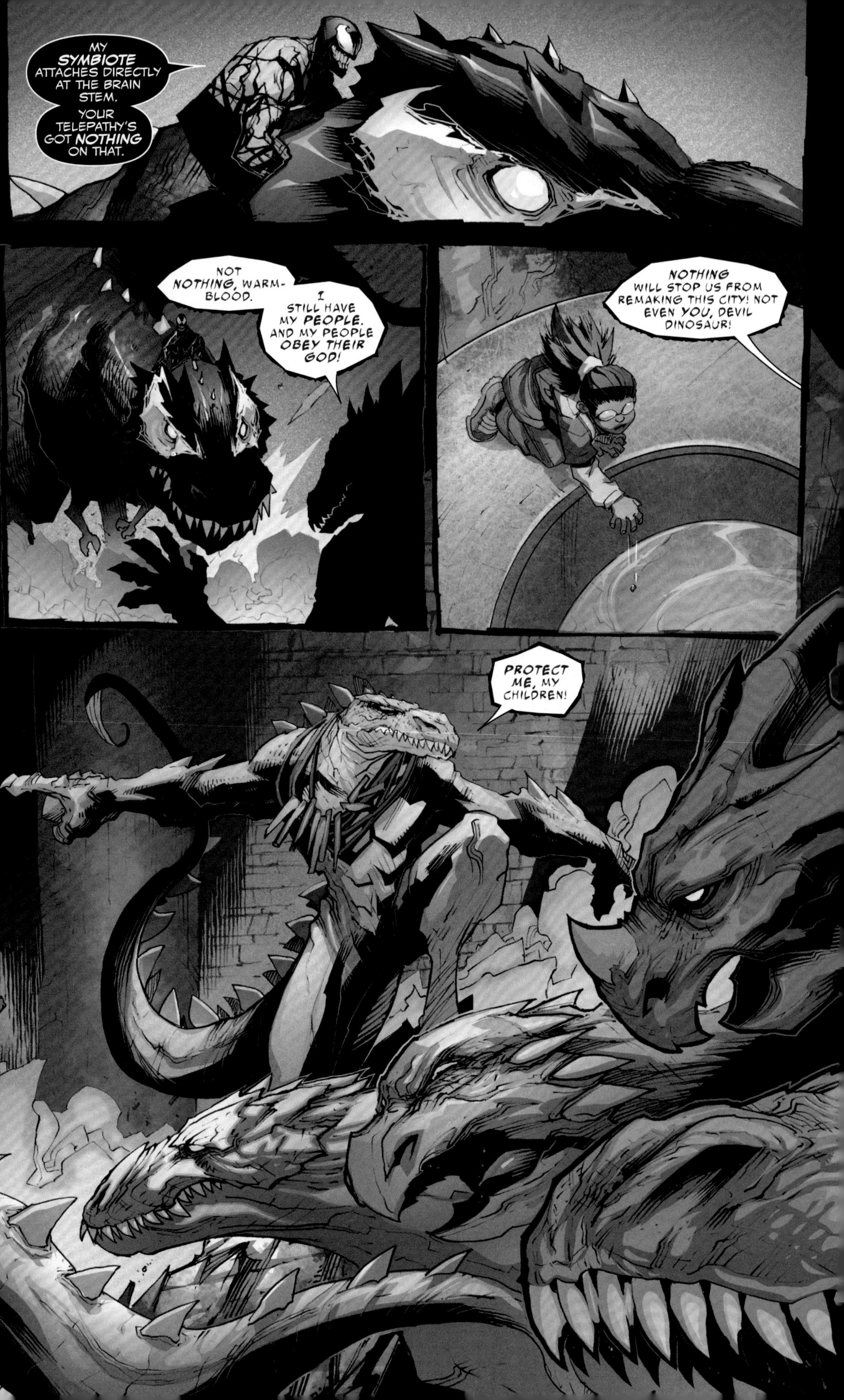
MY SYMBIOTE ATTACHES DIRECTLY AT THE BRAIN STEM.
YOUR TELEPATHY'S GOT NOTHING ON THAT.
NOT NOTHING, WARM-BLOOD.
I STILL HAVE MY PEOPLE. AND MY PEOPLE OBEY THEIR GOD!
NOTHING WILL STOP US FROM REMAKING THIS CITY! NOT EVEN YOU, DEVIL DINOSAUR!
PROTECT ME, MY CHILDREN!

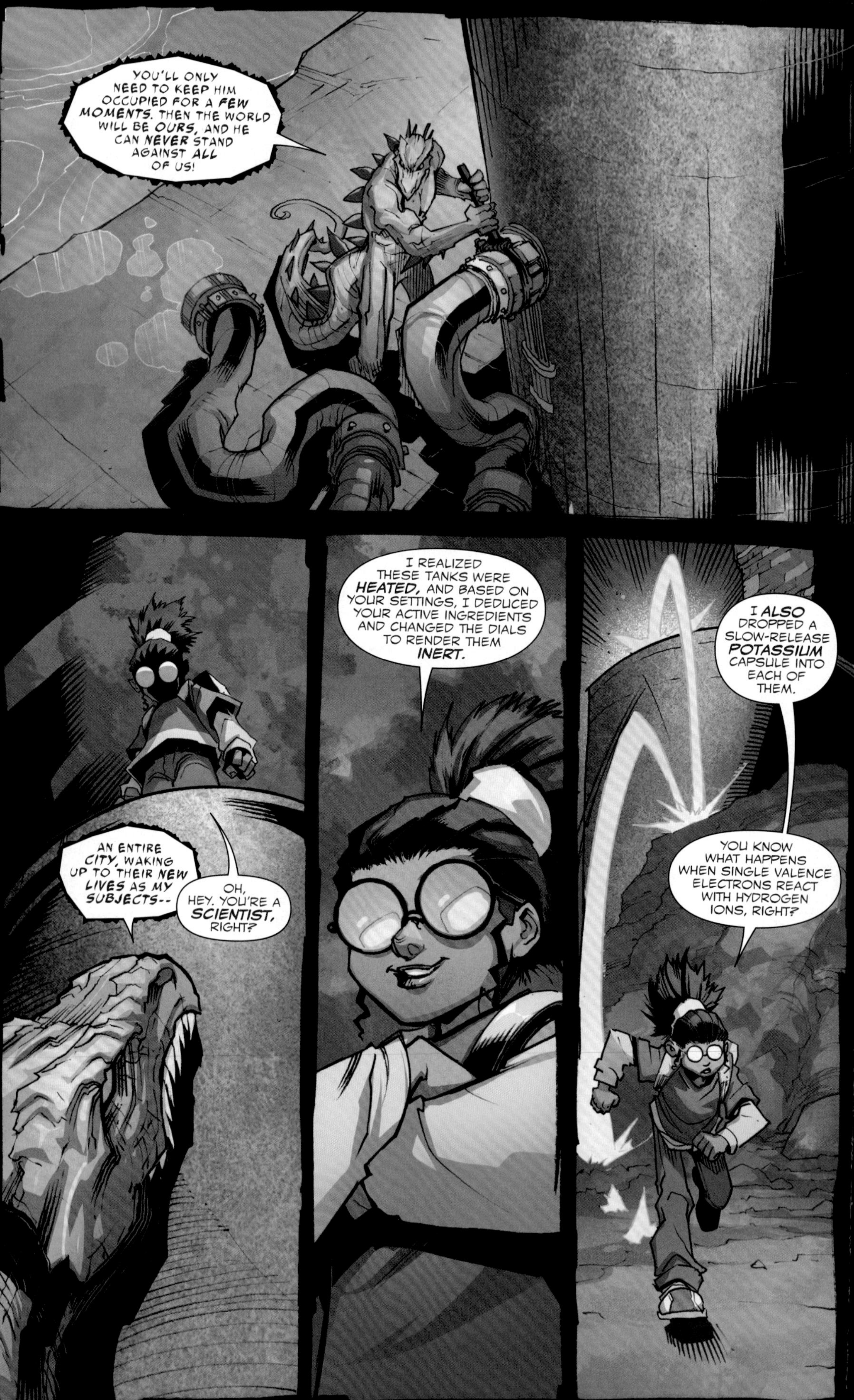
YOU'LL ONLY NEED TO KEEP HIM OCCUPIED FOR A FEW MOMENTS. THEN THE WORLD WILL BE OURS, AND HE CAN NEVER STAND AGAINST ALL OF US!
AN ENTIRE CITY, WAKING UP TO THEIR NEW LIVES AS MY SUBJECTS--
OH, HEY. YOU'RE A SCIENTIST, RIGHT?
I REALIZED THESE TANKS WERE HEATED, AND BASED ON YOUR SETTINGS, I DEDUCED YOUR ACTIVE INGREDIENTS AND CHANGED THE DIALS TO RENDER THEM INERT.
I ALSO DROPPED A SLOW-RELEASE POTASSIUM CAPSULE INTO EACH OF THEM.
YOU KNOW WHAT HAPPENS WHEN SINGLE VALENCE ELECTRONS REACT WITH HYDROGEN IONS, RIGHT?

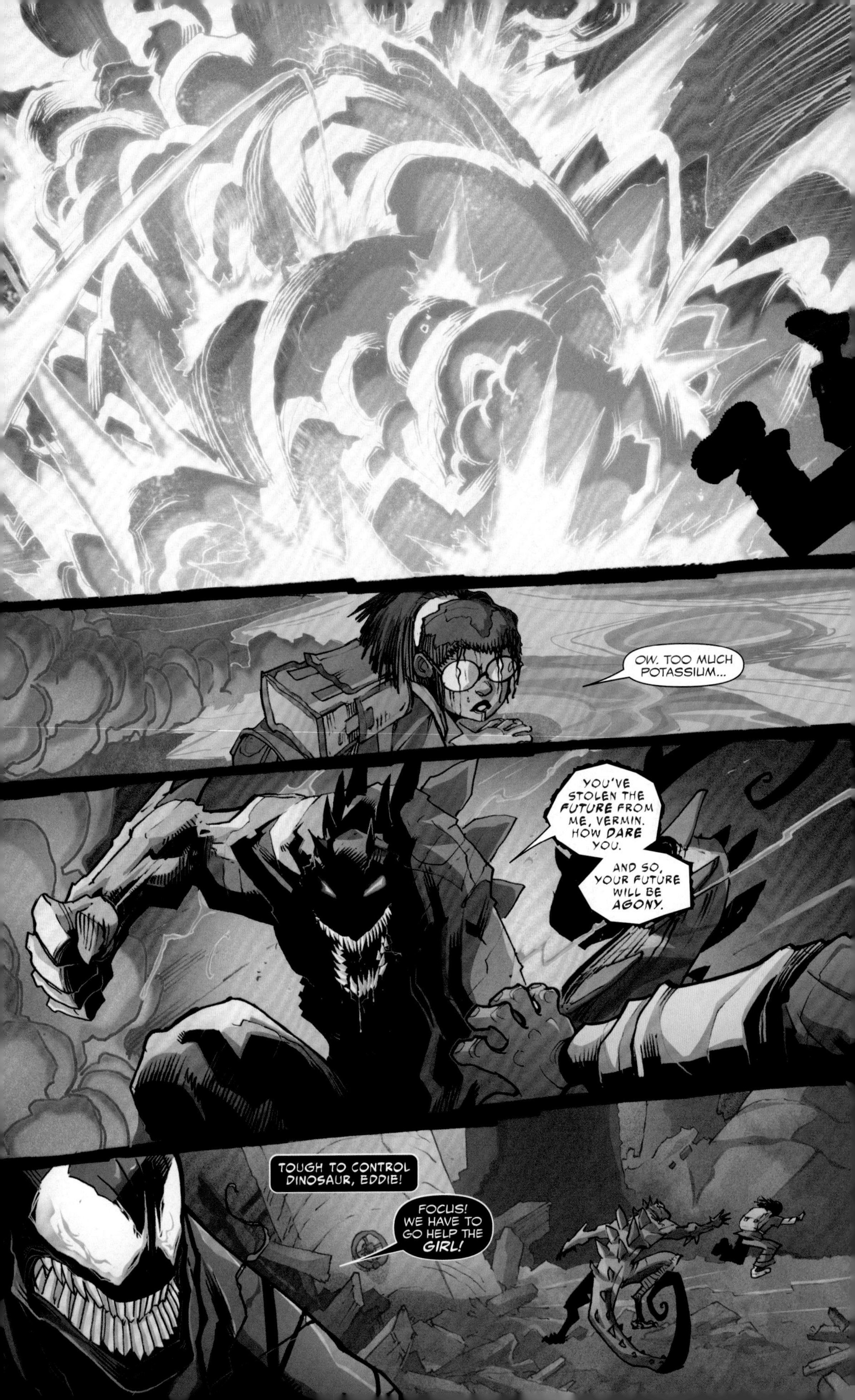
OW. TOO MUCH POTASSIUM...
YOU'VE STOLEN THE FUTURE FROM ME, VERMIN. HOW DARE YOU.
AND SO, YOUR FUTURE WILL BE AGONY.
TOUGH TO CONTROL DINOSAUR, EDDIE!
FOCUS! WE HAVE TO GO HELP THE GIRL!

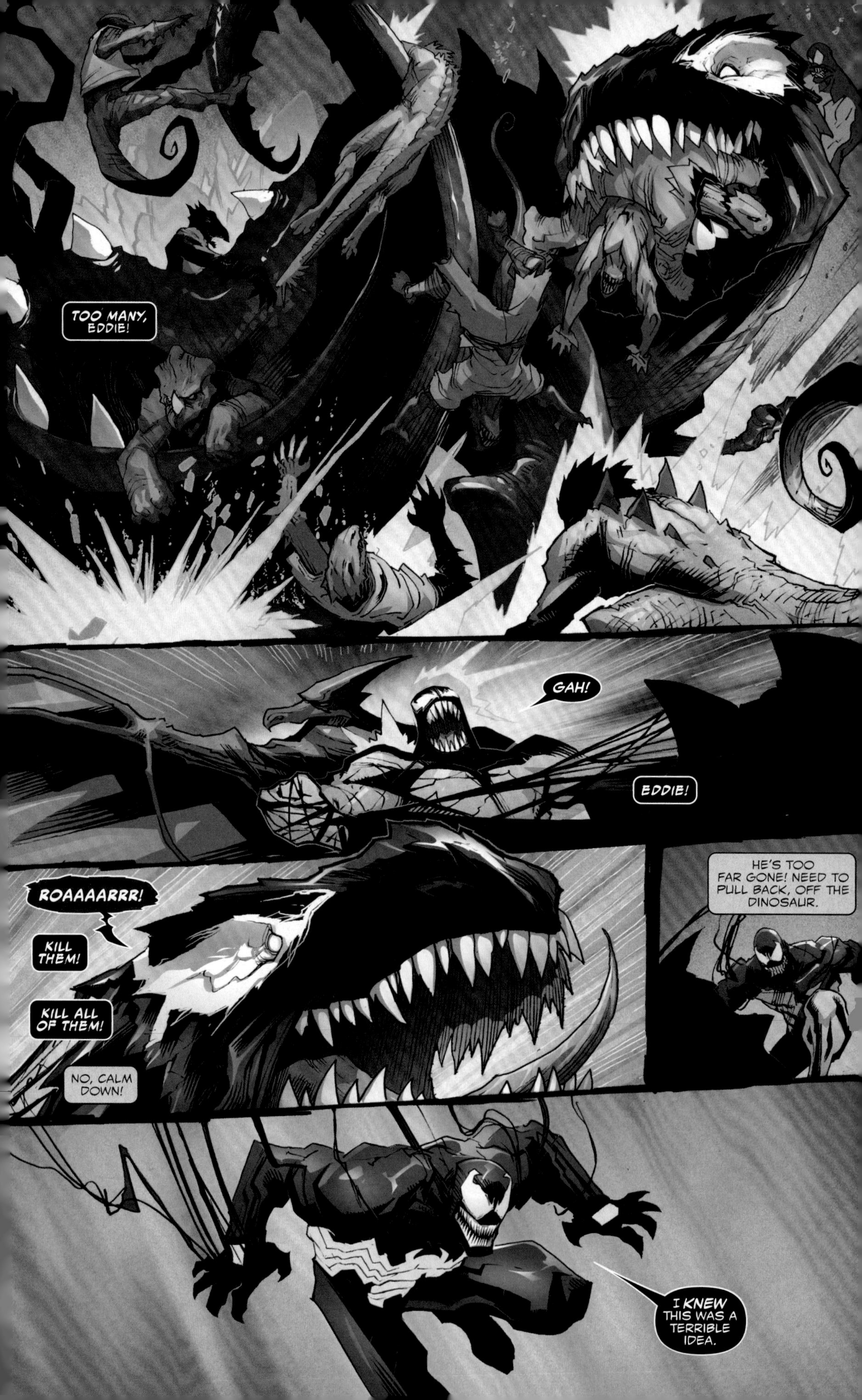
TOO MANY, EDDIE!
GAH!
EDDIE!
ROAAAARRR!
KILL THEM!
KILL ALL OF THEM!
NO, CALM DOWN!
HE'S TOO FAR GONE! NEED TO PULL BACK, OFF THE DINOSAUR.
I KNEW THIS WAS A TERRIBLE IDEA.

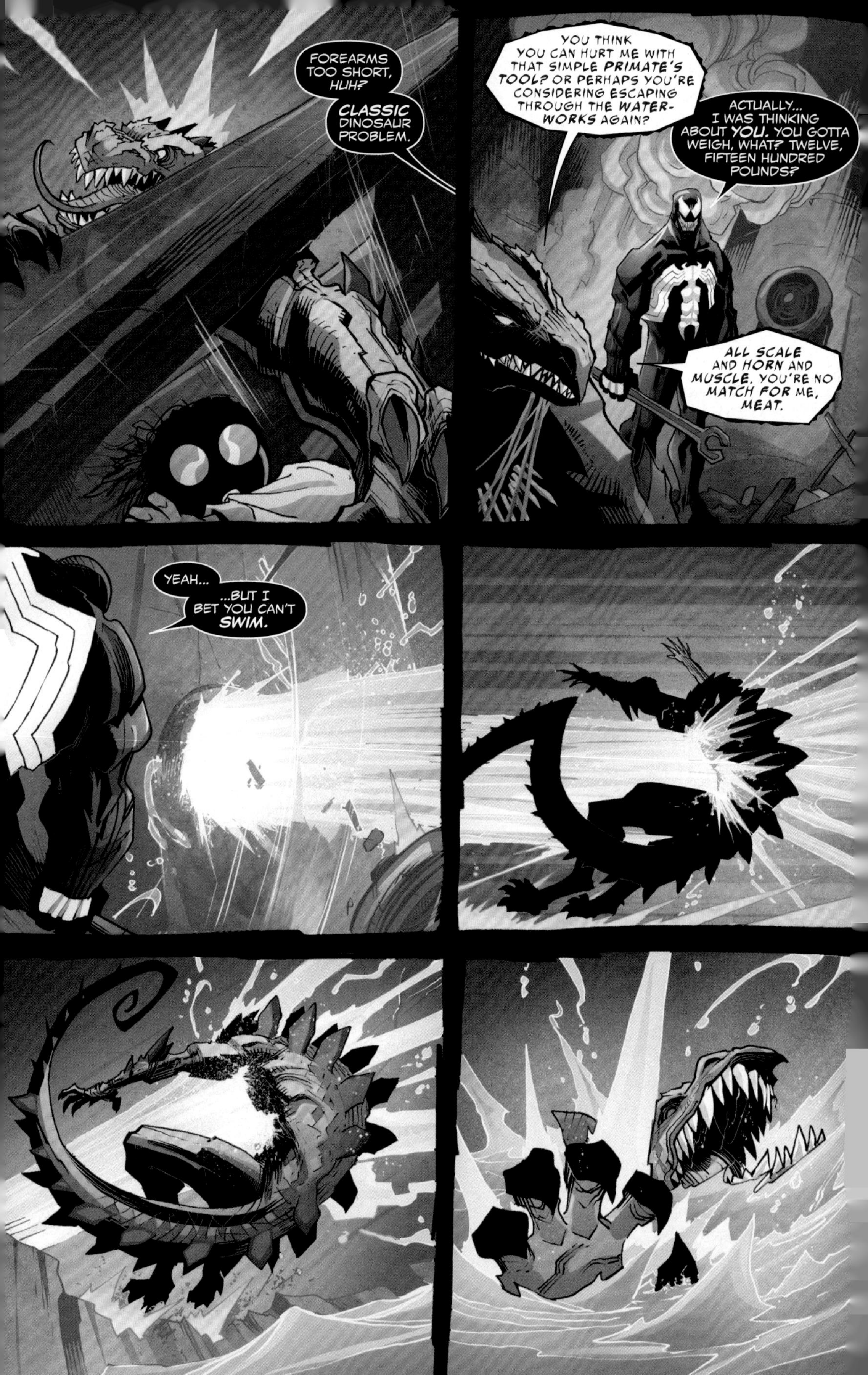
FOREARMS TOO SHORT, HUH?
CLASSIC DINOSAUR PROBLEM.
YOU THINK YOU CAN HURT ME WITH THAT SIMPLE PRIMATE'S TOOL? OR PERHAPS YOU'RE CONSIDERING ESCAPING THROUGH THE WATER-WORKS AGAIN?
ACTUALLY... I WAS THINKING ABOUT YOU. YOU GOTTA WEIGH, WHAT? TWELVE, FIFTEEN HUNDRED POUNDS?
ALL SCALE AND HORN AND MUSCLE. YOU'RE NO MATCH FOR ME, MEAT.
YEAH...
...BUT I BET YOU CAN'T SWIM.

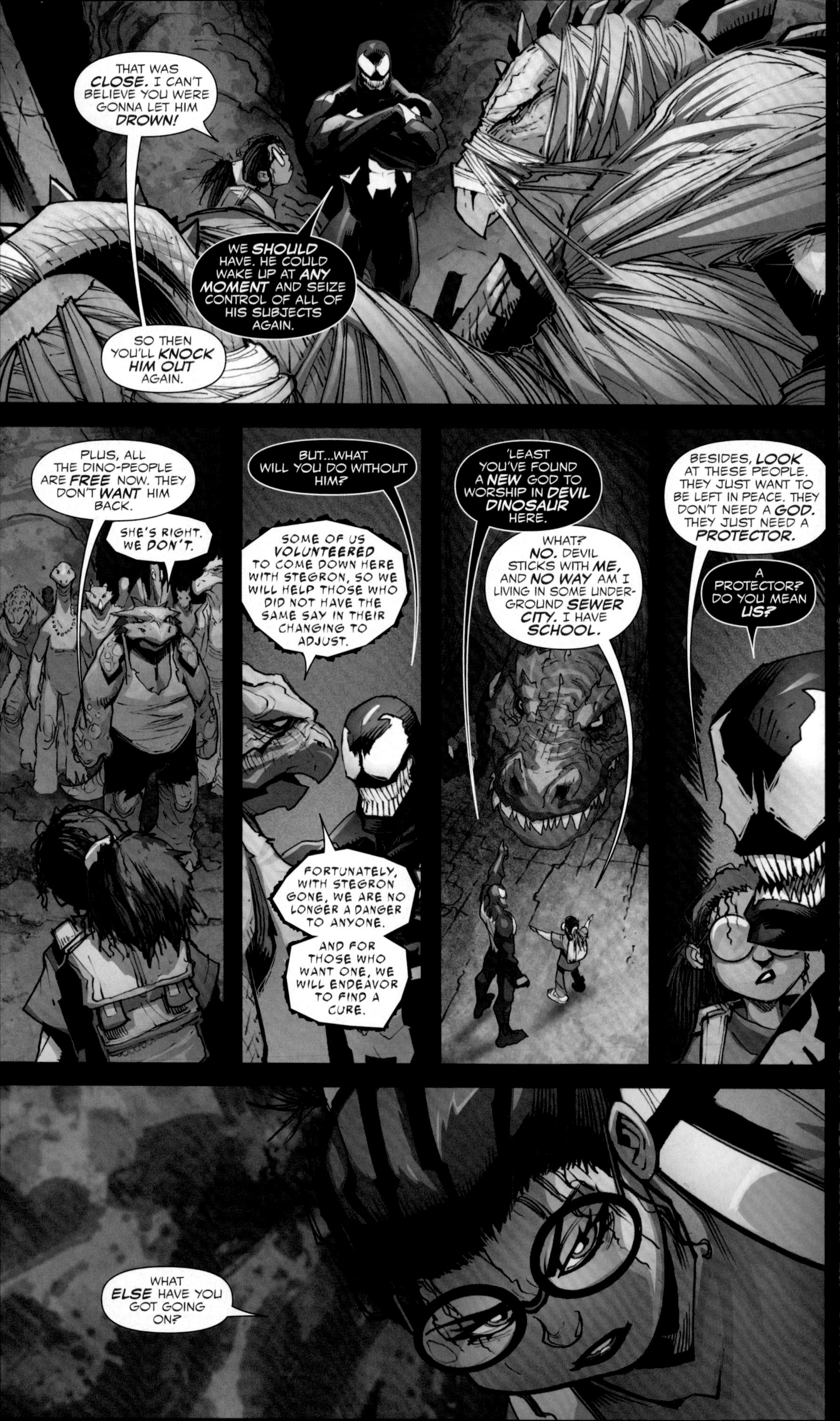
THAT WAS CLOSE. I CAN'T BELIEVE YOU WERE GONNA LET HIM DROWN!
WE SHOULD HAVE. HE COULD WAKE UP AT ANY MOMENT AND SEIZE CONTROL OF ALL OF HIS SUBJECTS AGAIN.
SO THEN YOU'LL KNOCK HIM OUT AGAIN.
PLUS, ALL THE DINO-PEOPLE ARE FREE NOW. THEY DON'T WANT HIM BACK.
SHE'S RIGHT. WE DON'T.
BUT...WHAT WILL YOU DO WITHOUT HIM?
SOME OF US VOLUNTEERED TO COME DOWN HERE WITH STEGRON, SO WE WILL HELP THOSE WHO DID NOT HAVE THE SAME SAY IN THEIR CHANGING TO ADJUST.
FORTUNATELY, WITH STEGRON GONE, WE ARE NO LONGER A DANGER TO ANYONE.
AND FOR THOSE WHO WANT ONE, WE WILL ENDEAVOR TO FIND A CURE.
'LEAST YOU'VE FOUND A NEW GOD TO WORSHIP IN DEVIL DINOSAUR HERE.
WHAT? NO. DEVIL STICKS WITH ME, AND NO WAY AM I LIVING IN SOME UNDER-GROUND SEWER CITY. I HAVE SCHOOL.
BESIDES, LOOK AT THESE PEOPLE. THEY JUST WANT TO BE LEFT IN PEACE. THEY DON'T NEED A GOD. THEY JUST NEED A PROTECTOR.
A PROTECTOR? DO YOU MEAN US?
WHAT ELSE HAVE YOU GOT GOING ON?

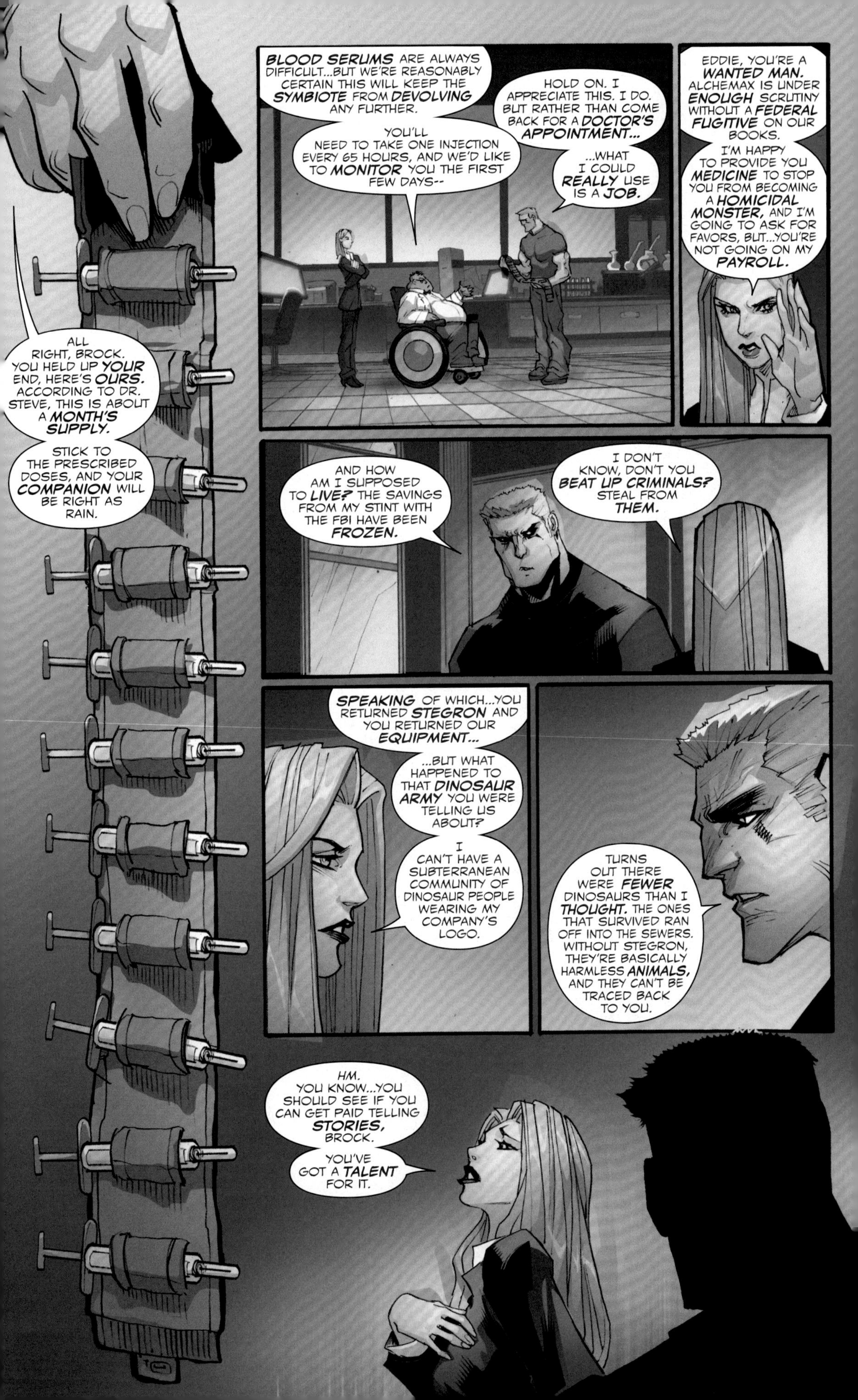

BLOOD SERUMS ARE ALWAYS DIFFICULT...BUT WE'RE REASONABLY CERTAIN THIS WILL KEEP THE SYMBIOTE FROM DEVOLVING ANY FURTHER.
YOU'LL NEED TO TAKE ONE INJECTION EVERY 65 HOURS, AND WE'D LIKE TO MONITOR YOU THE FIRST FEW DAYS--
HOLD ON. I APPRECIATE THIS. I DO. BUT RATHER THAN COME BACK FOR A DOCTOR'S APPOINTMENT...
...WHAT I COULD REALLY USE IS A JOB.
EDDIE, YOU'RE A WANTED MAN. ALCHEMAX IS UNDER ENOUGH SCRUTINY WITHOUT A FEDERAL FUGITIVE ON OUR BOOKS.
I'M HAPPY TO PROVIDE YOU MEDICINE TO STOP YOU FROM BECOMING A HOMICIDAL MONSTER, AND I'M GOING TO ASK FOR FAVORS, BUT...YOU'RE NOT GOING ON MY PAYROLL.
AND HOW AM I SUPPOSED TO LIVE? THE SAVINGS FROM MY STINT WITH THE FBI HAVE BEEN FROZEN.
I DON'T KNOW, DON'T YOU BEAT UP CRIMINALS? STEAL FROM THEM.
SPEAKING OF WHICH...YOU RETURNED STEGRON AND YOU RETURNED OUR EQUIPMENT...
...BUT WHAT HAPPENED TO THAT DINOSAUR ARMY YOU WERE TELLING US ABOUT?
I CAN'T HAVE A SUBTERRANEAN COMMUNITY OF DINOSAUR PEOPLE WEARING MY COMPANY'S LOGO.
TURNS OUT THERE WERE FEWER DINOSAURS THAN I THOUGHT. THE ONES THAT SURVIVED RAN OFF INTO THE SEWERS. WITHOUT STEGRON, THEY'RE BASICALLY HARMLESS ANIMALS, AND THEY CAN'T BE TRACED BACK TO YOU.
ALL RIGHT, BROCK. YOU HELD UP YOUR END, HERE'S OURS. ACCORDING TO DR. STEVE, THIS IS ABOUT A MONTH'S SUPPLY.
STICK TO THE PRESCRIBED DOSES, AND YOUR COMPANION WILL BE RIGHT AS RAIN.
HM. YOU KNOW...YOU SHOULD SEE IF YOU CAN GET PAID TELLING STORIES, BROCK.
YOU'VE GOT A TALENT FOR IT.

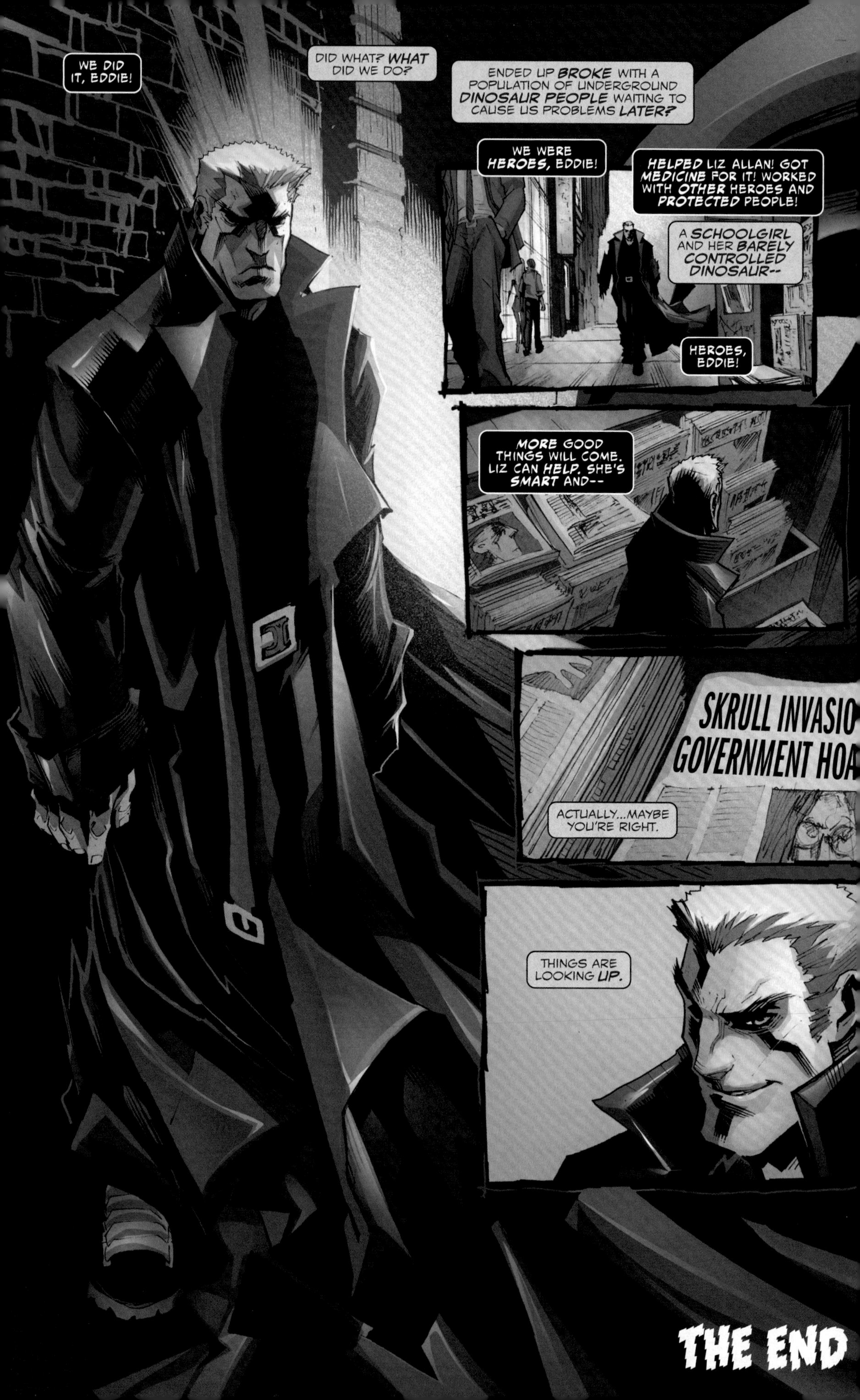
WE DID IT, EDDIE!
DID WHAT? WHAT DID WE DO?
ENDED UP BROKE WITH A POPULATION OF UNDERGROUND DINOSAUR PEOPLE WAITING TO CAUSE US PROBLEMS LATER?
WE WERE HEROES, EDDIE!
HELPED LIZ ALLAN! GOT MEDICINE FOR IT! WORKED WITH OTHER HEROES AND PROTECTED PEOPLE!
A SCHOOLGIRL AND HER BARELY CONTROLLED DINOSAUR--
HEROES, EDDIE!
MORE GOOD THINGS WILL COME. LIZ CAN HELP. SHE'S SMART AND--
SKRULL INVASIO
GOVERNMENT HOA
ACTUALLY...MAYBE YOU'RE RIGHT.
THINGS ARE LOOKING UP.
THE END

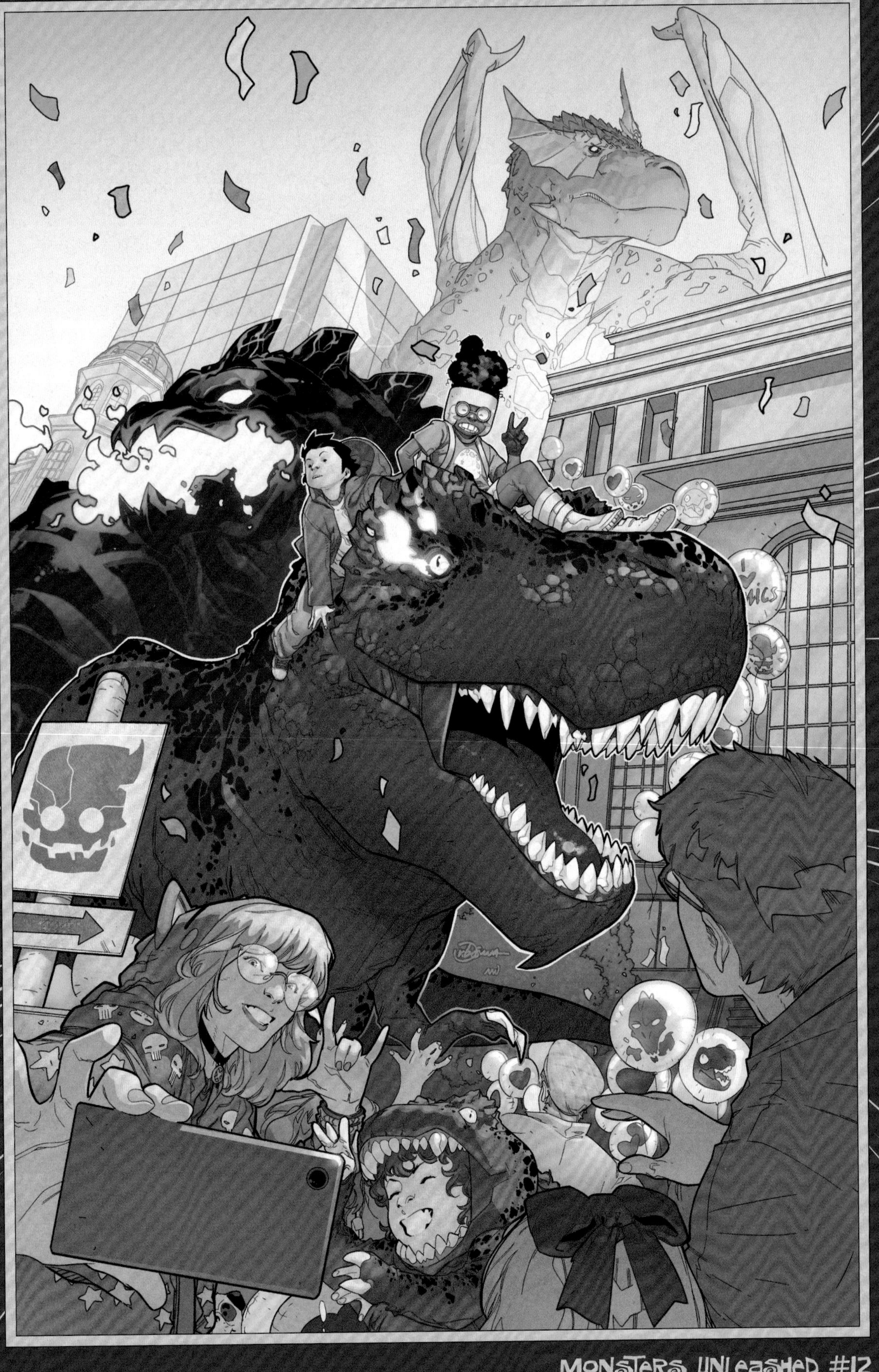

MONSTERS UNLEASHED #12

MONSTERS UNLEASHED!

KNOWN TO THE WORLD AS KID KAIJU, KEI KAWADE HAS THE INHUMAN ABILITY TO SUMMON AND CREATE MONSTERS SIMPLY BY DRAWING THEM. KID KAIJU AND HIS TEAM PROTECT THE WORLD FROM MONSTERS GONE BAD.

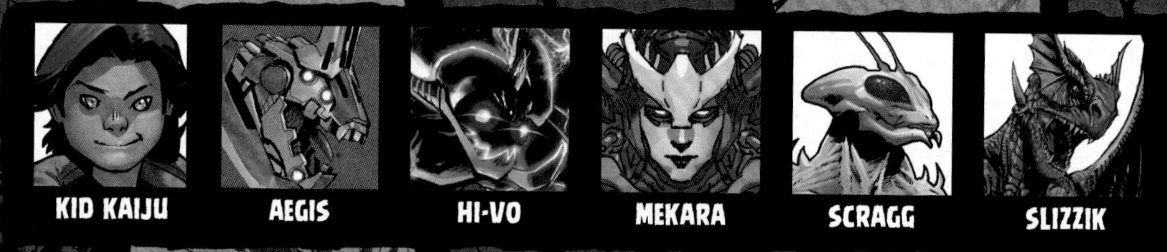
KID KAIJU
AEGIS
HI-VO
MEKARA
SCRAGG
SLIZZIK

KEI'S BEEN ON SOME ADVENTURES WITH HIS KAIJU BUDDIES LATELY--HE AND SCRAGG RESCUED A HIVE OF GIANT BEES; AEGIS SAVED THE WORLD FROM AN ANCIENT SEA-FARING MONOLITH; AND MEKARA TRAVELED TO THE MOON TO PLACATE A WORLD-DESTROYING ALIEN THAT JUST NEEDED A TIME-OUT.

LEARNING CURVE, PART FOUR
"KID KAIJU VERSUS MISS MECH"

JUSTIN JORDAN
WRITER

ALBERTO ALBURQUERQUE
ARTIST

CHRIS SOTOMAYOR
COLOR ARTIST

VC'S TRAVIS LANHAM
LETTERER

R.B. SILVA & NOLAN WOODARD
COVER ARTISTS

CHRISTINA HARRINGTON
EDITOR

MARK PANICCIA
SENIOR EDITOR

C.B. CEBULSKI
EDITOR IN CHIEF

JOE QUESADA
CHIEF CREATIVE OFFICER

DAN BUCKLEY
PRESIDENT

ALAN FINE
EXECUTIVE PRODUCER

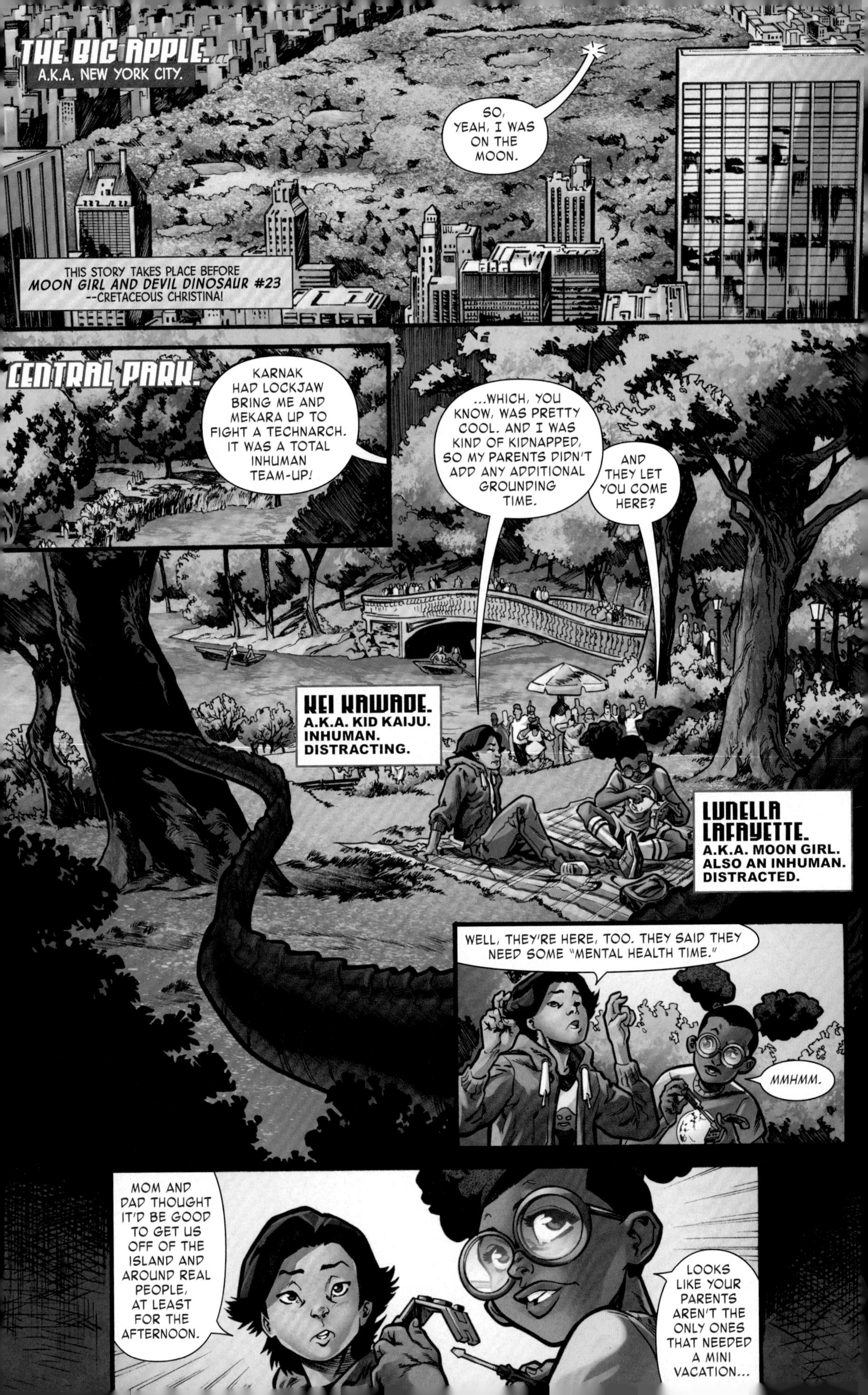
THE BIG APPLE.
A.K.A. NEW YORK CITY.
SO, YEAH, I WAS ON THE MOON.
THIS STORY TAKES PLACE BEFORE MOON GIRL AND DEVIL DINOSAUR #23 --CRETACEOUS CHRISTINA!
CENTRAL PARK.
KARNAK HAD LOCKJAW BRING ME AND MEKARA UP TO FIGHT A TECHNARCH. IT WAS A TOTAL INHUMAN TEAM-UP!
...WHICH, YOU KNOW, WAS PRETTY COOL. AND I WAS KIND OF KIDNAPPED, SO MY PARENTS DIDN'T ADD ANY ADDITIONAL GROUNDING TIME.
AND THEY LET YOU COME HERE?
KEI KAWADE. A.K.A. KID KAIJU. INHUMAN. DISTRACTING.
LUNELLA LAFAYETTE. A.K.A. MOON GIRL. ALSO AN INHUMAN. DISTRACTED.
WELL, THEY'RE HERE, TOO. THEY SAID THEY NEED SOME "MENTAL HEALTH TIME."
MMHMM.
MOM AND DAD THOUGHT IT'D BE GOOD TO GET US OFF OF THE ISLAND AND AROUND REAL PEOPLE, AT LEAST FOR THE AFTERNOON.
LOOKS LIKE YOUR PARENTS AREN'T THE ONLY ONES THAT NEEDED A MINI VACATION...

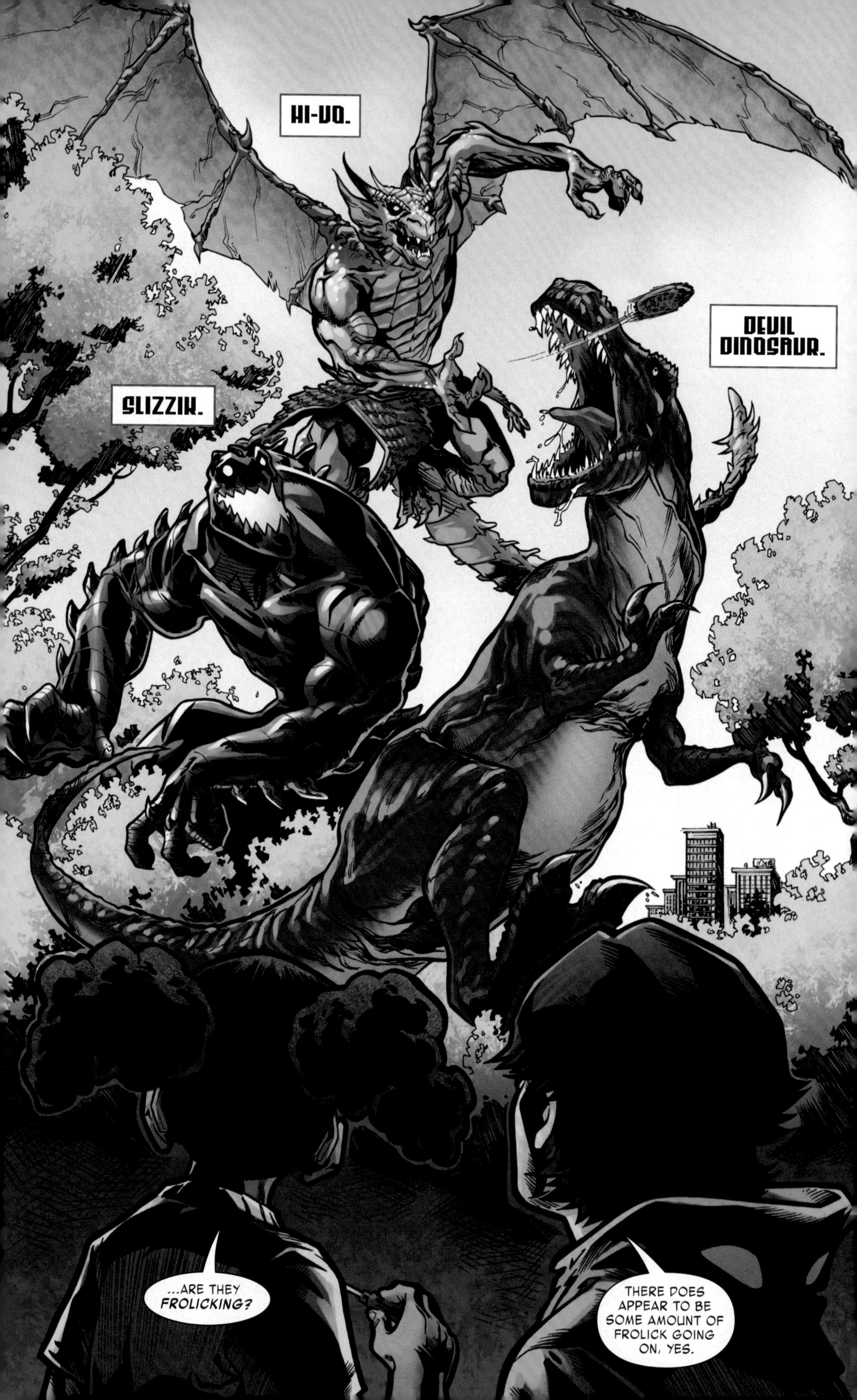
HI-VO.
SLIZZIK.
DEVIL DINOSAUR.
...ARE THEY *FROLICKING?*
THERE DOES APPEAR TO BE SOME AMOUNT OF FROLICK GOING ON, YES.

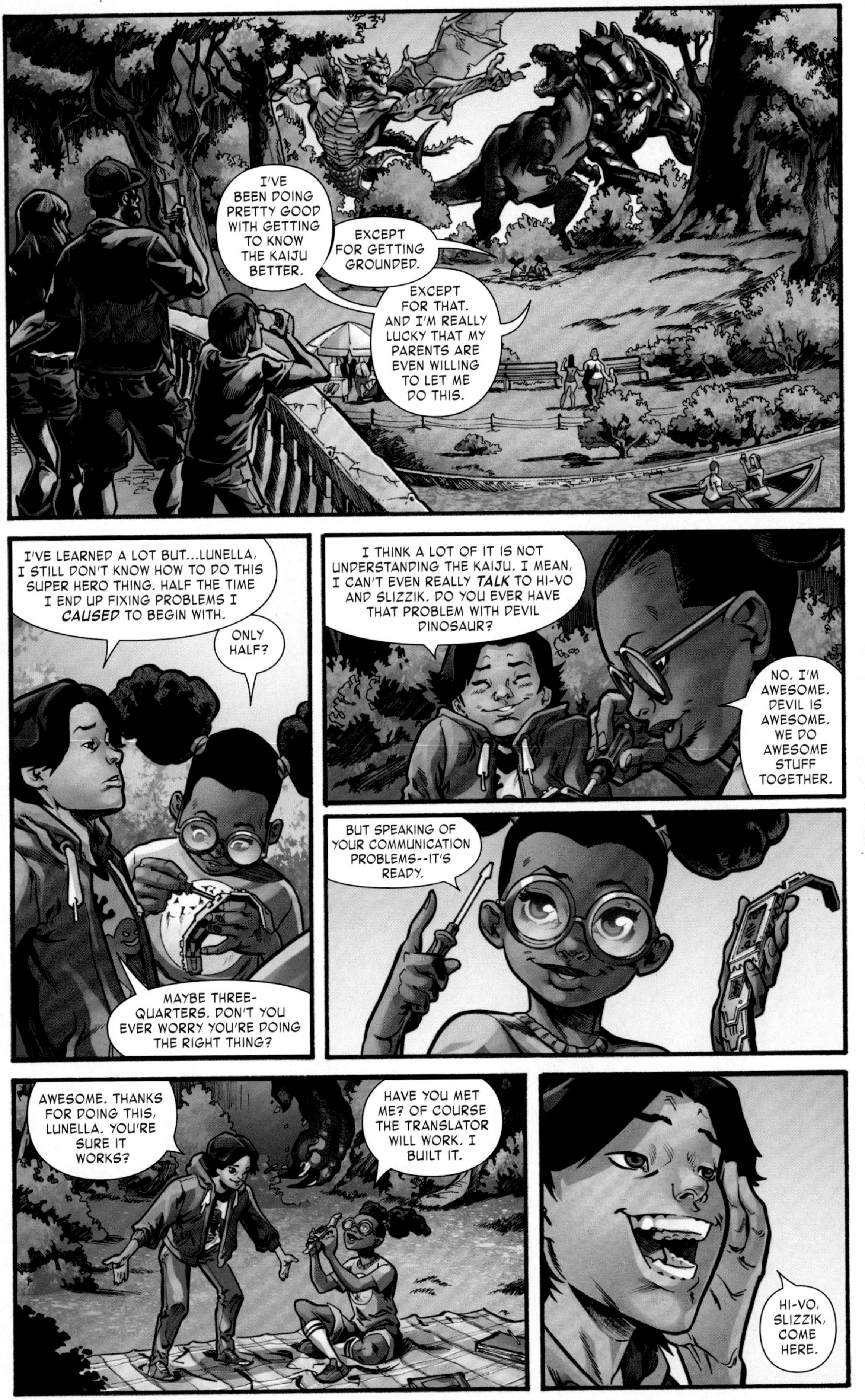
I'VE BEEN DOING PRETTY GOOD WITH GETTING TO KNOW THE KAIJU BETTER.
EXCEPT FOR GETTING GROUNDED.
EXCEPT FOR THAT. AND I'M REALLY LUCKY THAT MY PARENTS ARE EVEN WILLING TO LET ME DO THIS.
I'VE LEARNED A LOT BUT...LUNELLA, I STILL DON'T KNOW HOW TO DO THIS SUPER HERO THING. HALF THE TIME I END UP FIXING PROBLEMS I CAUSED TO BEGIN WITH.
ONLY HALF?
MAYBE THREE-QUARTERS. DON'T YOU EVER WORRY YOU'RE DOING THE RIGHT THING?
I THINK A LOT OF IT IS NOT UNDERSTANDING THE KAIJU. I MEAN, I CAN'T EVEN REALLY TALK TO HI-VO AND SLIZZIK. DO YOU EVER HAVE THAT PROBLEM WITH DEVIL DINOSAUR?
NO. I'M AWESOME. DEVIL IS AWESOME. WE DO AWESOME STUFF TOGETHER.
BUT SPEAKING OF YOUR COMMUNICATION PROBLEMS--IT'S READY.
AWESOME. THANKS FOR DOING THIS, LUNELLA. YOU'RE SURE IT WORKS?
HAVE YOU MET ME? OF COURSE THE TRANSLATOR WILL WORK. I BUILT IT.
HI-VO, SLIZZIK, COME HERE.

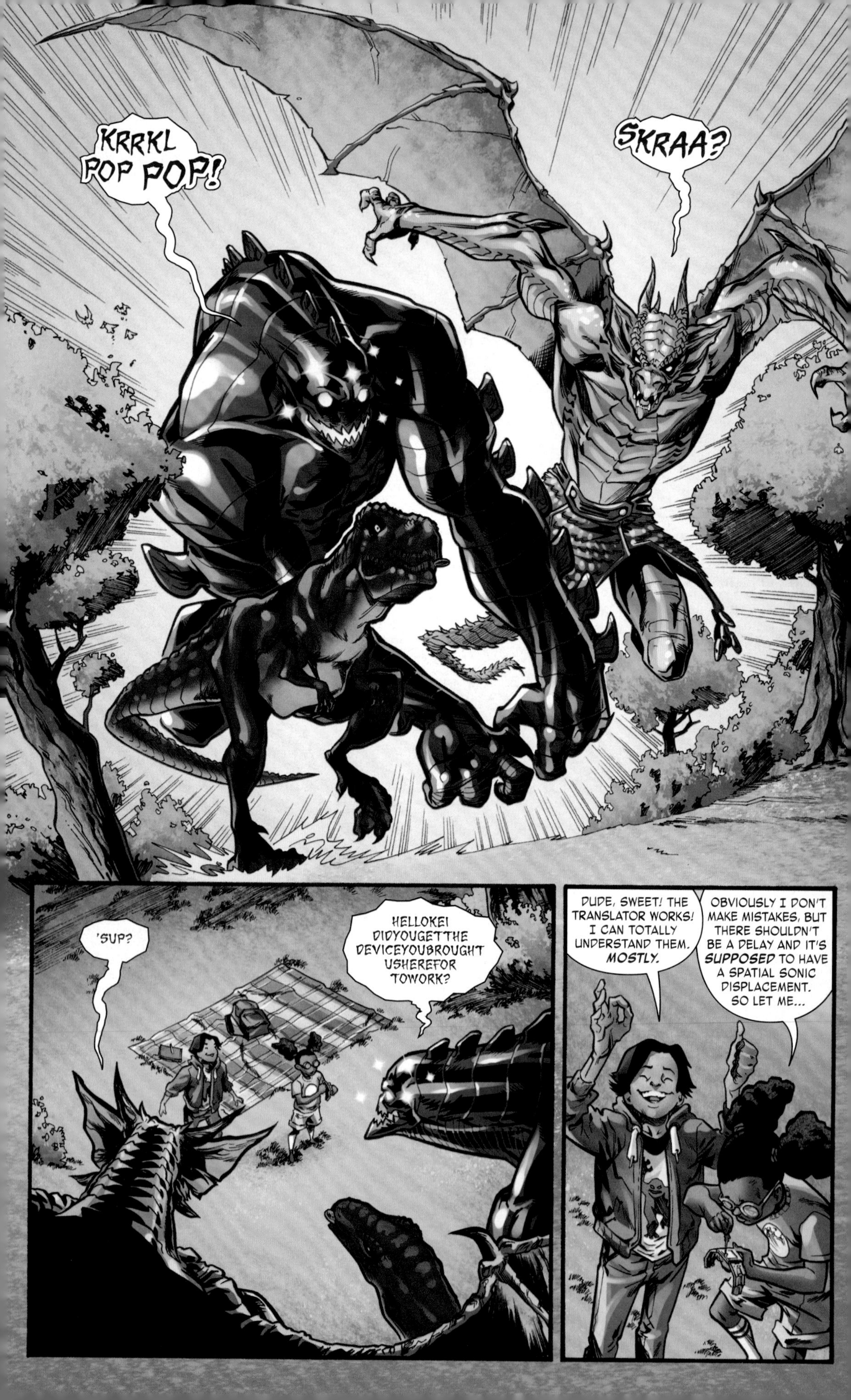
KRRKL POP POP!
SKRAA?
'SUP?
HELLOKEI DIDYOUGETTHE DEVICEYOUBROUGHT USHEREFOR TOWORK?
DUDE, SWEET! THE TRANSLATOR WORKS! I CAN TOTALLY UNDERSTAND THEM. MOSTLY.
OBVIOUSLY I DON'T MAKE MISTAKES, BUT THERE SHOULDN'T BE A DELAY AND IT'S SUPPOSED TO HAVE A SPATIAL SONIC DISPLACEMENT. SO LET ME...

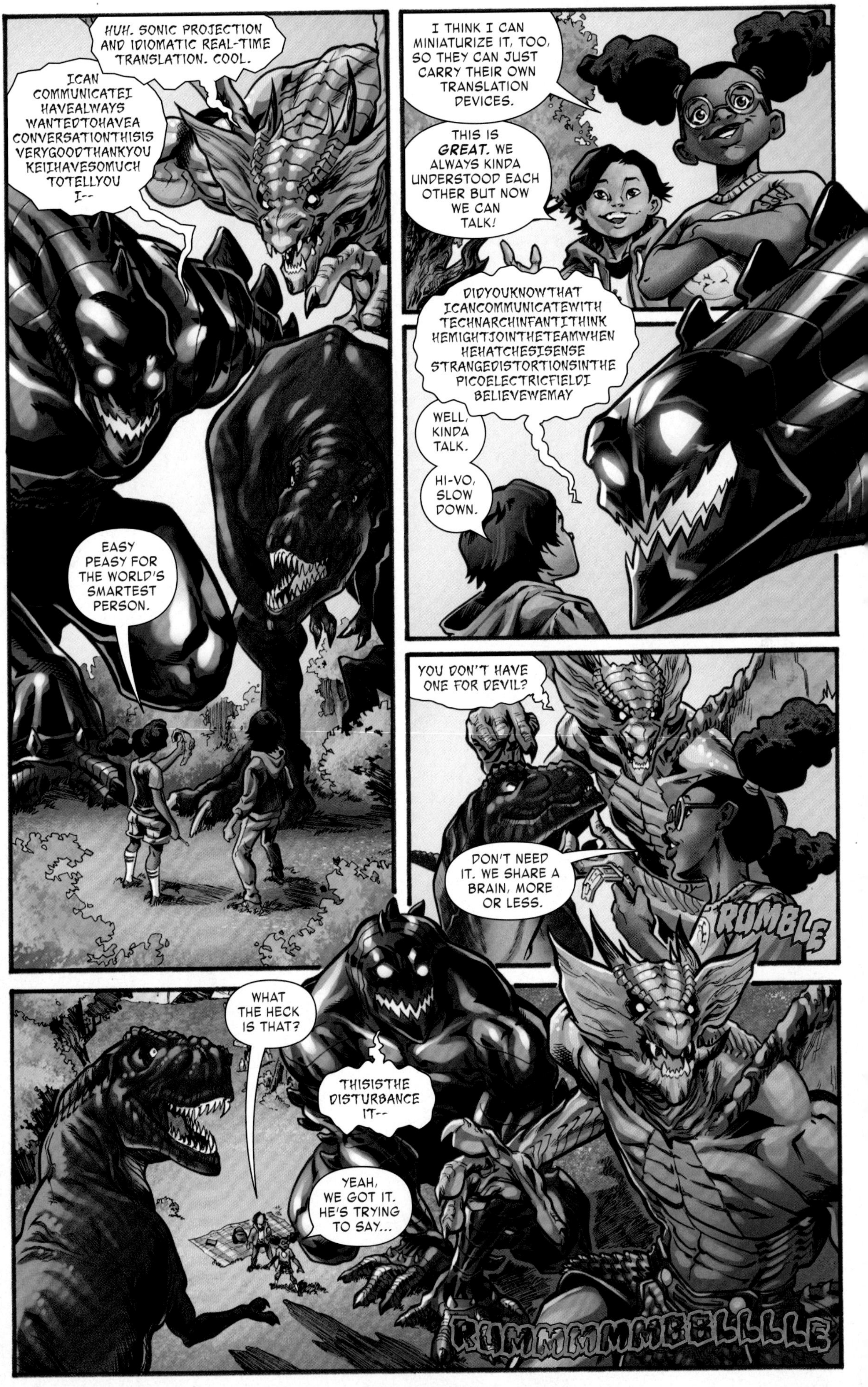
HUH. SONIC PROJECTION AND IDIOMATIC REAL-TIME TRANSLATION. COOL.
ICAN COMMUNICATEI HAVEALWAYS WANTEDTOHAVEA CONVERSATIONTHISIS VERYGOODTHANKYOU KEIIHAVESOMUCH TOTELLYOU I--
EASY PEASY FOR THE WORLD'S SMARTEST PERSON.
I THINK I CAN MINIATURIZE IT, TOO, SO THEY CAN JUST CARRY THEIR OWN TRANSLATION DEVICES.
THIS IS GREAT. WE ALWAYS KINDA UNDERSTOOD EACH OTHER BUT NOW WE CAN TALK!
DIDYOUKNOWTHAT ICANCOMMUNICATEWITH TECHNARCHINFANTITHINK HEMIGHTJOINTHETEAMWHEN HEHATCHESISENSE STRANGEDISTORTIONSINTHE PICOELECTRICFIELDI BELIEVEWEMAY
WELL, KINDA TALK.
HI-VO, SLOW DOWN.
YOU DON'T HAVE ONE FOR DEVIL?
DON'T NEED IT. WE SHARE A BRAIN, MORE OR LESS.
RUMBLE
WHAT THE HECK IS THAT?
THISISTHE DISTURBANCE IT--
YEAH, WE GOT IT. HE'S TRYING TO SAY...
RUMMMMMMBBLLLLE

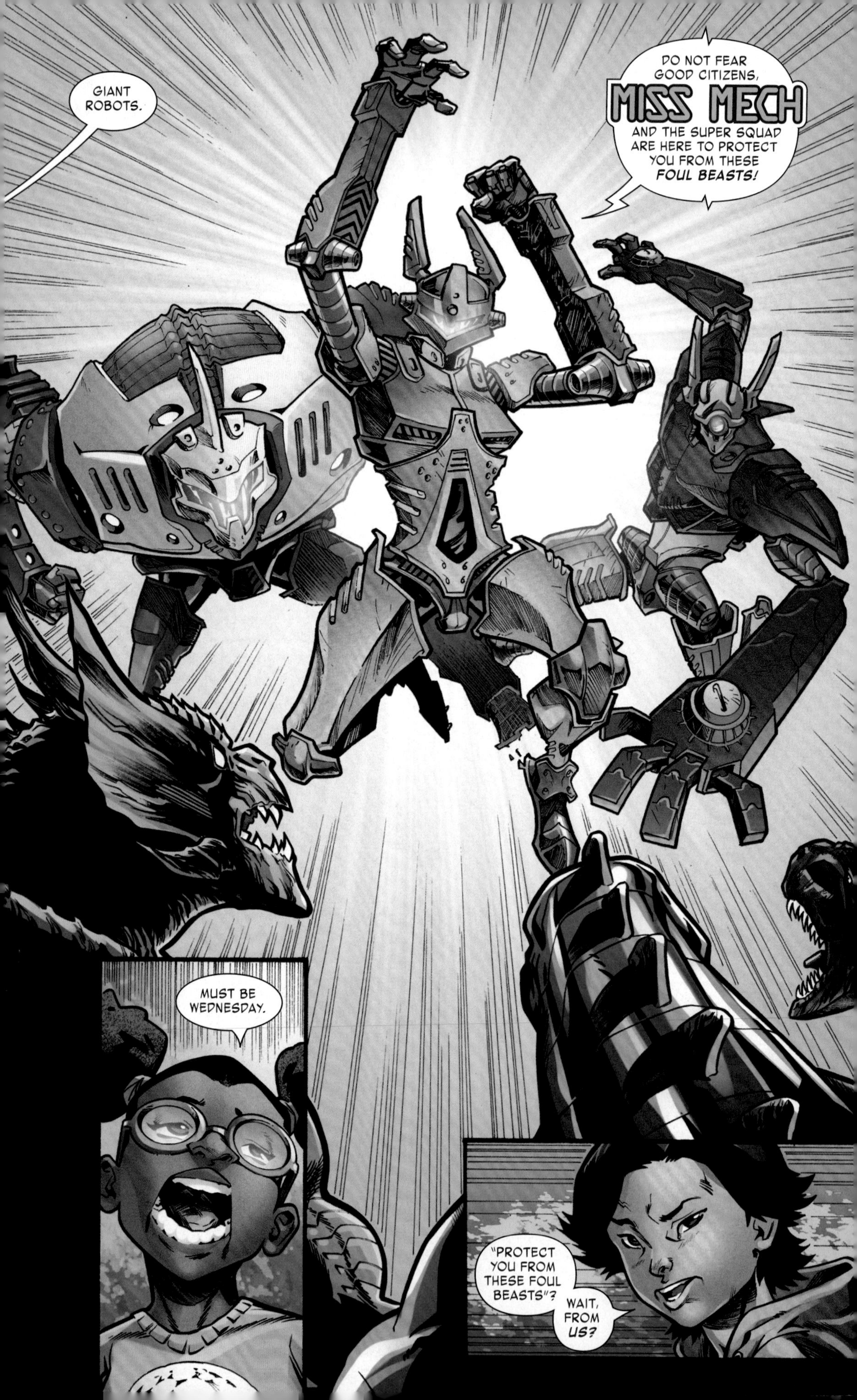
GIANT ROBOTS.
DO NOT FEAR GOOD CITIZENS, MISS MECH AND THE SUPER SQUAD ARE HERE TO PROTECT YOU FROM THESE FOUL BEASTS!
MUST BE WEDNESDAY.
"PROTECT YOU FROM THESE FOUL BEASTS"?
WAIT, FROM US?

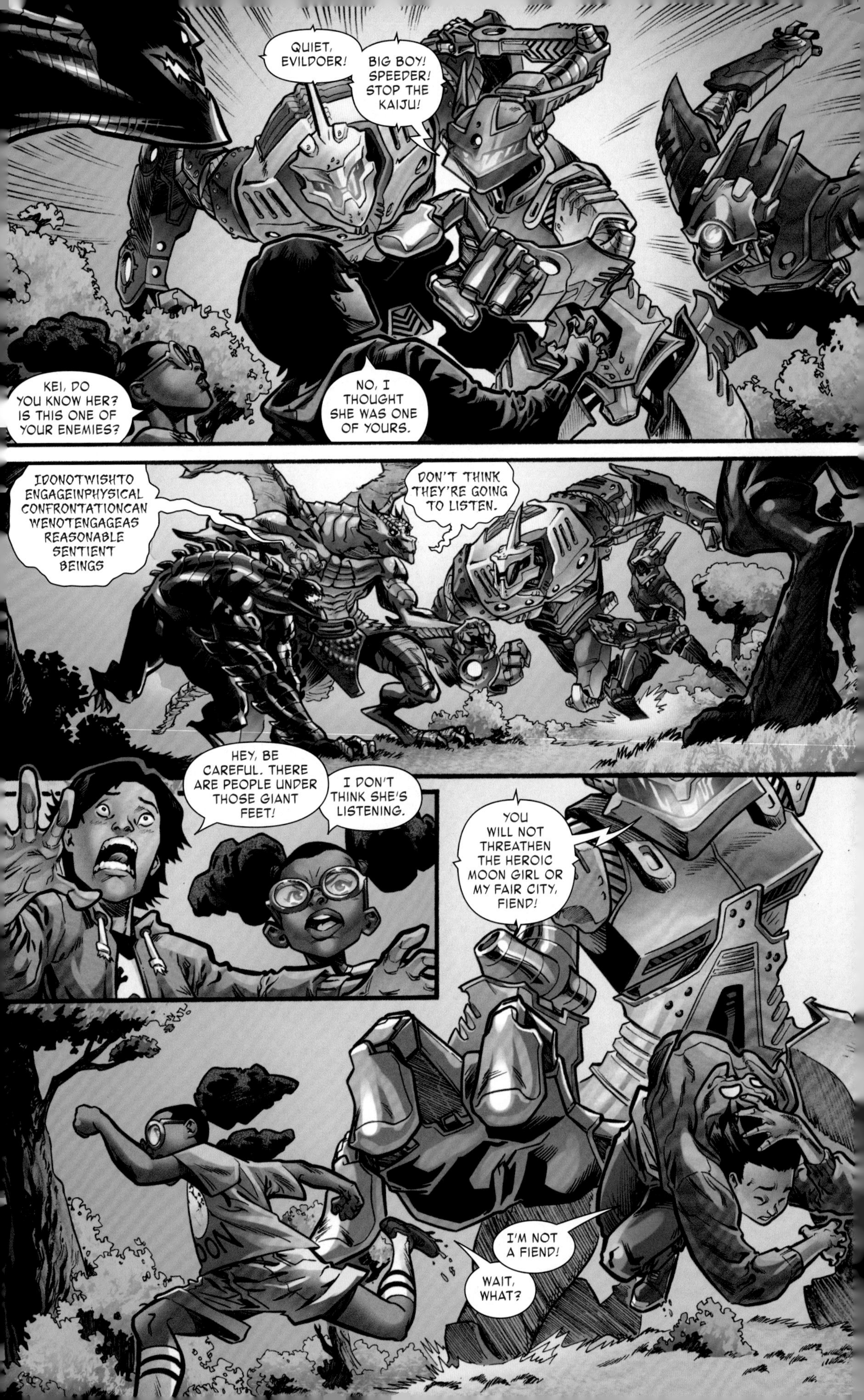
QUIET, EVILDOER!
BIG BOY! SPEEDER! STOP THE KAIJU!
KEI, DO YOU KNOW HER? IS THIS ONE OF YOUR ENEMIES?
NO, I THOUGHT SHE WAS ONE OF YOURS.
IDONOTWISHTO ENGAGEINPHYSICAL CONFRONTATIONCAN WENOTENGAGEAS REASONABLE SENTIENT BEINGS
DON'T THINK THEY'RE GOING TO LISTEN.
HEY, BE CAREFUL. THERE ARE PEOPLE UNDER THOSE GIANT FEET!
I DON'T THINK SHE'S LISTENING.
YOU WILL NOT THREATHEN THE HEROIC MOON GIRL OR MY FAIR CITY, FIEND!
I'M NOT A FIEND!
WAIT, WHAT?

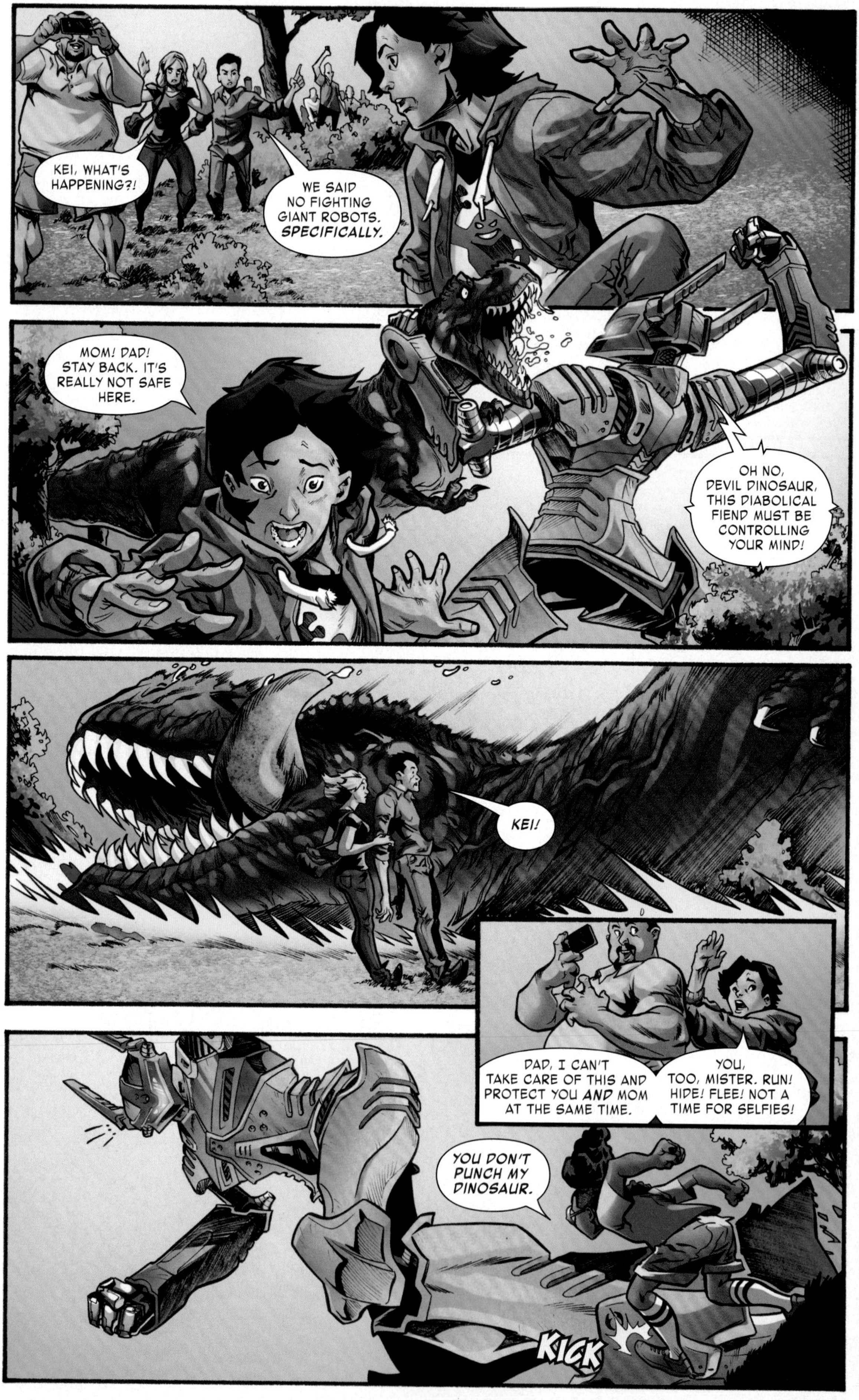
KEI, WHAT'S HAPPENING?!
WE SAID NO FIGHTING GIANT ROBOTS. *SPECIFICALLY.*
MOM! DAD! STAY BACK. IT'S REALLY NOT SAFE HERE.
OH NO, DEVIL DINOSAUR, THIS DIABOLICAL FIEND MUST BE CONTROLLING YOUR MIND!
KEI!
DAD, I CAN'T TAKE CARE OF THIS AND PROTECT YOU *AND* MOM AT THE SAME TIME.
YOU, TOO, MISTER. RUN! HIDE! FLEE! NOT A TIME FOR SELFIES!
YOU DON'T PUNCH MY DINOSAUR.
KICK

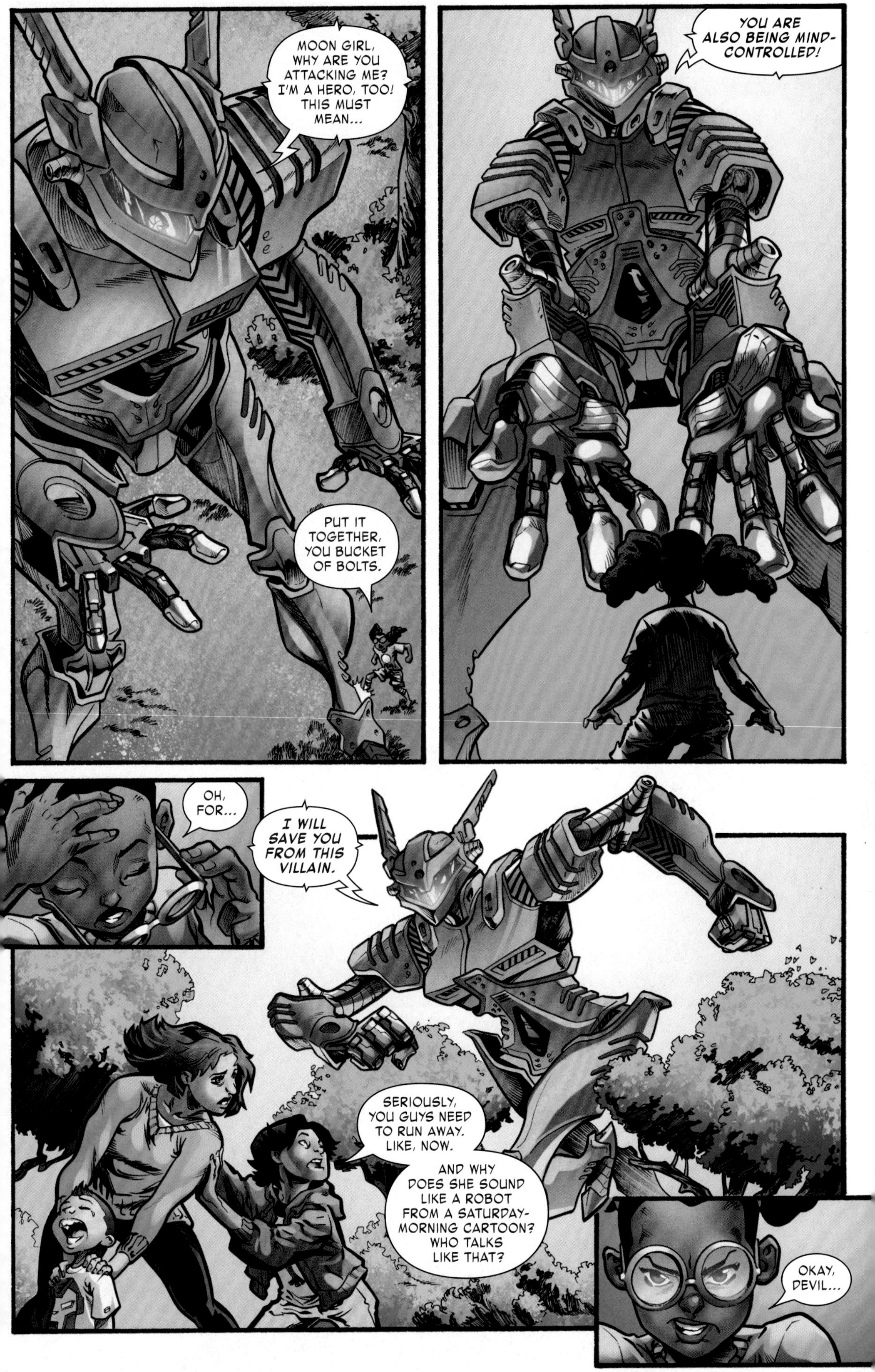
MOON GIRL, WHY ARE YOU ATTACKING ME? I'M A HERO, TOO! THIS MUST MEAN...
PUT IT TOGETHER, YOU BUCKET OF BOLTS.
YOU ARE ALSO BEING MIND-CONTROLLED!
OH, FOR...
I WILL SAVE YOU FROM THIS VILLAIN.
SERIOUSLY, YOU GUYS NEED TO RUN AWAY. LIKE, NOW.
AND WHY DOES SHE SOUND LIKE A ROBOT FROM A SATURDAY-MORNING CARTOON? WHO TALKS LIKE THAT?
OKAY, DEVIL...

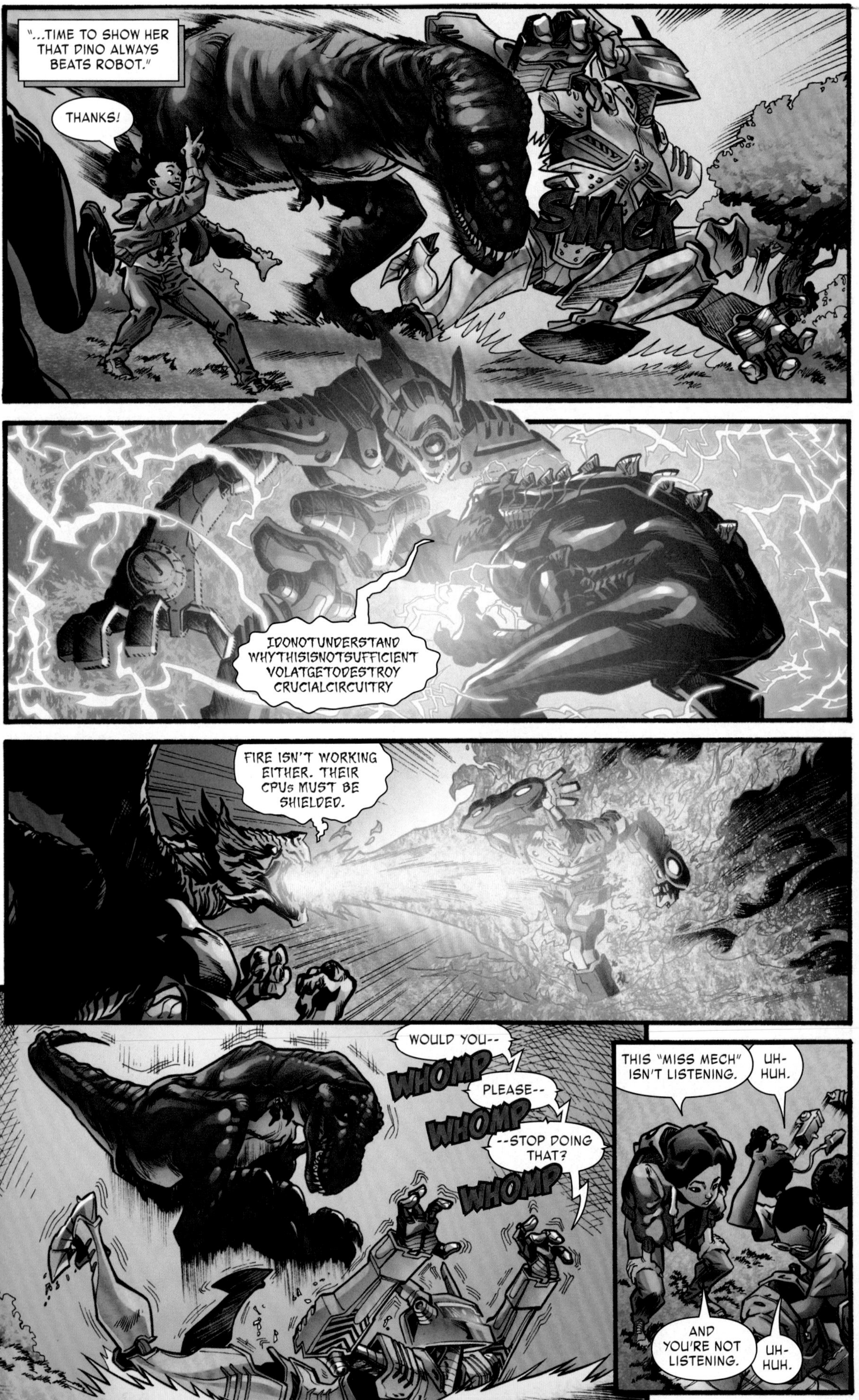
"...TIME TO SHOW HER THAT DINO ALWAYS BEATS ROBOT."
THANKS!
SMACK
IDONOTUNDERSTAND WHYTHISISNOTSUFFICIENT VOLATGETODESTROY CRUCIALCIRCUITRY
FIRE ISN'T WORKING EITHER. THEIR CPUs MUST BE SHIELDED.
WOULD YOU--
WHOMP
PLEASE--
WHOMP
--STOP DOING THAT?
WHOMP
THIS "MISS MECH" ISN'T LISTENING.
UH-HUH.
AND YOU'RE NOT LISTENING.
UH-HUH.

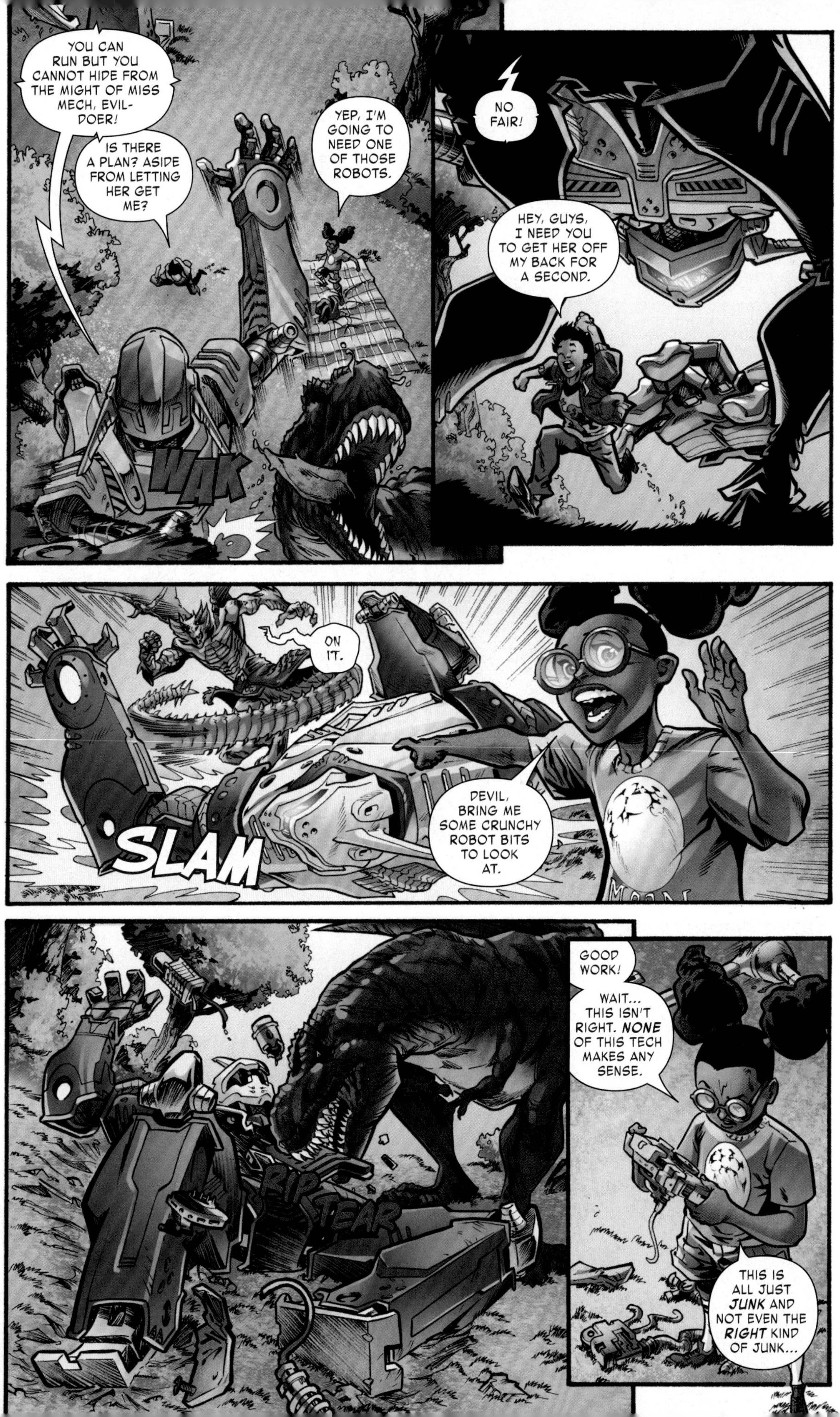
YOU CAN RUN BUT YOU CANNOT HIDE FROM THE MIGHT OF MISS MECH, EVIL-DOER!
IS THERE A PLAN? ASIDE FROM LETTING HER GET ME?
YEP, I'M GOING TO NEED ONE OF THOSE ROBOTS.
WAK
NO FAIR!
HEY, GUYS, I NEED YOU TO GET HER OFF MY BACK FOR A SECOND.
ON IT.
DEVIL, BRING ME SOME CRUNCHY ROBOT BITS TO LOOK AT.
SLAM
RIP
TEAR
GOOD WORK!
WAIT... THIS ISN'T RIGHT. NONE OF THIS TECH MAKES ANY SENSE.
THIS IS ALL JUST JUNK AND NOT EVEN THE RIGHT KIND OF JUNK...

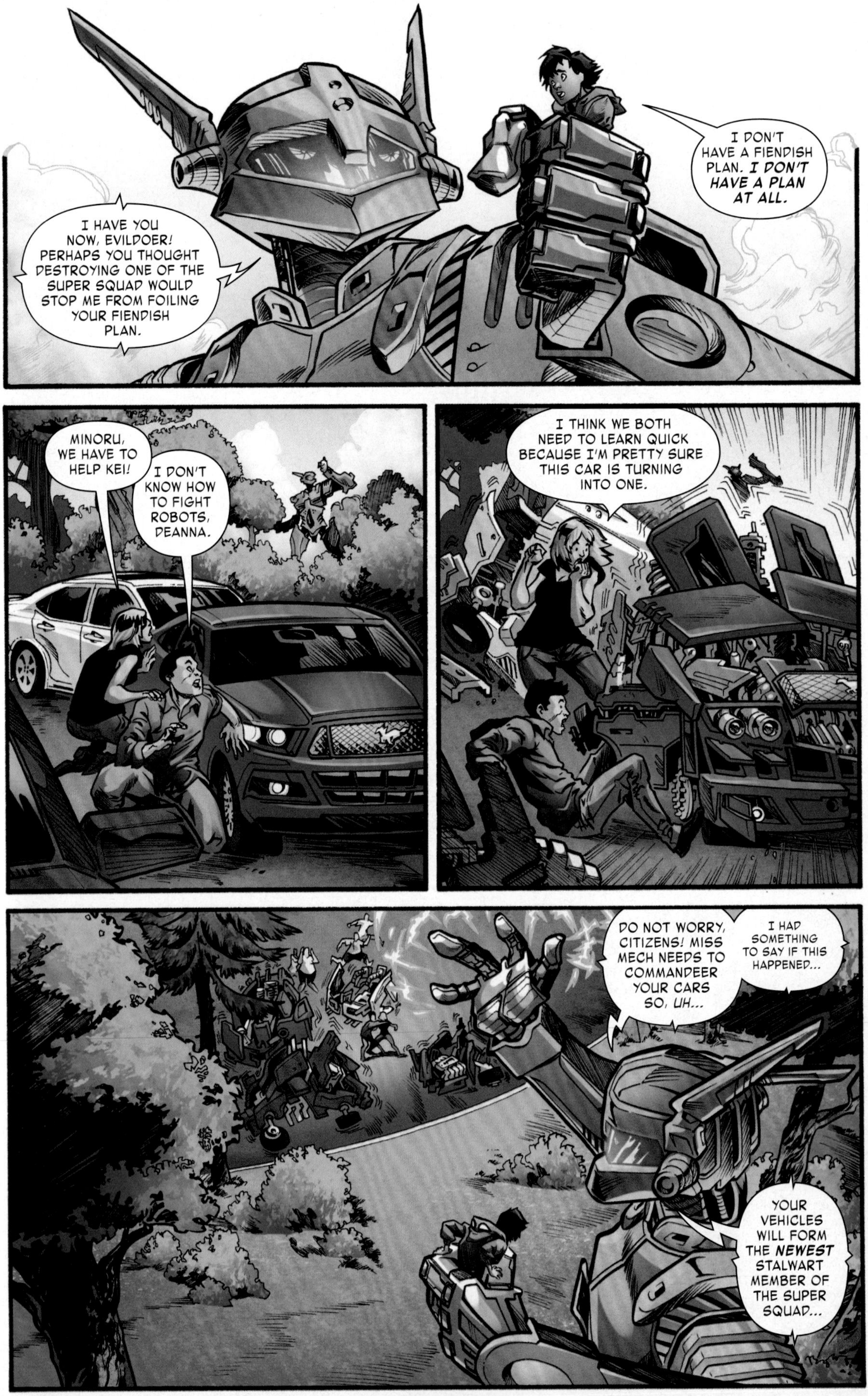
I HAVE YOU NOW, EVILDOER! PERHAPS YOU THOUGHT DESTROYING ONE OF THE SUPER SQUAD WOULD STOP ME FROM FOILING YOUR FIENDISH PLAN.
I DON'T HAVE A FIENDISH PLAN. I DON'T HAVE A PLAN AT ALL.
MINORU, WE HAVE TO HELP KEI!
I DON'T KNOW HOW TO FIGHT ROBOTS, DEANNA.
I THINK WE BOTH NEED TO LEARN QUICK BECAUSE I'M PRETTY SURE THIS CAR IS TURNING INTO ONE.
DO NOT WORRY, CITIZENS! MISS MECH NEEDS TO COMMANDEER YOUR CARS SO, UH...
I HAD SOMETHING TO SAY IF THIS HAPPENED...
YOUR VEHICLES WILL FORM THE NEWEST STALWART MEMBER OF THE SUPER SQUAD...

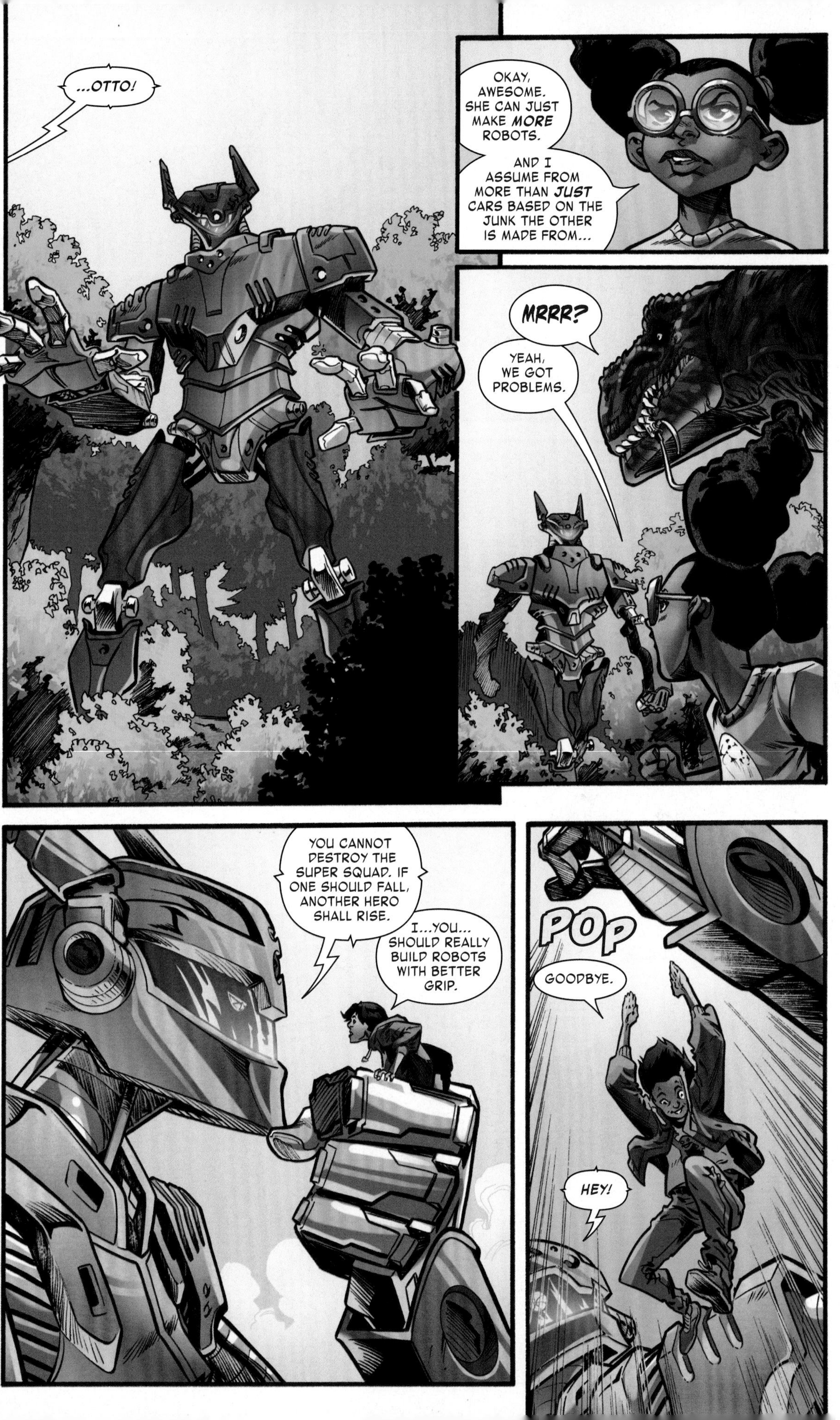
...OTTO!
OKAY, AWESOME. SHE CAN JUST MAKE MORE ROBOTS.
AND I ASSUME FROM MORE THAN JUST CARS BASED ON THE JUNK THE OTHER IS MADE FROM...
MRRR?
YEAH, WE GOT PROBLEMS.
YOU CANNOT DESTROY THE SUPER SQUAD. IF ONE SHOULD FALL, ANOTHER HERO SHALL RISE.
I...YOU... SHOULD REALLY BUILD ROBOTS WITH BETTER GRIP.
POP
GOODBYE.
HEY!

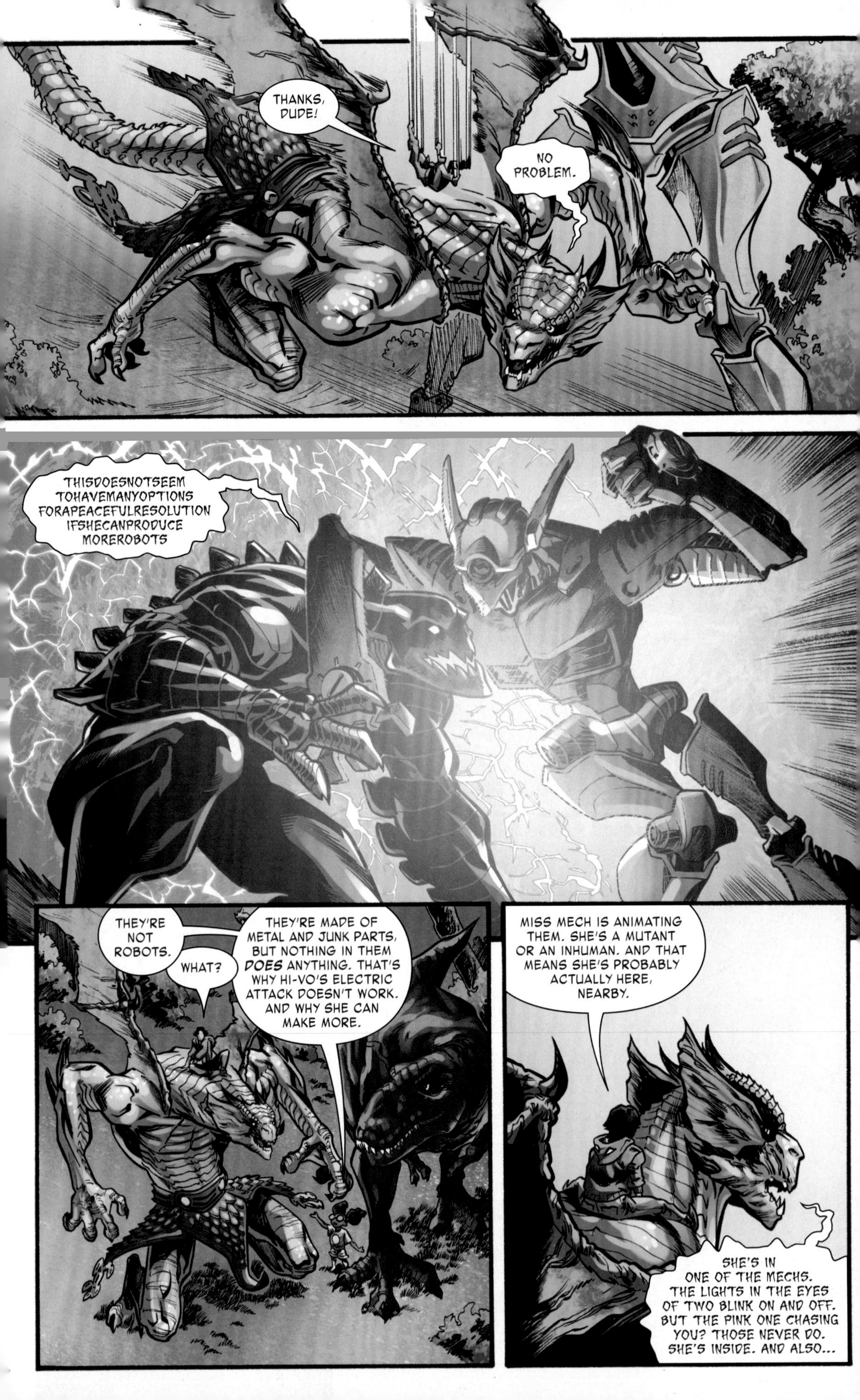
THANKS, DUDE!
NO PROBLEM.
THISDOESNOTSEEM TOHAVEMANYOPTIONS FORAPEACEFULRESOLUTION IFSHECANPRODUCE MOREROBOTS
THEY'RE NOT ROBOTS.
WHAT?
THEY'RE MADE OF METAL AND JUNK PARTS, BUT NOTHING IN THEM DOES ANYTHING. THAT'S WHY HI-VO'S ELECTRIC ATTACK DOESN'T WORK. AND WHY SHE CAN MAKE MORE.
MISS MECH IS ANIMATING THEM. SHE'S A MUTANT OR AN INHUMAN. AND THAT MEANS SHE'S PROBABLY ACTUALLY HERE, NEARBY.
SHE'S IN ONE OF THE MECHS. THE LIGHTS IN THE EYES OF TWO BLINK ON AND OFF. BUT THE PINK ONE CHASING YOU? THOSE NEVER DO. SHE'S INSIDE. AND ALSO...

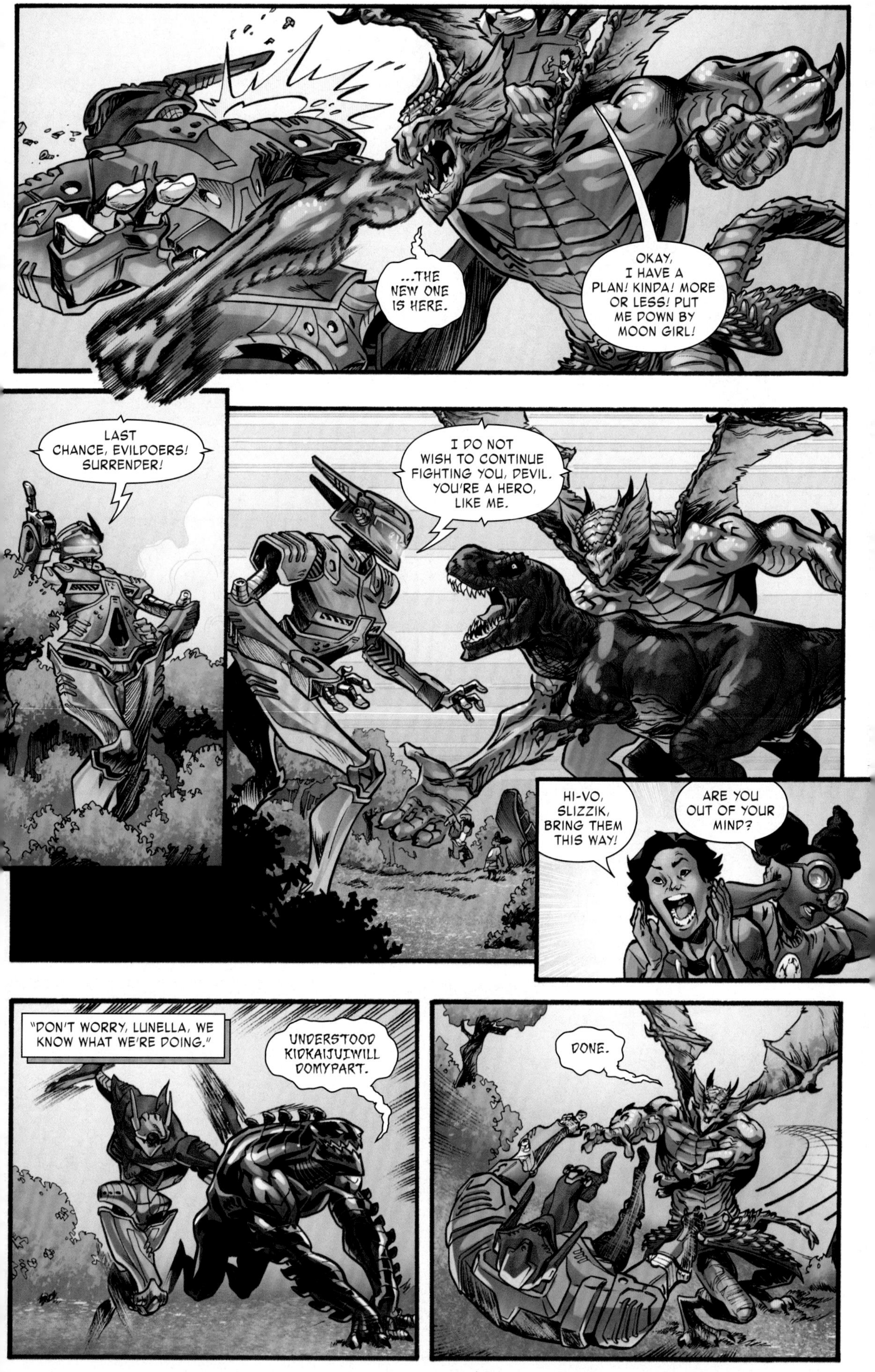
...THE NEW ONE IS HERE.
OKAY, I HAVE A PLAN! KINDA! MORE OR LESS! PUT ME DOWN BY MOON GIRL!
LAST CHANCE, EVILDOERS! SURRENDER!
I DO NOT WISH TO CONTINUE FIGHTING YOU, DEVIL. YOU'RE A HERO, LIKE ME.
HI-VO, SLIZZIK, BRING THEM THIS WAY!
ARE YOU OUT OF YOUR MIND?
"DON'T WORRY, LUNELLA, WE KNOW WHAT WE'RE DOING."
UNDERSTOOD KIDKAIJUIWILL DOMYPART.
DONE.

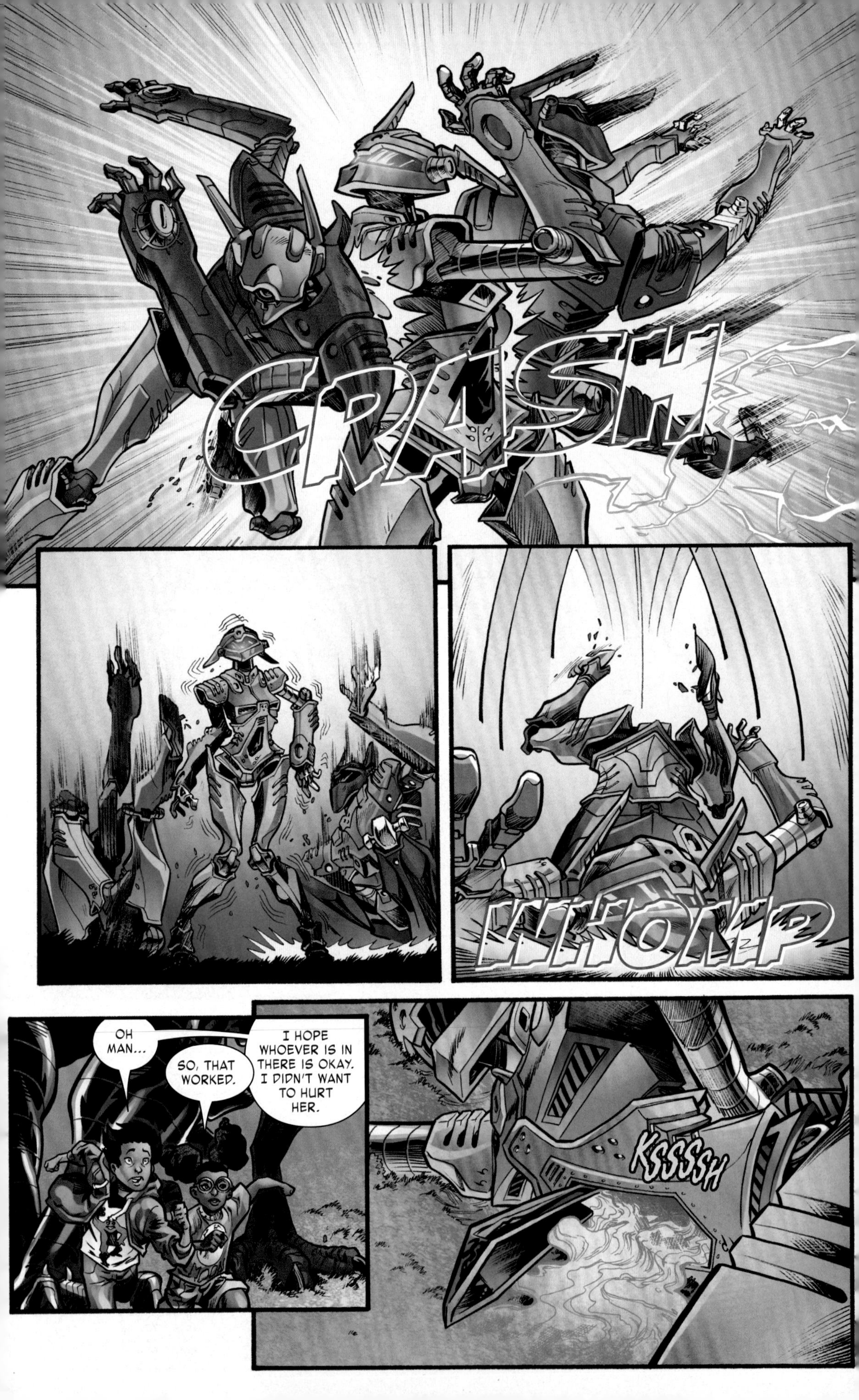
CRASH
WHOMP
OH MAN...
I HOPE WHOEVER IS IN THERE IS OKAY. I DIDN'T WANT TO HURT HER.
SO, THAT WORKED.
KSSSSH

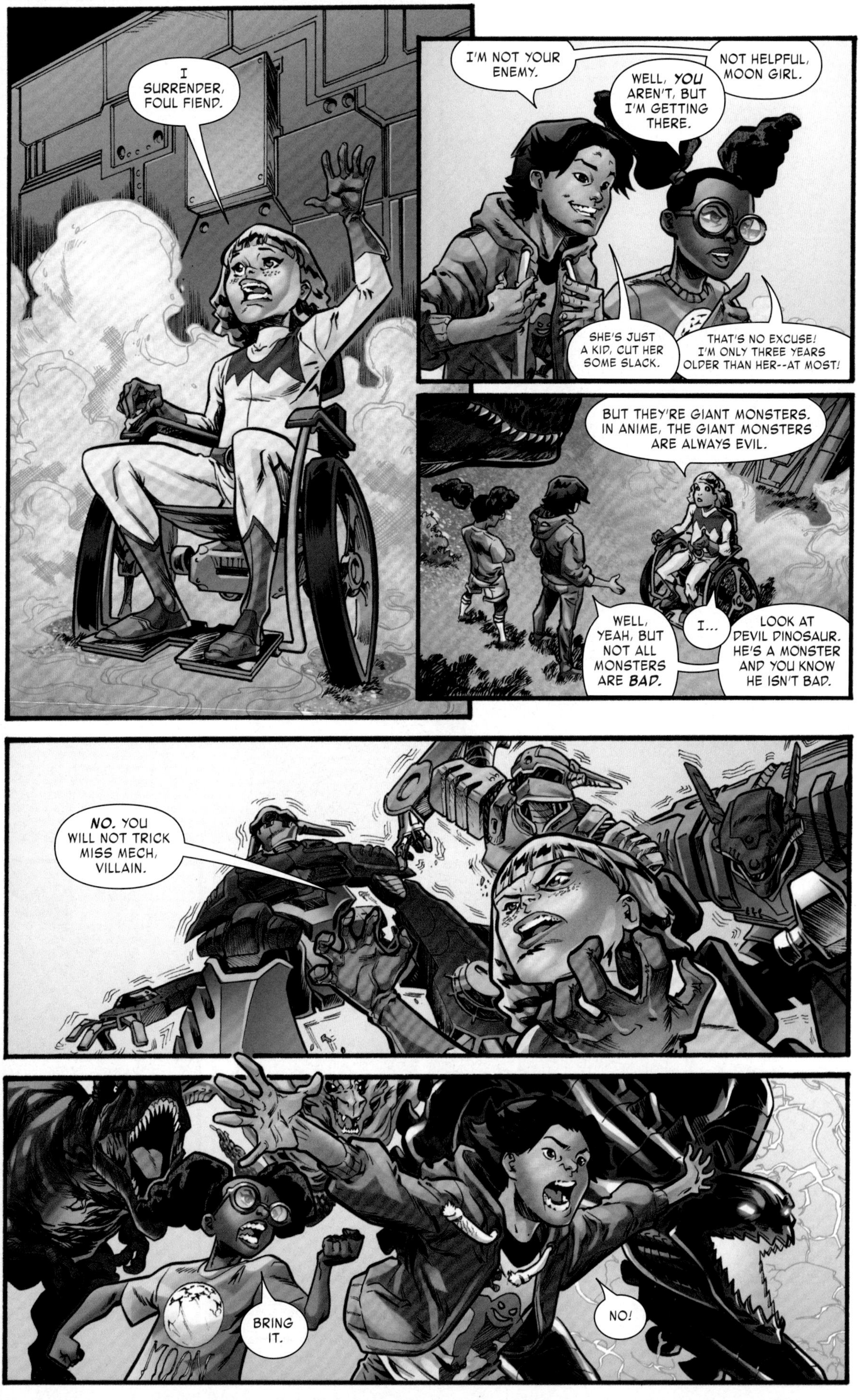
I SURRENDER, FOUL FIEND.
I'M NOT YOUR ENEMY.
NOT HELPFUL, MOON GIRL.
WELL, YOU AREN'T, BUT I'M GETTING THERE.
SHE'S JUST A KID, CUT HER SOME SLACK.
THAT'S NO EXCUSE! I'M ONLY THREE YEARS OLDER THAN HER--AT MOST!
BUT THEY'RE GIANT MONSTERS. IN ANIME, THE GIANT MONSTERS ARE ALWAYS EVIL.
WELL, YEAH, BUT NOT ALL MONSTERS ARE BAD.
I...
LOOK AT DEVIL DINOSAUR. HE'S A MONSTER AND YOU KNOW HE ISN'T BAD.
NO. YOU WILL NOT TRICK MISS MECH, VILLAIN.
BRING IT.
NO!

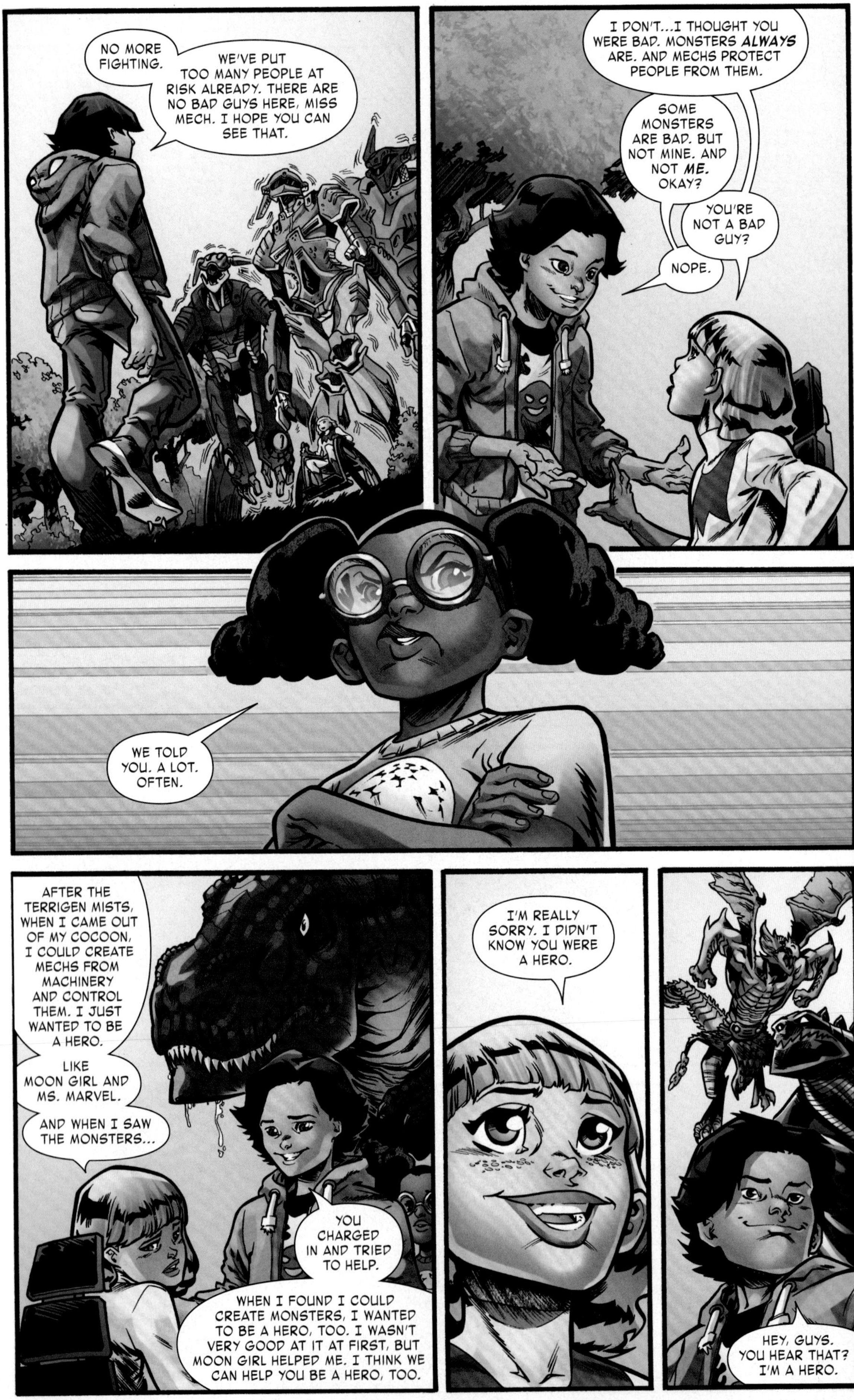

NO MORE FIGHTING.
WE'VE PUT TOO MANY PEOPLE AT RISK ALREADY. THERE ARE NO BAD GUYS HERE, MISS MECH. I HOPE YOU CAN SEE THAT.
I DON'T...I THOUGHT YOU WERE BAD. MONSTERS ALWAYS ARE. AND MECHS PROTECT PEOPLE FROM THEM.
SOME MONSTERS ARE BAD. BUT NOT MINE. AND NOT ME. OKAY?
YOU'RE NOT A BAD GUY?
NOPE.
WE TOLD YOU. A LOT. OFTEN.
AFTER THE TERRIGEN MISTS, WHEN I CAME OUT OF MY COCOON, I COULD CREATE MECHS FROM MACHINERY AND CONTROL THEM. I JUST WANTED TO BE A HERO.
LIKE MOON GIRL AND MS. MARVEL.
AND WHEN I SAW THE MONSTERS...
YOU CHARGED IN AND TRIED TO HELP.
WHEN I FOUND I COULD CREATE MONSTERS, I WANTED TO BE A HERO, TOO. I WASN'T VERY GOOD AT IT AT FIRST, BUT MOON GIRL HELPED ME. I THINK WE CAN HELP YOU BE A HERO, TOO.
I'M REALLY SORRY. I DIDN'T KNOW YOU WERE A HERO.
HEY, GUYS. YOU HEAR THAT? I'M A HERO.

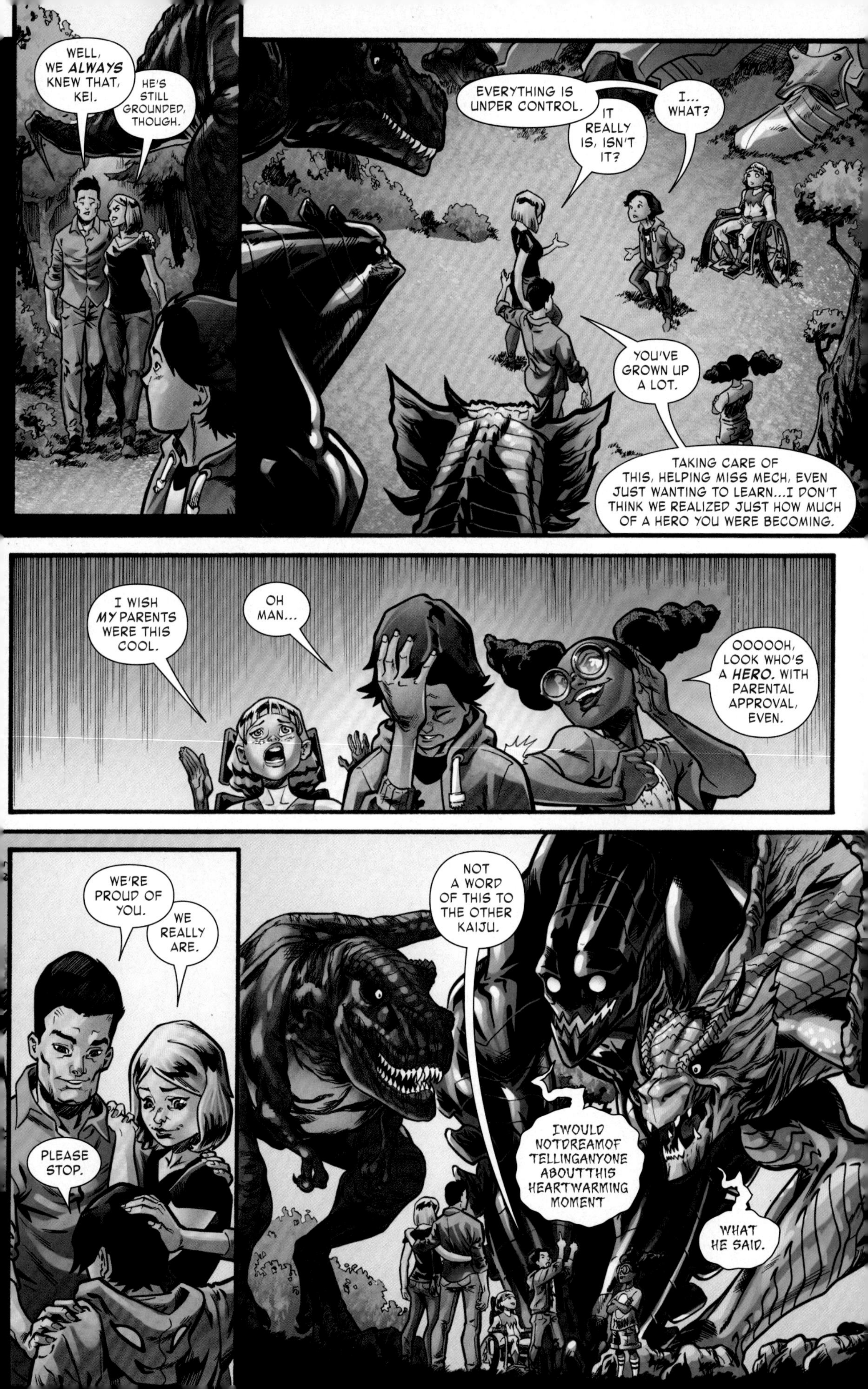
WELL, WE ALWAYS KNEW THAT, KEI.
HE'S STILL GROUNDED, THOUGH.
EVERYTHING IS UNDER CONTROL.
IT REALLY IS, ISN'T IT?
I... WHAT?
YOU'VE GROWN UP A LOT.
TAKING CARE OF THIS, HELPING MISS MECH, EVEN JUST WANTING TO LEARN...I DON'T THINK WE REALIZED JUST HOW MUCH OF A HERO YOU WERE BECOMING.
I WISH MY PARENTS WERE THIS COOL.
OH MAN...
OOOOOH, LOOK WHO'S A HERO. WITH PARENTAL APPROVAL, EVEN.
WE'RE PROUD OF YOU.
WE REALLY ARE.
PLEASE STOP.
NOT A WORD OF THIS TO THE OTHER KAIJU.
IWOULD NOTDREAMOF TELLINGANYONE ABOUTTHIS HEARTWARMING MOMENT
WHAT HE SAID.

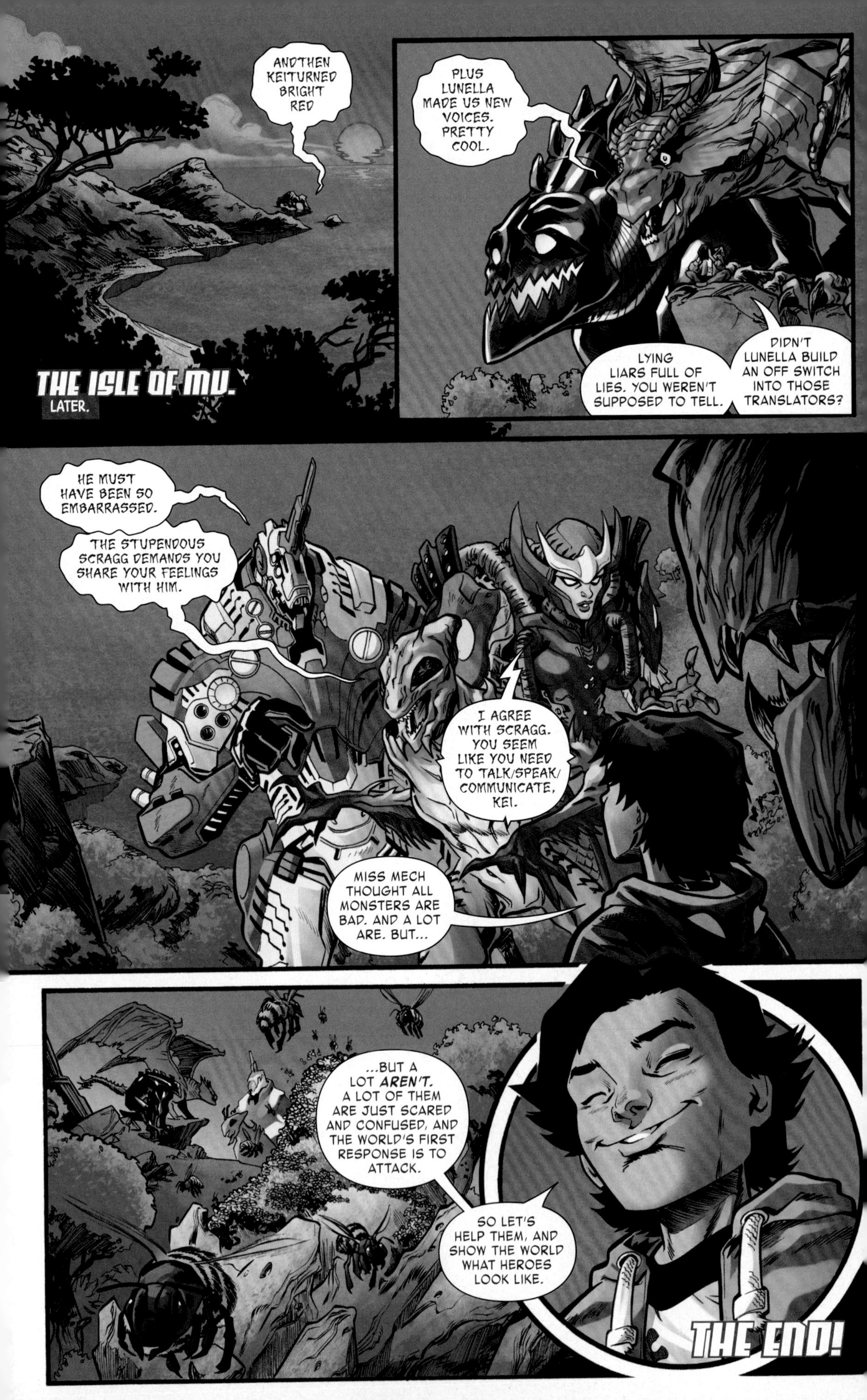
AND THEN KEI TURNED BRIGHT RED
THE ISLE OF MU.
LATER.
PLUS LUNELLA MADE US NEW VOICES. PRETTY COOL.
LYING LIARS FULL OF LIES. YOU WEREN'T SUPPOSED TO TELL.
DIDN'T LUNELLA BUILD AN OFF SWITCH INTO THOSE TRANSLATORS?
HE MUST HAVE BEEN SO EMBARRASSED.
THE STUPENDOUS SCRAGG DEMANDS YOU SHARE YOUR FEELINGS WITH HIM.
I AGREE WITH SCRAGG. YOU SEEM LIKE YOU NEED TO TALK/SPEAK/COMMUNICATE, KEI.
MISS MECH THOUGHT ALL MONSTERS ARE BAD. AND A LOT ARE. BUT...
...BUT A LOT AREN'T. A LOT OF THEM ARE JUST SCARED AND CONFUSED, AND THE WORLD'S FIRST RESPONSE IS TO ATTACK.
SO LET'S HELP THEM, AND SHOW THE WORLD WHAT HEROES LOOK LIKE.
THE END!

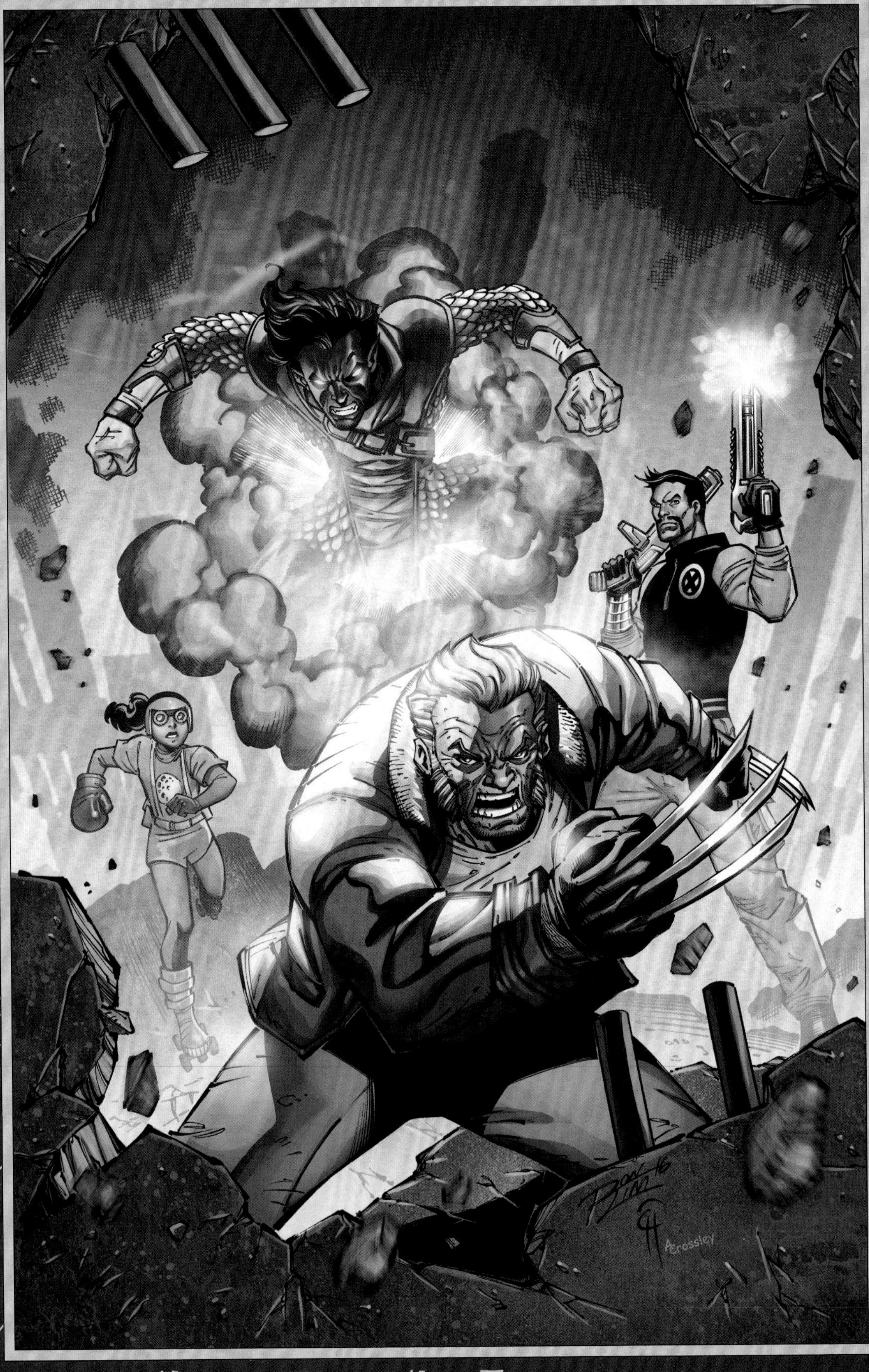
Ron Lim '16
CH
A.Crossley

EXTRAORDINARY X-MEN ANNUAL #1 VARIANT
BY RON LIM, CORY HAMSCHER & ANDREW CROSSLEY

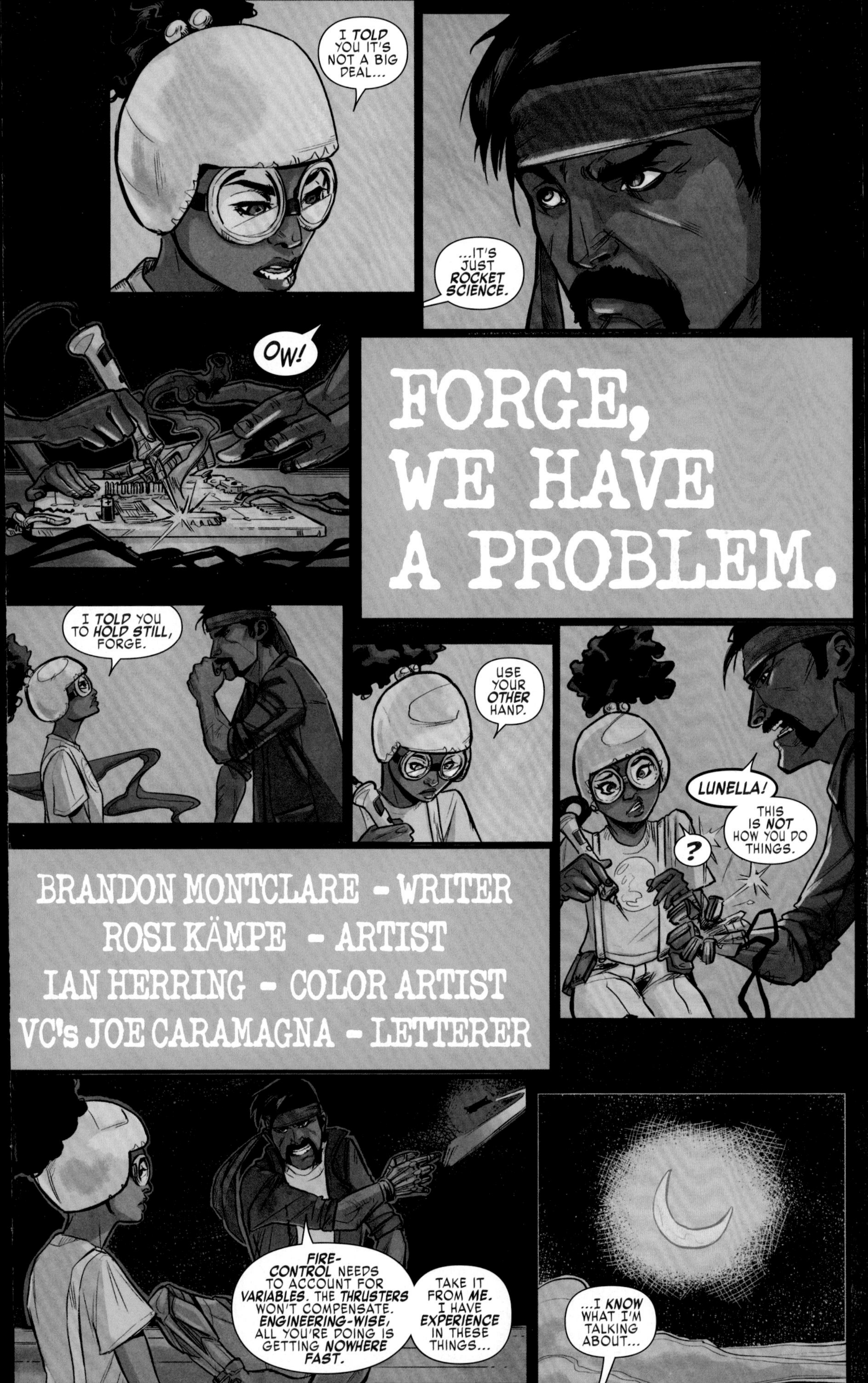
I TOLD YOU IT'S NOT A BIG DEAL...
...IT'S JUST ROCKET SCIENCE.
OW!
FORGE, WE HAVE A PROBLEM.
I TOLD YOU TO HOLD STILL, FORGE.
USE YOUR OTHER HAND.
LUNELLA!
THIS IS NOT HOW YOU DO THINGS.
?
BRANDON MONTCLARE - WRITER
ROSI KÄMPE - ARTIST
IAN HERRING - COLOR ARTIST
VC's JOE CARAMAGNA - LETTERER
FIRE-CONTROL NEEDS TO ACCOUNT FOR VARIABLES. THE THRUSTERS WON'T COMPENSATE. ENGINEERING-WISE, ALL YOU'RE DOING IS GETTING NOWHERE FAST.
TAKE IT FROM ME. I HAVE EXPERIENCE IN THESE THINGS...
...I KNOW WHAT I'M TALKING ABOUT...

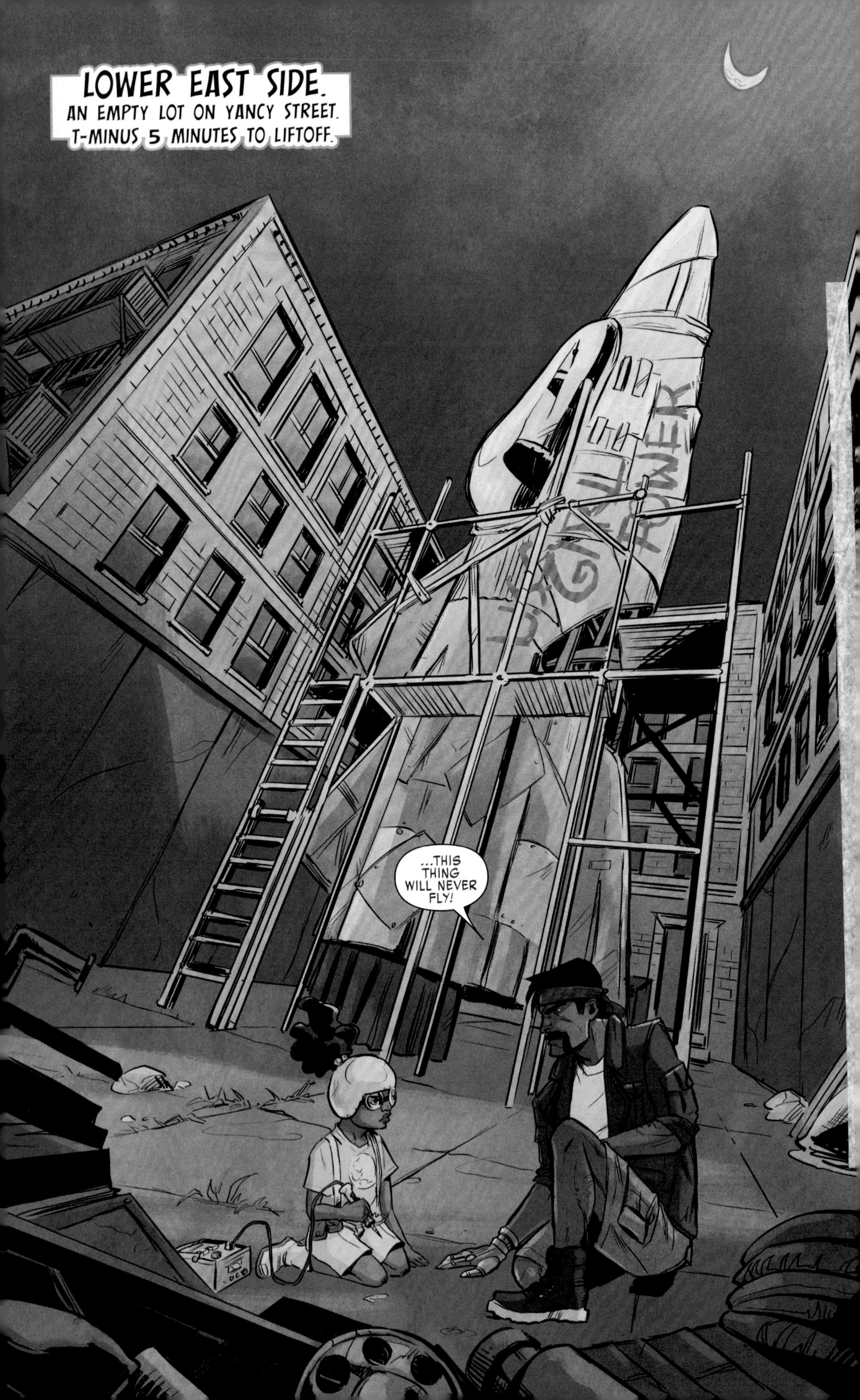
LOWER EAST SIDE.
AN EMPTY LOT ON YANCY STREET.
T-MINUS 5 MINUTES TO LIFTOFF.
...THIS THING WILL NEVER FLY!

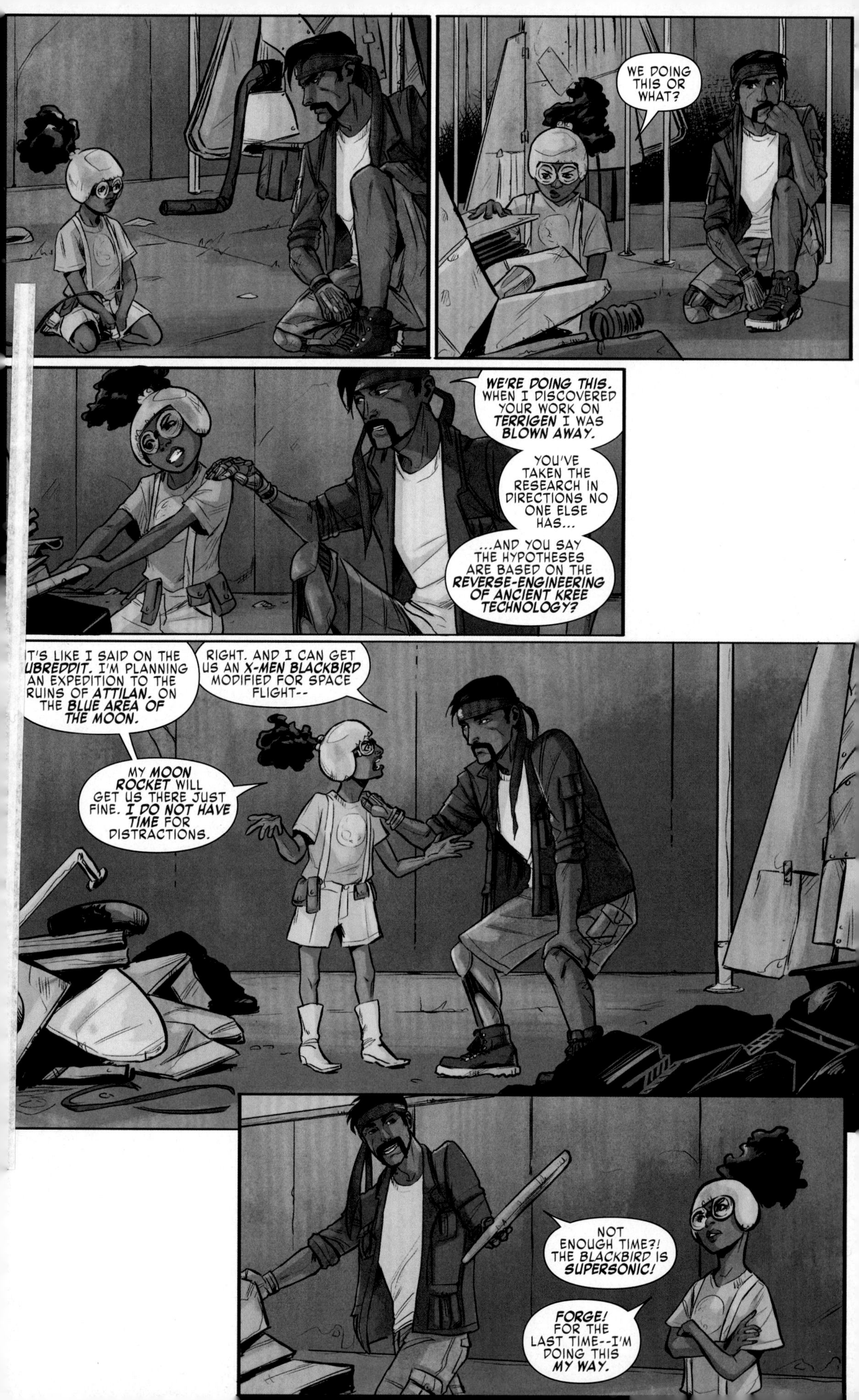
WE DOING THIS OR WHAT?
WE'RE DOING THIS. WHEN I DISCOVERED YOUR WORK ON TERRIGEN I WAS BLOWN AWAY.
YOU'VE TAKEN THE RESEARCH IN DIRECTIONS NO ONE ELSE HAS...
...AND YOU SAY THE HYPOTHESES ARE BASED ON THE REVERSE-ENGINEERING OF ANCIENT KREE TECHNOLOGY?
IT'S LIKE I SAID ON THE SUBREDDIT. I'M PLANNING AN EXPEDITION TO THE RUINS OF ATTILAN. ON THE BLUE AREA OF THE MOON.
RIGHT. AND I CAN GET US AN X-MEN BLACKBIRD MODIFIED FOR SPACE FLIGHT--
MY MOON ROCKET WILL GET US THERE JUST FINE. I DO NOT HAVE TIME FOR DISTRACTIONS.
NOT ENOUGH TIME?! THE BLACKBIRD IS SUPERSONIC!
FORGE! FOR THE LAST TIME--I'M DOING THIS MY WAY.

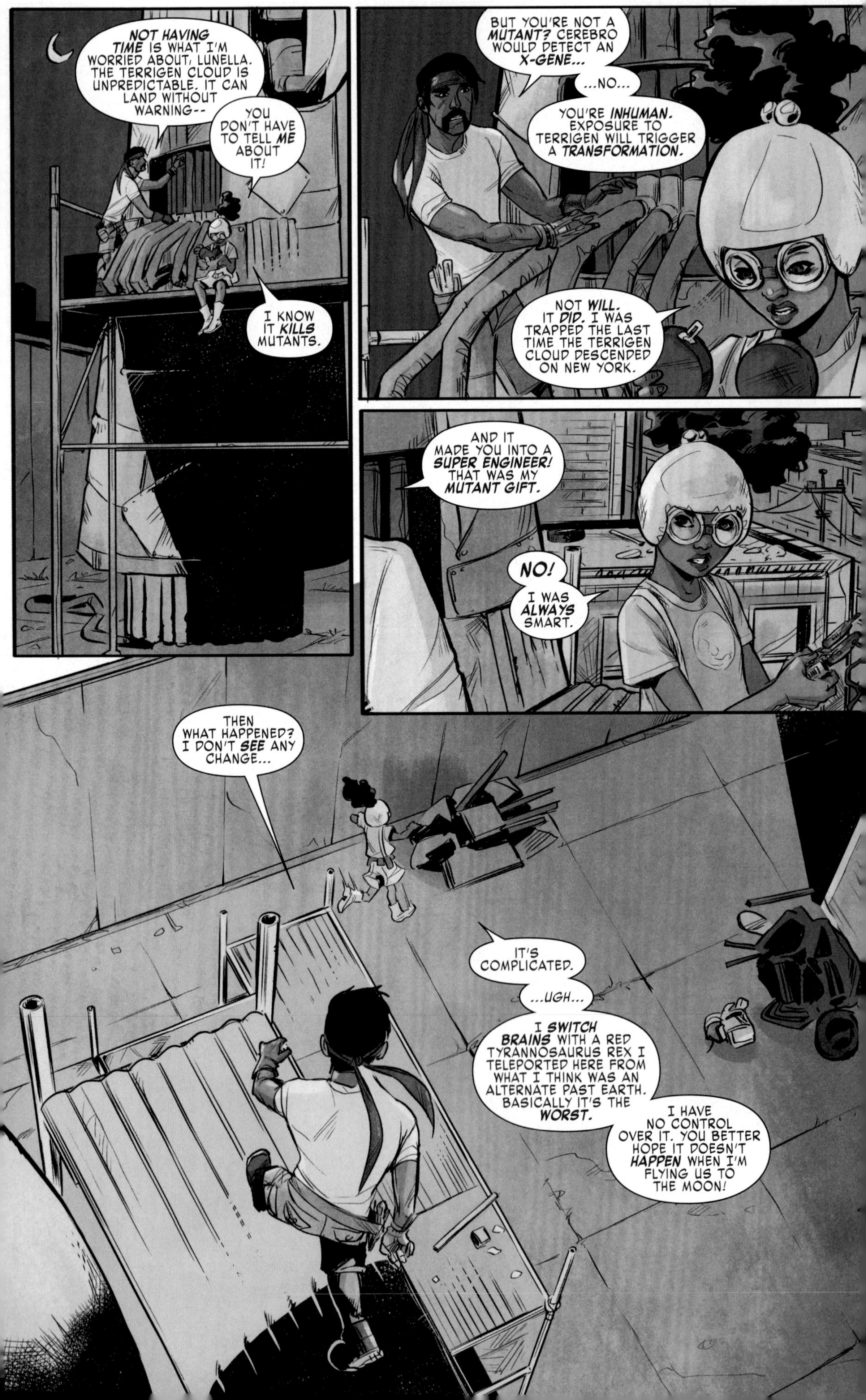
NOT HAVING TIME IS WHAT I'M WORRIED ABOUT, LUNELLA. THE TERRIGEN CLOUD IS UNPREDICTABLE. IT CAN LAND WITHOUT WARNING--
YOU DON'T HAVE TO TELL ME ABOUT IT!
I KNOW IT KILLS MUTANTS.
BUT YOU'RE NOT A MUTANT? CEREBRO WOULD DETECT AN X-GENE...
...NO...
YOU'RE INHUMAN. EXPOSURE TO TERRIGEN WILL TRIGGER A TRANSFORMATION.
NOT WILL. IT DID. I WAS TRAPPED THE LAST TIME THE TERRIGEN CLOUD DESCENDED ON NEW YORK.
AND IT MADE YOU INTO A SUPER ENGINEER! THAT WAS MY MUTANT GIFT.
NO!
I WAS ALWAYS SMART.
THEN WHAT HAPPENED? I DON'T SEE ANY CHANGE...
IT'S COMPLICATED.
...UGH...
I SWITCH BRAINS WITH A RED TYRANNOSAURUS REX I TELEPORTED HERE FROM WHAT I THINK WAS AN ALTERNATE PAST EARTH. BASICALLY IT'S THE WORST.
I HAVE NO CONTROL OVER IT. YOU BETTER HOPE IT DOESN'T HAPPEN WHEN I'M FLYING US TO THE MOON!

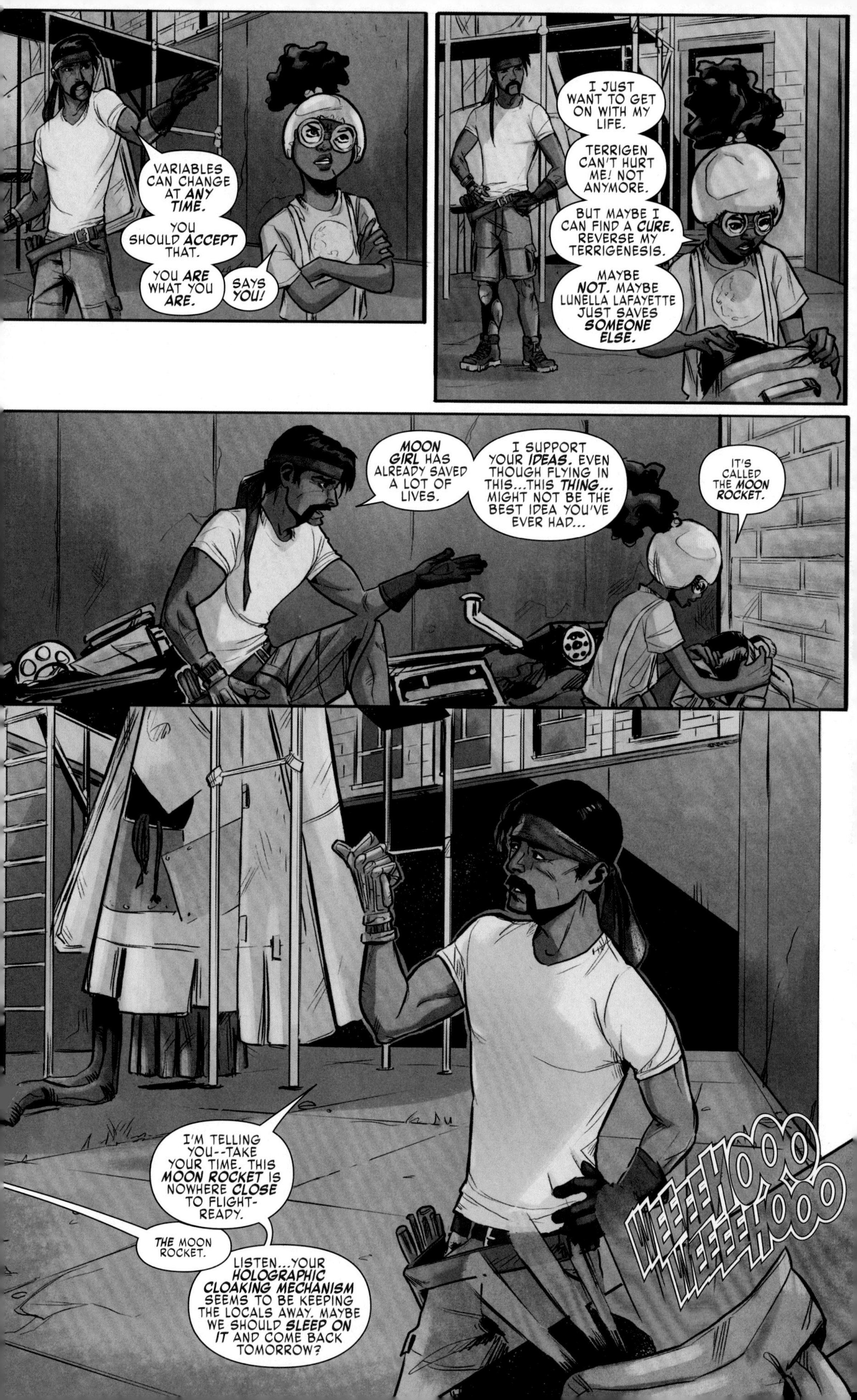
VARIABLES CAN CHANGE AT ANY TIME.
YOU SHOULD ACCEPT THAT.
YOU ARE WHAT YOU ARE.
SAYS YOU!
I JUST WANT TO GET ON WITH MY LIFE.
TERRIGEN CAN'T HURT ME! NOT ANYMORE.
BUT MAYBE I CAN FIND A CURE. REVERSE MY TERRIGENESIS.
MAYBE NOT. MAYBE LUNELLA LAFAYETTE JUST SAVES SOMEONE ELSE.
MOON GIRL HAS ALREADY SAVED A LOT OF LIVES.
I SUPPORT YOUR IDEAS. EVEN THOUGH FLYING IN THIS...THIS THING... MIGHT NOT BE THE BEST IDEA YOU'VE EVER HAD...
IT'S CALLED THE MOON ROCKET.
I'M TELLING YOU--TAKE YOUR TIME. THIS MOON ROCKET IS NOWHERE CLOSE TO FLIGHT-READY.
THE MOON ROCKET.
LISTEN...YOUR HOLOGRAPHIC CLOAKING MECHANISM SEEMS TO BE KEEPING THE LOCALS AWAY. MAYBE WE SHOULD SLEEP ON IT AND COME BACK TOMORROW?
WEEEEHOOO WEEEEHOOO

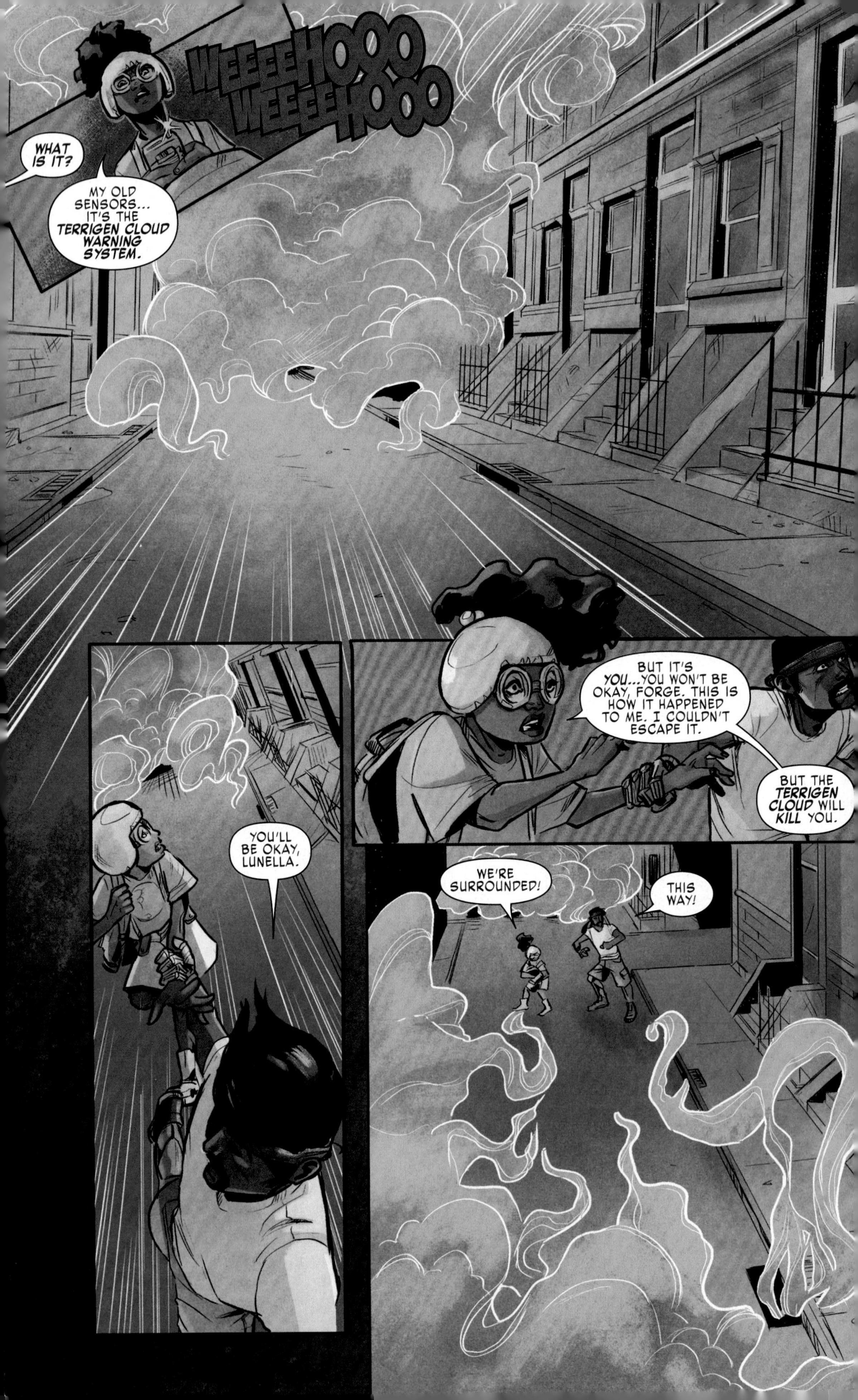
WEEEEHOOO WEEEEHOOO
WHAT IS IT?
MY OLD SENSORS... IT'S THE TERRIGEN CLOUD WARNING SYSTEM.
YOU'LL BE OKAY, LUNELLA.
BUT IT'S YOU...YOU WON'T BE OKAY, FORGE. THIS IS HOW IT HAPPENED TO ME. I COULDN'T ESCAPE IT.
BUT THE TERRIGEN CLOUD WILL KILL YOU.
WE'RE SURROUNDED!
THIS WAY!

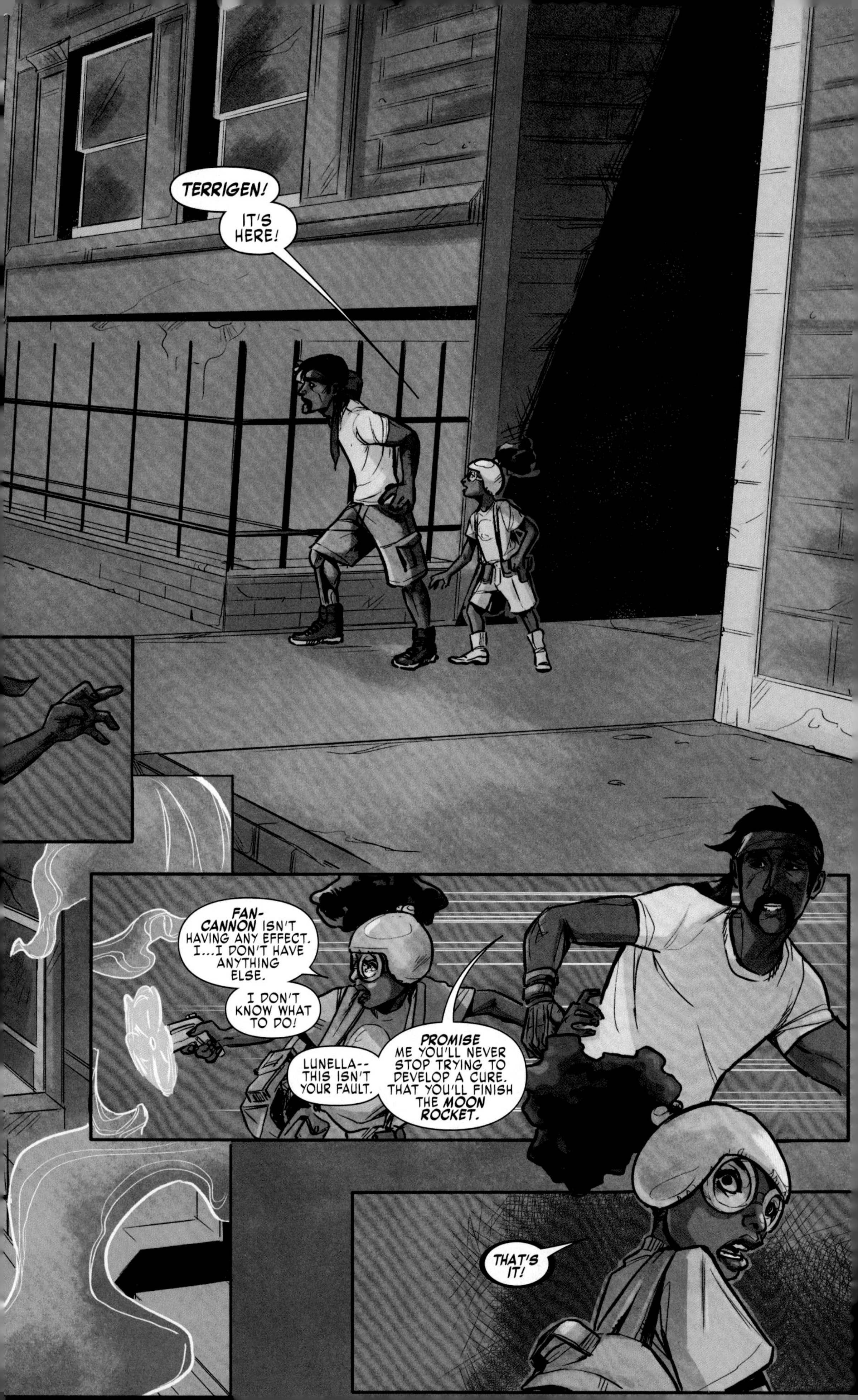
TERRIGEN!
IT'S HERE!
FAN-CANNON ISN'T HAVING ANY EFFECT. I...I DON'T HAVE ANYTHING ELSE.
I DON'T KNOW WHAT TO DO!
LUNELLA-- THIS ISN'T YOUR FAULT.
PROMISE ME YOU'LL NEVER STOP TRYING TO DEVELOP A CURE. THAT YOU'LL FINISH THE MOON ROCKET.
THAT'S IT!

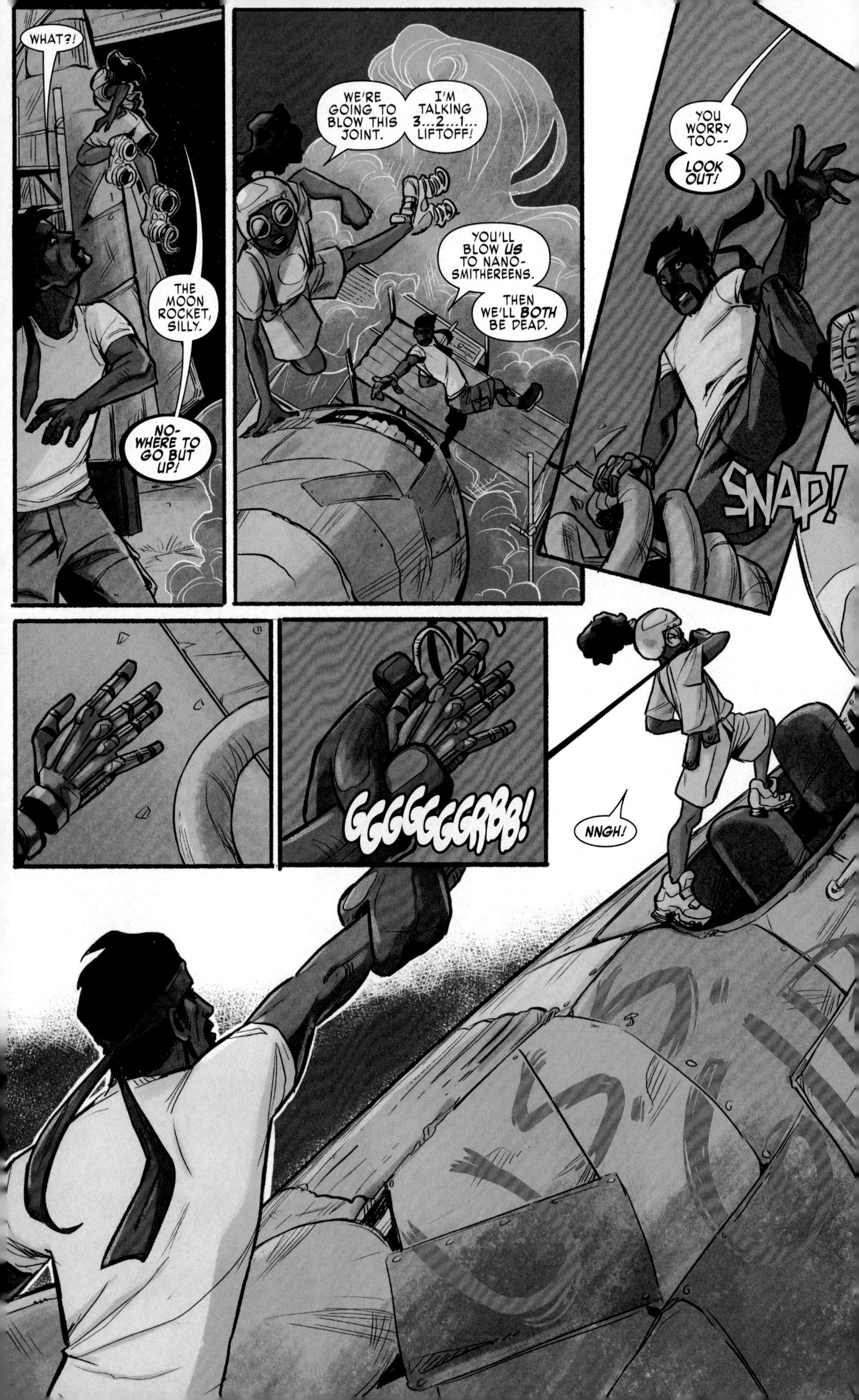

WHAT?!
THE MOON ROCKET, SILLY.
NO-WHERE TO GO BUT UP!
WE'RE GOING TO BLOW THIS JOINT.
I'M TALKING 3...2...1... LIFTOFF!
YOU'LL BLOW US TO NANO-SMITHEREENS.
THEN WE'LL BOTH BE DEAD.
YOU WORRY TOO--
LOOK OUT!
SNAP!
GGGGGGGRBB!
NNGH!

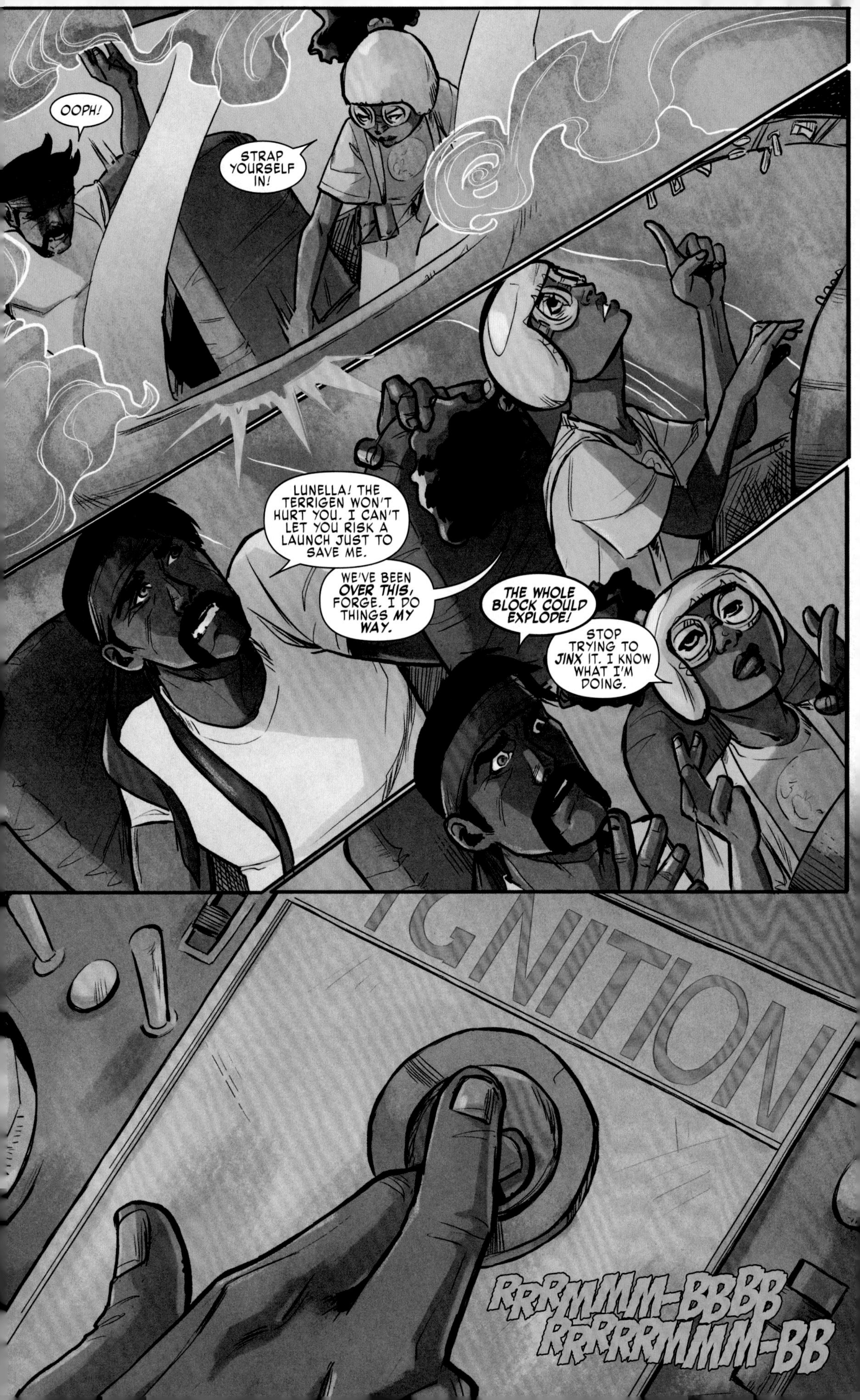
OOPH!
STRAP YOURSELF IN!
LUNELLA! THE TERRIGEN WON'T HURT YOU. I CAN'T LET YOU RISK A LAUNCH JUST TO SAVE ME.
WE'VE BEEN OVER THIS, FORGE. I DO THINGS MY WAY.
THE WHOLE BLOCK COULD EXPLODE!
STOP TRYING TO JINX IT. I KNOW WHAT I'M DOING.
IGNITION
RRRMMM-BBBB
RRRRRMMMM-BB

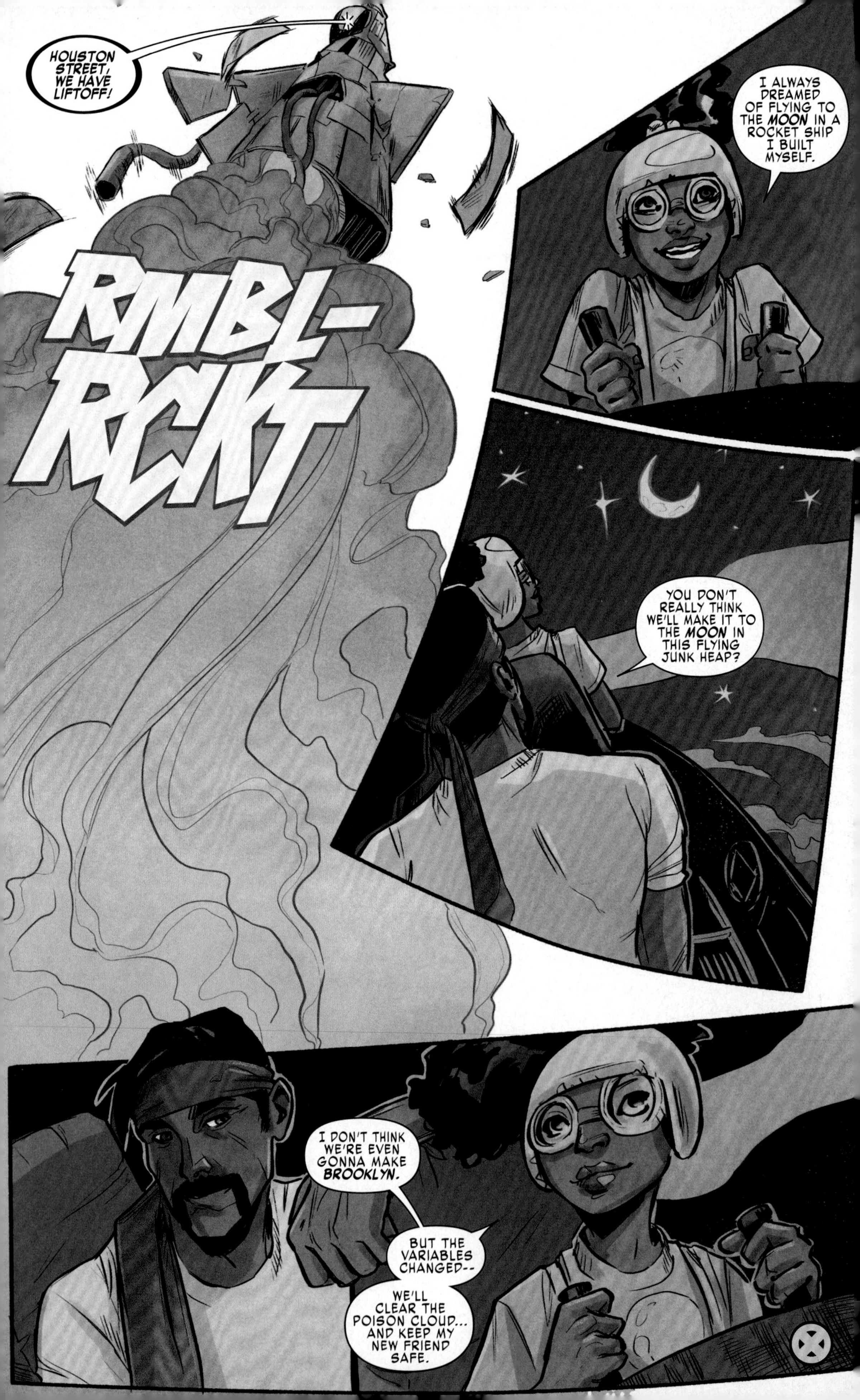
HOUSTON STREET, WE HAVE LIFTOFF!
RMBL-RCKT
I ALWAYS DREAMED OF FLYING TO THE *MOON* IN A ROCKET SHIP I BUILT MYSELF.
YOU DON'T REALLY THINK WE'LL MAKE IT TO THE *MOON* IN THIS FLYING JUNK HEAP?
I DON'T THINK WE'RE EVEN GONNA MAKE *BROOKLYN*.
BUT THE VARIABLES CHANGED--
WE'LL CLEAR THE POISON CLOUD... AND KEEP MY NEW FRIEND SAFE.

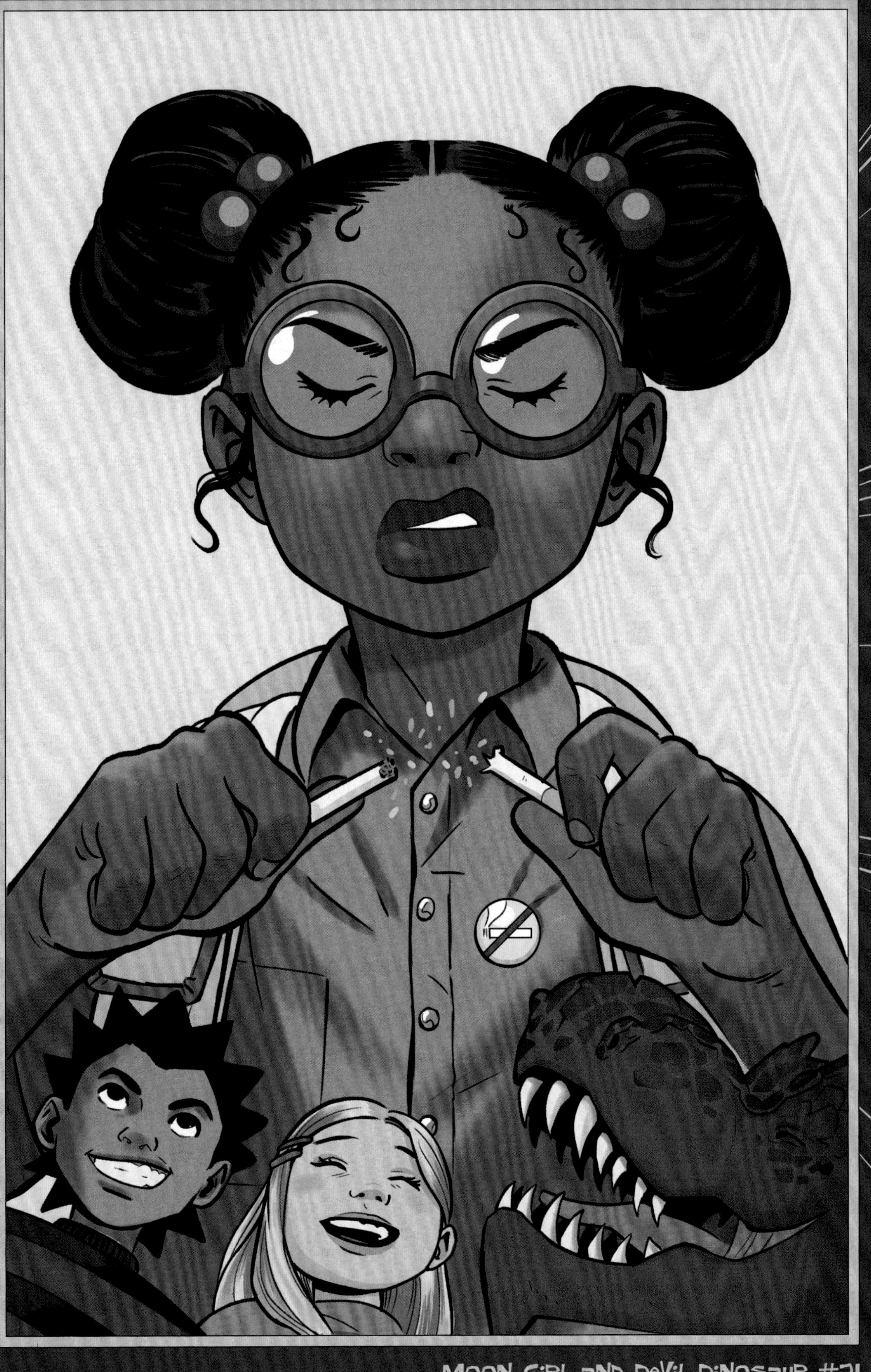

MOON GIRL AND DEVIL DINOSAUR #31

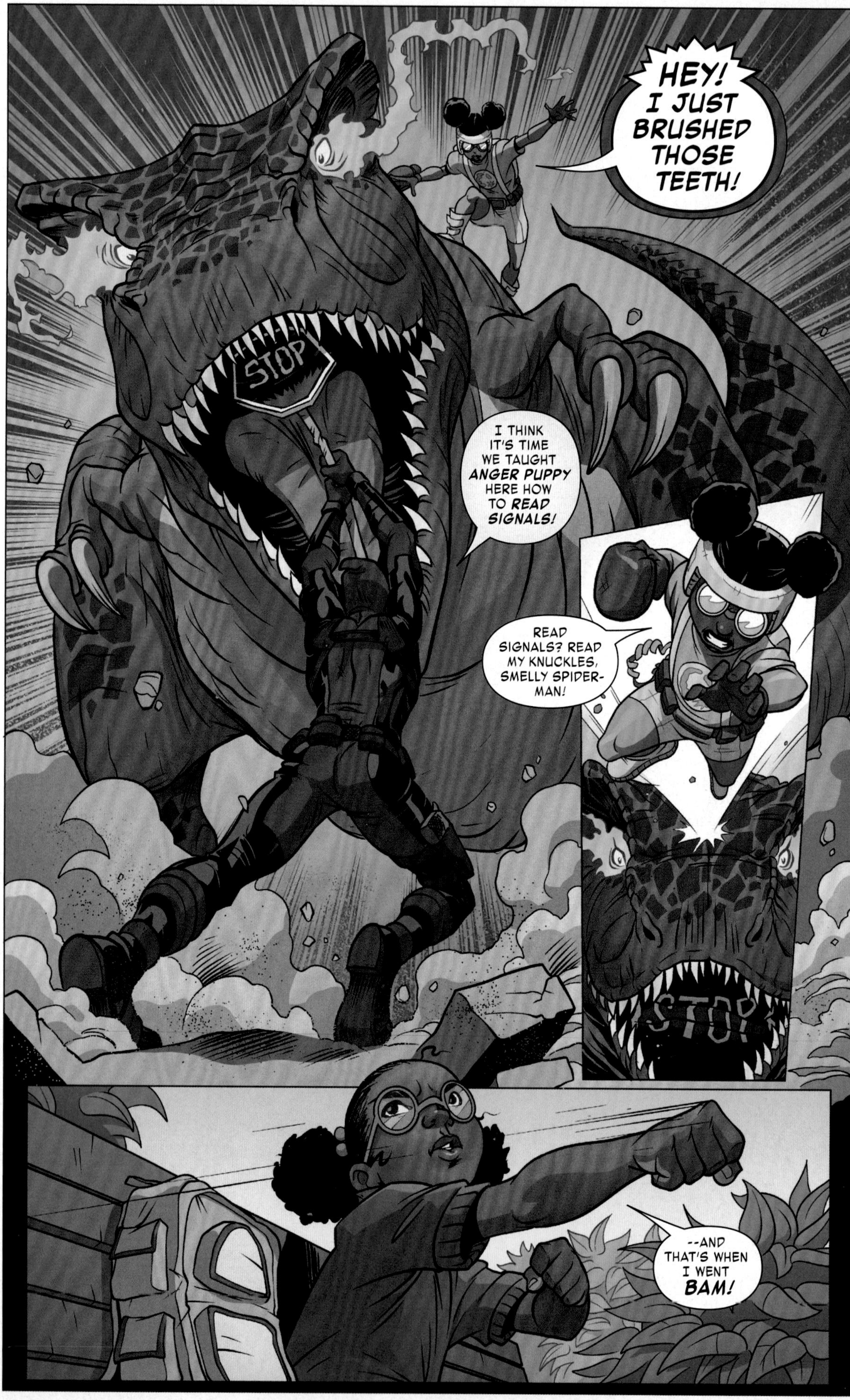
HEY! I JUST BRUSHED THOSE TEETH!
STOP
I THINK IT'S TIME WE TAUGHT ANGER PUPPY HERE HOW TO READ SIGNALS!
READ SIGNALS? READ MY KNUCKLES, SMELLY SPIDER-MAN!
STOP
--AND THAT'S WHEN I WENT BAM!

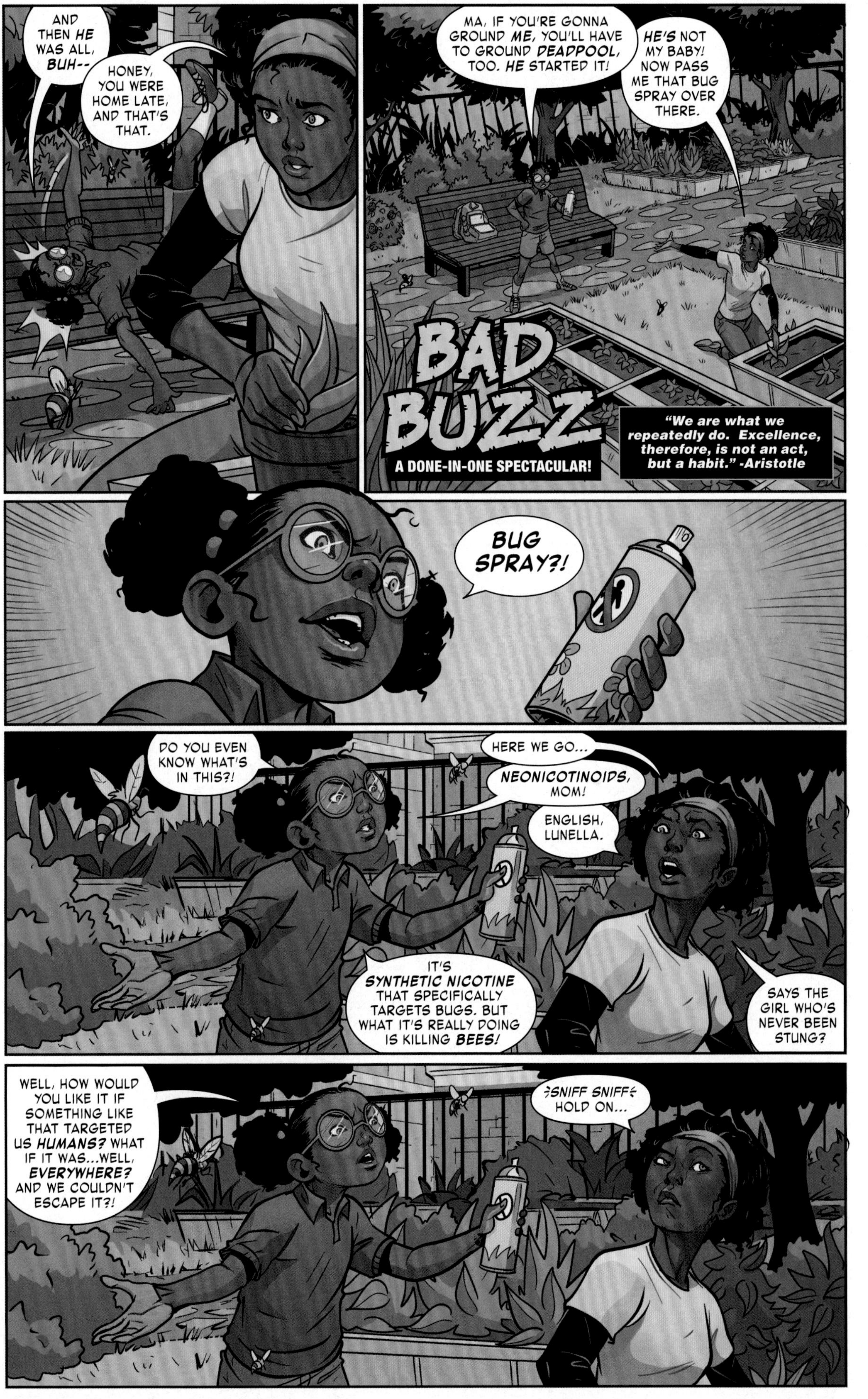

AND THEN HE WAS ALL, BUH--
HONEY, YOU WERE HOME LATE, AND THAT'S THAT.
MA, IF YOU'RE GONNA GROUND ME, YOU'LL HAVE TO GROUND DEADPOOL, TOO. HE STARTED IT!
HE'S NOT MY BABY! NOW PASS ME THAT BUG SPRAY OVER THERE.
BAD BUZZ
A DONE-IN-ONE SPECTACULAR!
"We are what we repeatedly do. Excellence, therefore, is not an act, but a habit." -Aristotle
BUG SPRAY?!
DO YOU EVEN KNOW WHAT'S IN THIS?!
HERE WE GO...
NEONICOTINOIDS, MOM!
ENGLISH, LUNELLA.
IT'S SYNTHETIC NICOTINE THAT SPECIFICALLY TARGETS BUGS. BUT WHAT IT'S REALLY DOING IS KILLING BEES!
SAYS THE GIRL WHO'S NEVER BEEN STUNG?
WELL, HOW WOULD YOU LIKE IT IF SOMETHING LIKE THAT TARGETED US HUMANS? WHAT IF IT WAS...WELL, EVERYWHERE? AND WE COULDN'T ESCAPE IT?!
SNIFF SNIFF HOLD ON...

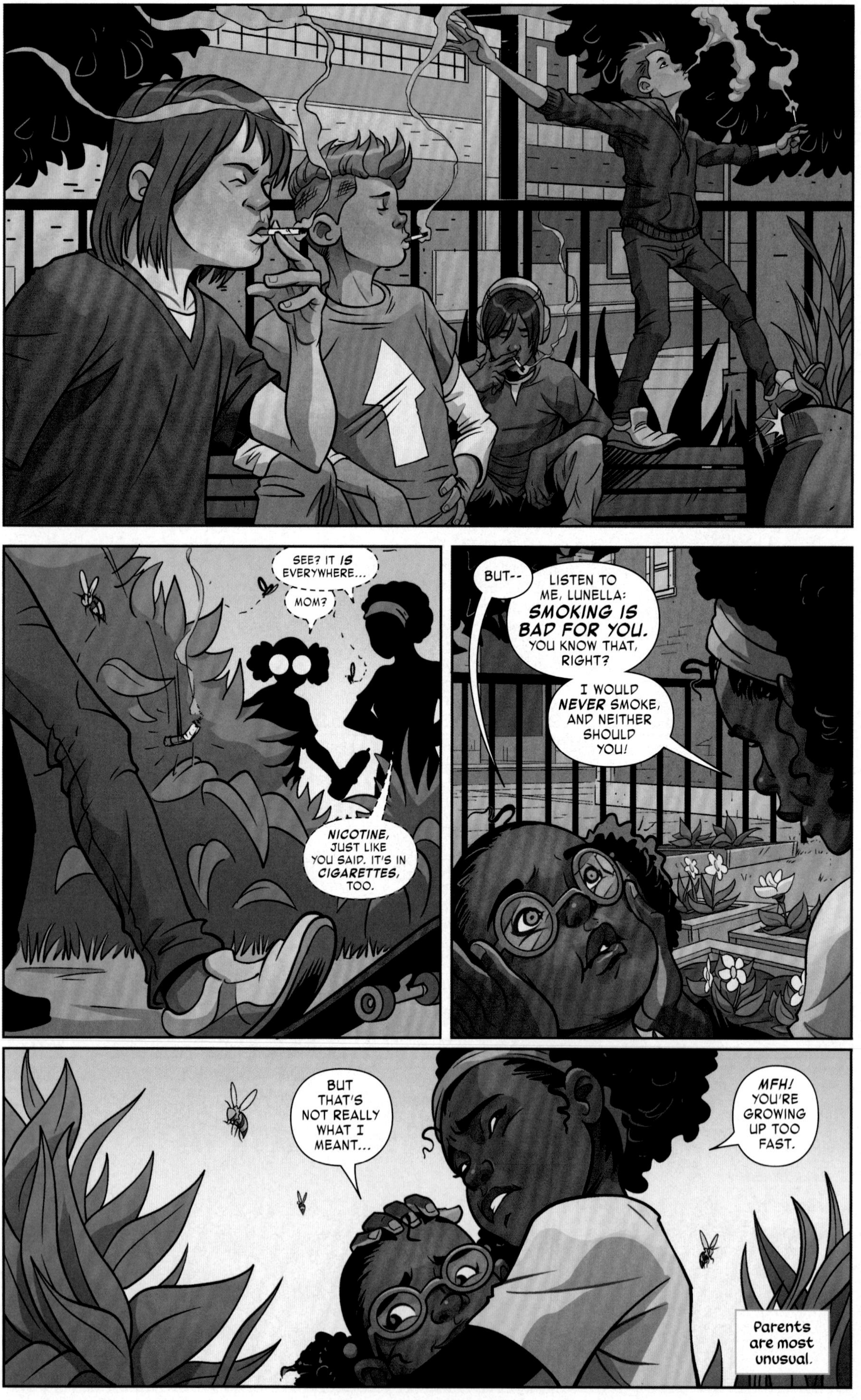
SEE? IT IS EVERYWHERE...
MOM?
NICOTINE, JUST LIKE YOU SAID. IT'S IN CIGARETTES, TOO.
BUT--
LISTEN TO ME, LUNELLA: SMOKING IS BAD FOR YOU. YOU KNOW THAT, RIGHT?
I WOULD NEVER SMOKE, AND NEITHER SHOULD YOU!
BUT THAT'S NOT REALLY WHAT I MEANT...
MFH! YOU'RE GROWING UP TOO FAST.
Parents are most unusual.

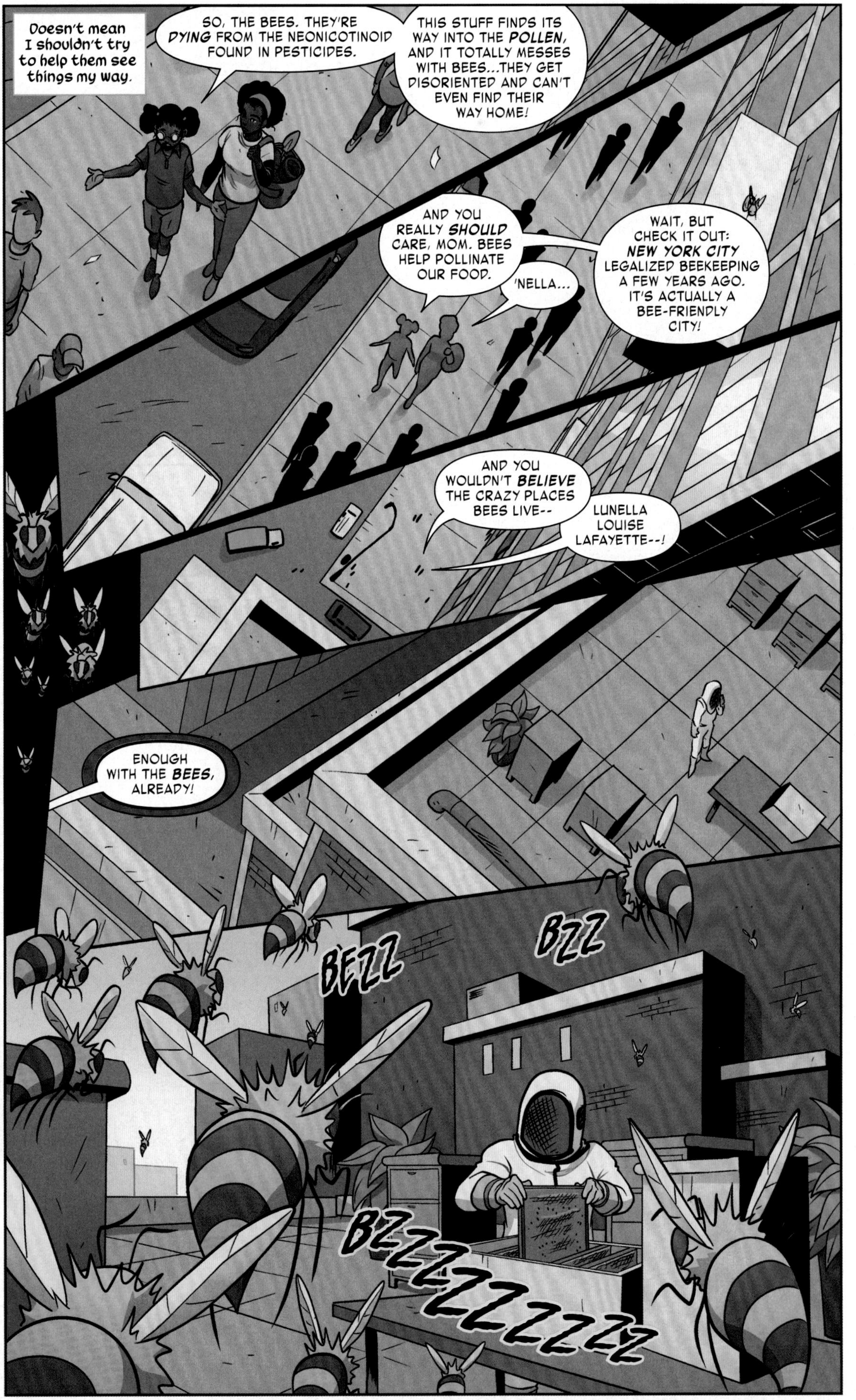
Doesn't mean I shouldn't try to help them see things my way.
SO, THE BEES. THEY'RE *DYING* FROM THE NEONICOTINOID FOUND IN PESTICIDES.
THIS STUFF FINDS ITS WAY INTO THE *POLLEN*, AND IT TOTALLY MESSES WITH BEES...THEY GET DISORIENTED AND CAN'T EVEN FIND THEIR WAY HOME!
AND YOU REALLY *SHOULD* CARE, MOM. BEES HELP POLLINATE OUR FOOD.
'NELLA...
WAIT, BUT CHECK IT OUT: *NEW YORK CITY* LEGALIZED BEEKEEPING A FEW YEARS AGO. IT'S ACTUALLY A BEE-FRIENDLY CITY!
AND YOU WOULDN'T *BELIEVE* THE CRAZY PLACES BEES LIVE--
LUNELLA LOUISE LAFAYETTE--!
ENOUGH WITH THE *BEES*, ALREADY!
BEZZ
BZZ
BZZZZZZZZZZZZ

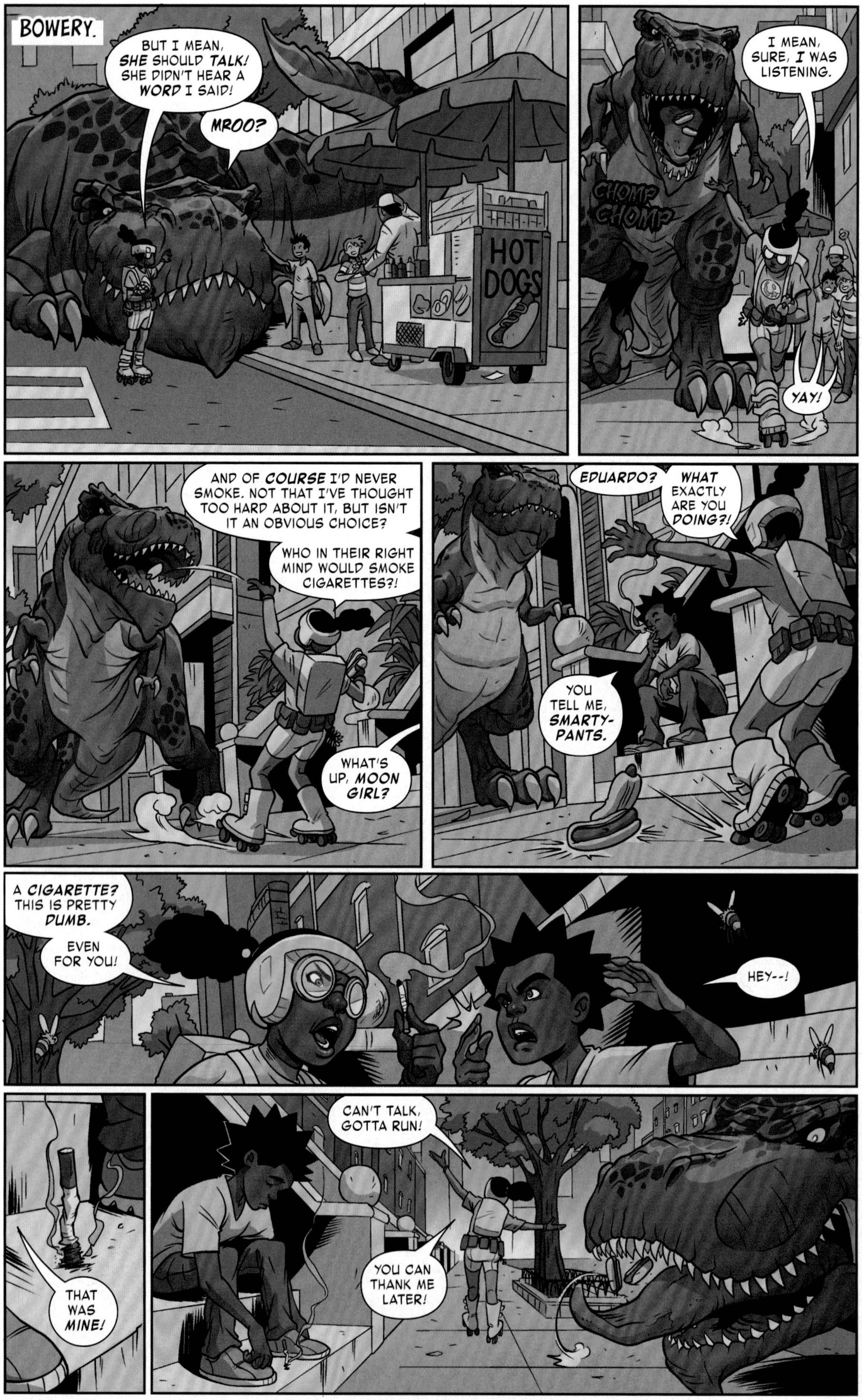
BOWERY.
BUT I MEAN, SHE SHOULD TALK! SHE DIDN'T HEAR A WORD I SAID!
MROO?
HOT DOGS
I MEAN, SURE, I WAS LISTENING.
CHOMP CHOMP
YAY!
AND OF COURSE I'D NEVER SMOKE. NOT THAT I'VE THOUGHT TOO HARD ABOUT IT, BUT ISN'T IT AN OBVIOUS CHOICE?
WHO IN THEIR RIGHT MIND WOULD SMOKE CIGARETTES?!
WHAT'S UP, MOON GIRL?
EDUARDO?
WHAT EXACTLY ARE YOU DOING?!
YOU TELL ME, SMARTY-PANTS.
A CIGARETTE? THIS IS PRETTY DUMB.
EVEN FOR YOU!
HEY--!
THAT WAS MINE!
CAN'T TALK, GOTTA RUN!
YOU CAN THANK ME LATER!

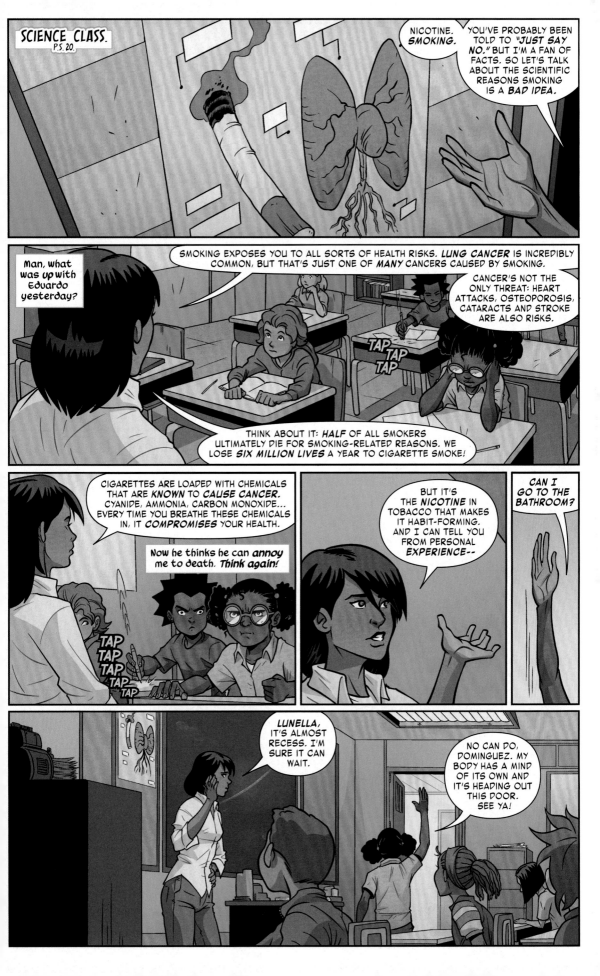

SCIENCE CLASS.
P.S. 20.

NICOTINE. *SMOKING.*

YOU'VE PROBABLY BEEN TOLD TO *"JUST SAY NO."* BUT I'M A FAN OF FACTS. SO LET'S TALK ABOUT THE SCIENTIFIC REASONS SMOKING IS A *BAD IDEA.*

Man, what was up with Eduardo yesterday?

SMOKING EXPOSES YOU TO ALL SORTS OF HEALTH RISKS. *LUNG CANCER* IS INCREDIBLY COMMON, BUT THAT'S JUST ONE OF *MANY* CANCERS CAUSED BY SMOKING.

CANCER'S NOT THE ONLY THREAT: HEART ATTACKS, OSTEOPOROSIS, CATARACTS AND STROKE ARE ALSO RISKS.

TAP TAP TAP

THINK ABOUT IT: *HALF* OF ALL SMOKERS ULTIMATELY DIE FOR SMOKING-RELATED REASONS. WE LOSE *SIX MILLION LIVES* A YEAR TO CIGARETTE SMOKE!

CIGARETTES ARE LOADED WITH CHEMICALS THAT ARE *KNOWN* TO *CAUSE CANCER.* CYANIDE, AMMONIA, CARBON MONOXIDE... EVERY TIME YOU BREATHE THESE CHEMICALS IN, IT *COMPROMISES* YOUR HEALTH.

Now he thinks he can *annoy* me to death. *Think again!*

TAP TAP TAP TAP TAP

BUT IT'S THE *NICOTINE* IN TOBACCO THAT MAKES IT HABIT-FORMING. AND I CAN TELL YOU FROM PERSONAL *EXPERIENCE*--

CAN I GO TO THE BATHROOM?

LUNELLA, IT'S ALMOST RECESS. I'M SURE IT CAN WAIT.

NO CAN DO, DOMINGUEZ. MY BODY HAS A MIND OF ITS OWN AND IT'S HEADING OUT THIS DOOR. SEE YA!

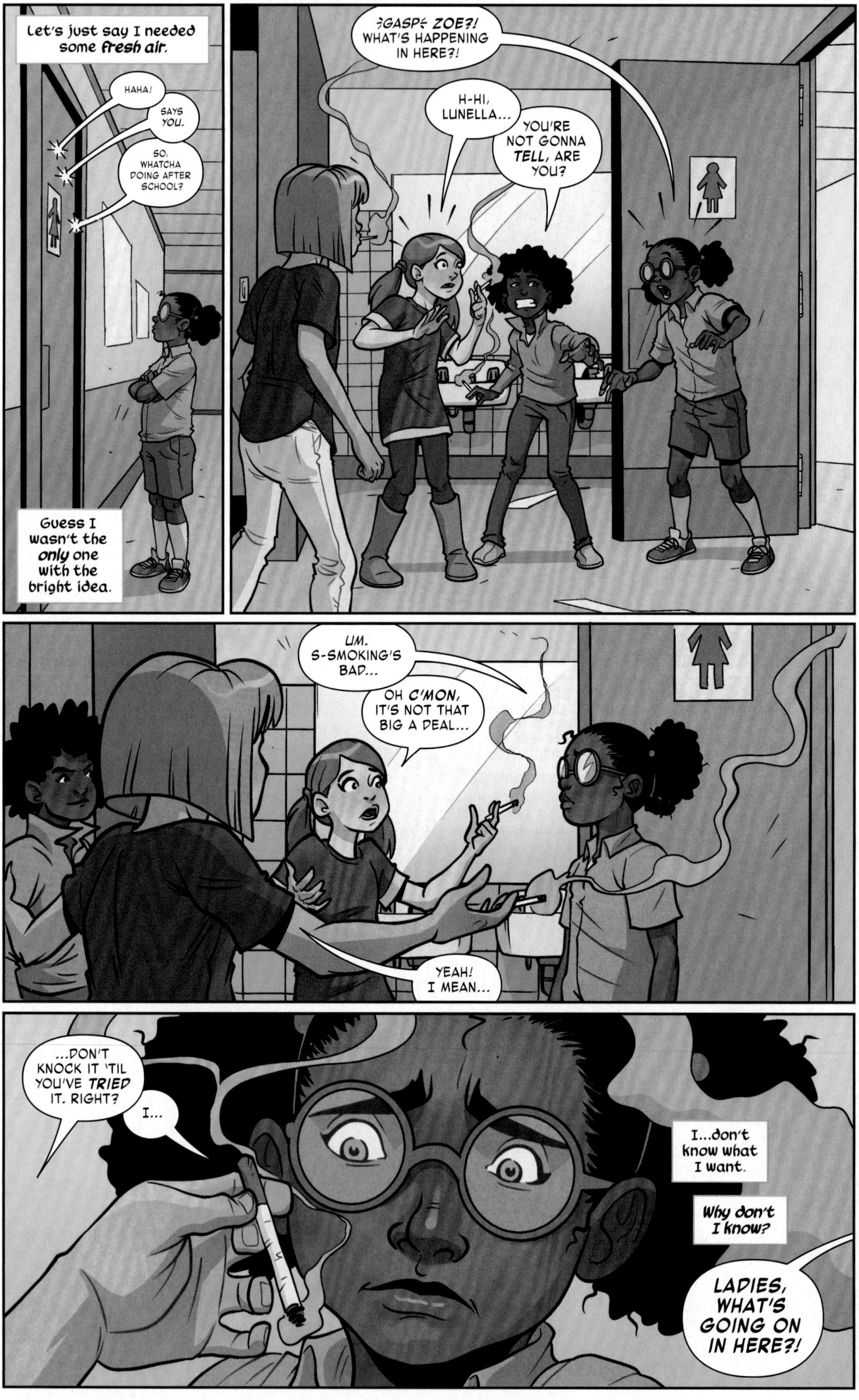
Let's just say I needed some fresh air.
HAHA!
SAYS YOU.
SO, WHATCHA DOING AFTER SCHOOL?
Guess I wasn't the only one with the bright idea.
GASP ZOE?! WHAT'S HAPPENING IN HERE?!
H-HI, LUNELLA...
YOU'RE NOT GONNA TELL, ARE YOU?
UM. S-SMOKING'S BAD...
OH C'MON, IT'S NOT THAT BIG A DEAL...
YEAH! I MEAN...
...DON'T KNOCK IT 'TIL YOU'VE TRIED IT. RIGHT?
I...
I...don't know what I want.
Why don't I know?
LADIES, WHAT'S GOING ON IN HERE?!

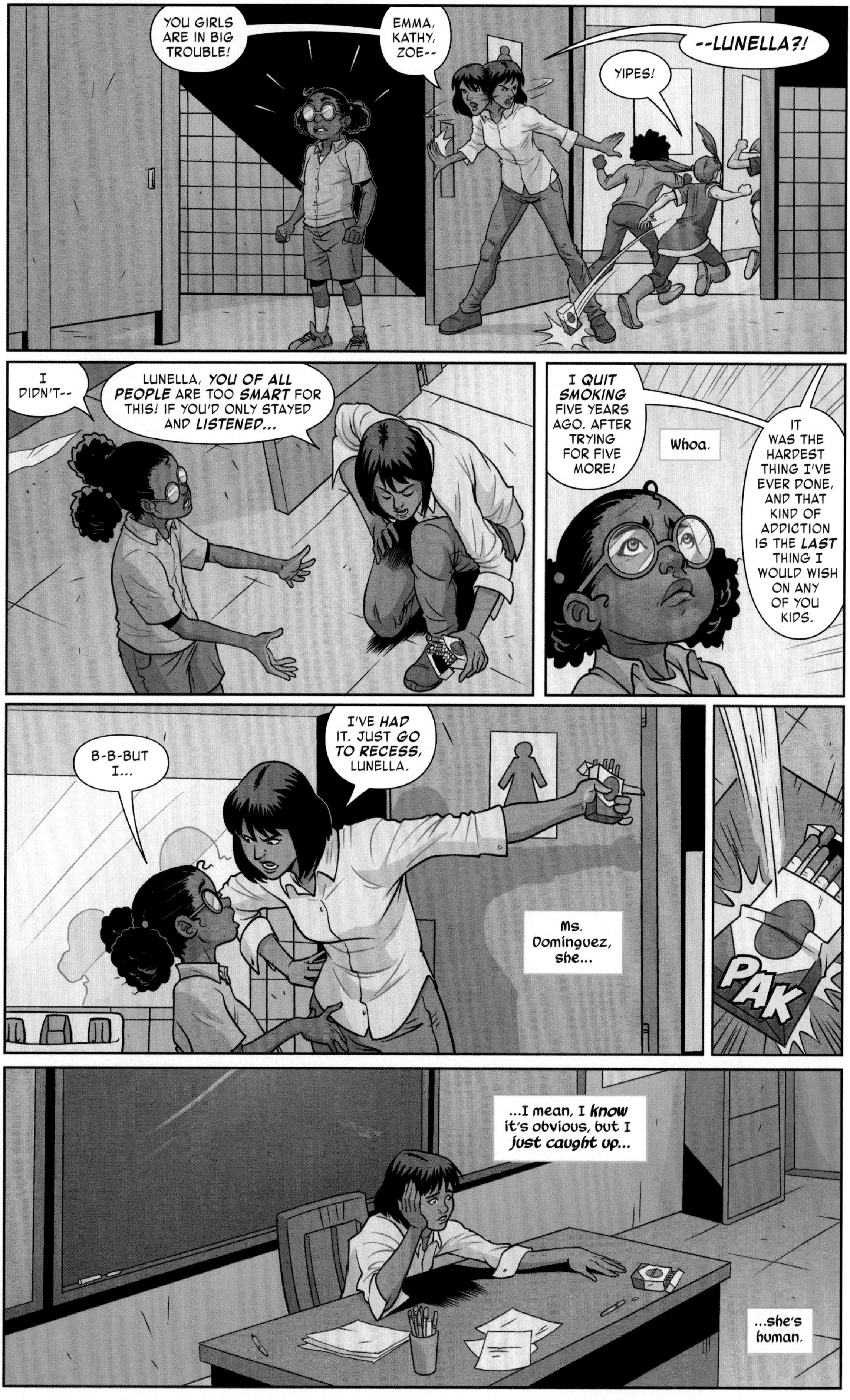
YOU GIRLS ARE IN BIG TROUBLE!
EMMA, KATHY, ZOE--
--LUNELLA?!
YIPES!
I DIDN'T--
LUNELLA, YOU OF ALL PEOPLE ARE TOO SMART FOR THIS! IF YOU'D ONLY STAYED AND LISTENED...
I QUIT SMOKING FIVE YEARS AGO. AFTER TRYING FOR FIVE MORE!
Whoa.
IT WAS THE HARDEST THING I'VE EVER DONE, AND THAT KIND OF ADDICTION IS THE LAST THING I WOULD WISH ON ANY OF YOU KIDS.
B-B-BUT I...
I'VE HAD IT. JUST GO TO RECESS, LUNELLA.
Ms. Dominguez, she...
PAK
...I mean, I know it's obvious, but I just caught up...
...she's human.

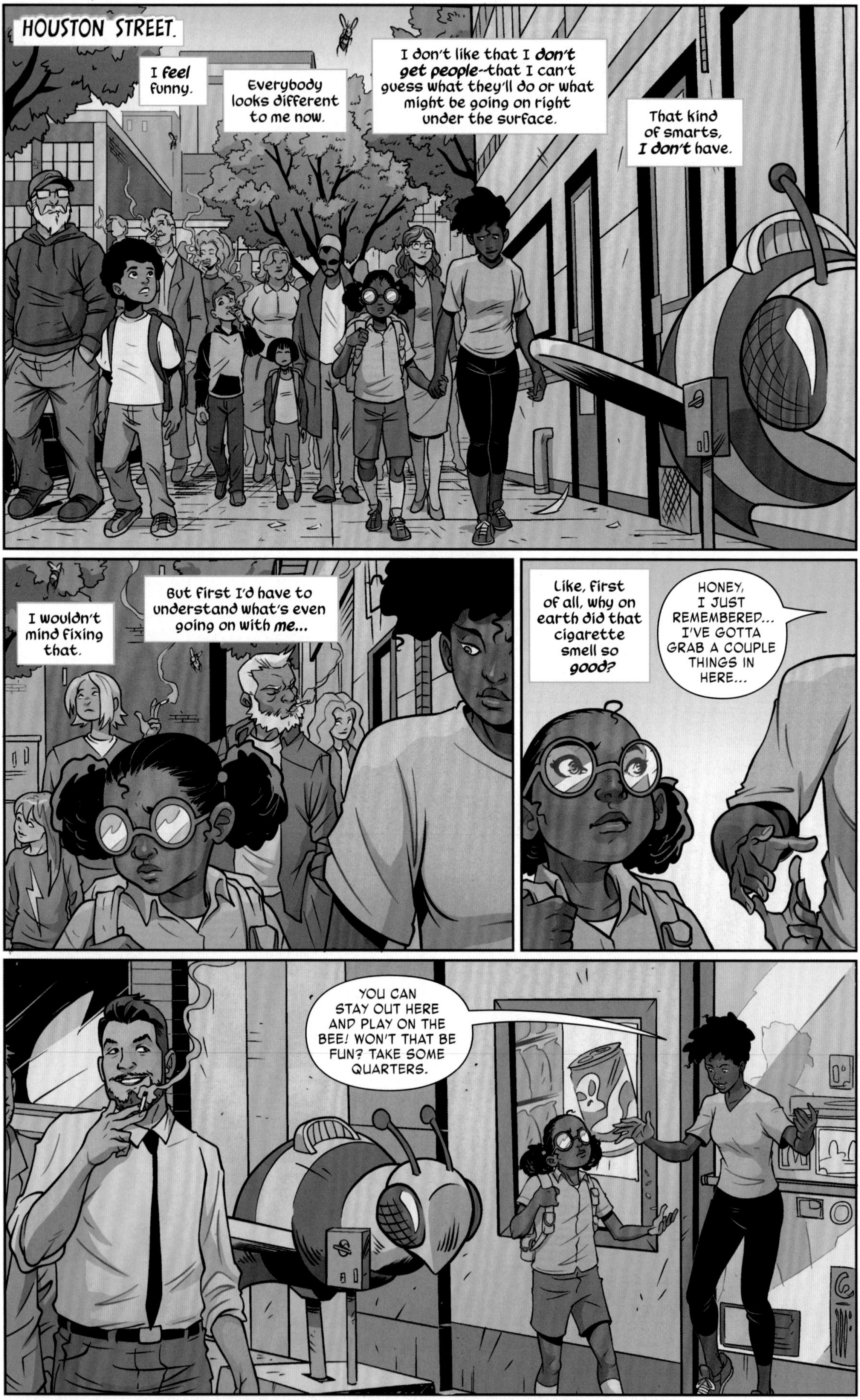
HOUSTON STREET.
I *feel* funny.
Everybody looks different to me now.
I don't like that I *don't get people*--that I can't guess what they'll do or what might be going on right under the surface.
That kind of smarts, *I don't* have.
I wouldn't mind fixing that.
But first I'd have to understand what's even going on with *me...*
Like, first of all, why on earth did that cigarette smell so *good?*
HONEY, I JUST REMEMBERED... I'VE GOTTA GRAB A COUPLE THINGS IN HERE...
YOU CAN STAY OUT HERE AND PLAY ON THE BEE! WON'T THAT BE FUN? TAKE SOME QUARTERS.

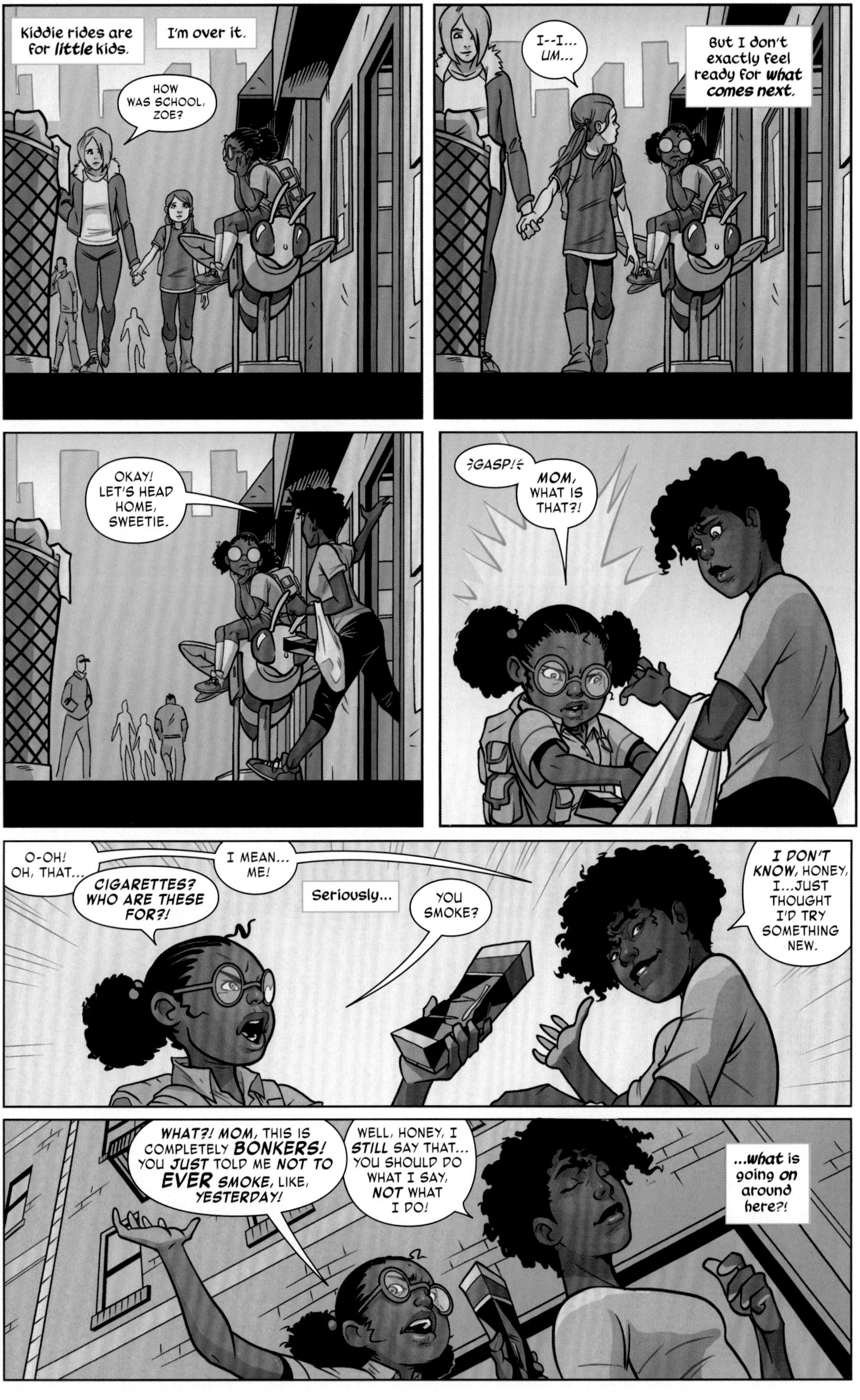

Kiddie rides are for *little* kids.
I'm over it.
HOW WAS SCHOOL, ZOE?
I--I... UM...
But I don't exactly feel ready for ***what comes next.***
OKAY! LET'S HEAD HOME, SWEETIE.
GASP!
MOM, WHAT IS THAT?!
O-OH! OH, THAT...
CIGARETTES? WHO ARE THESE FOR?!
I MEAN... ME!
Seriously...
YOU SMOKE?
I DON'T KNOW, HONEY, I...JUST THOUGHT I'D TRY SOMETHING NEW.
WHAT?! MOM, THIS IS COMPLETELY ***BONKERS!*** YOU ***JUST*** TOLD ME ***NOT TO EVER*** SMOKE, LIKE, ***YESTERDAY!***
WELL, HONEY, I ***STILL*** SAY THAT... YOU SHOULD DO WHAT I SAY, ***NOT*** WHAT I DO!
...what is going ***on*** around here?!

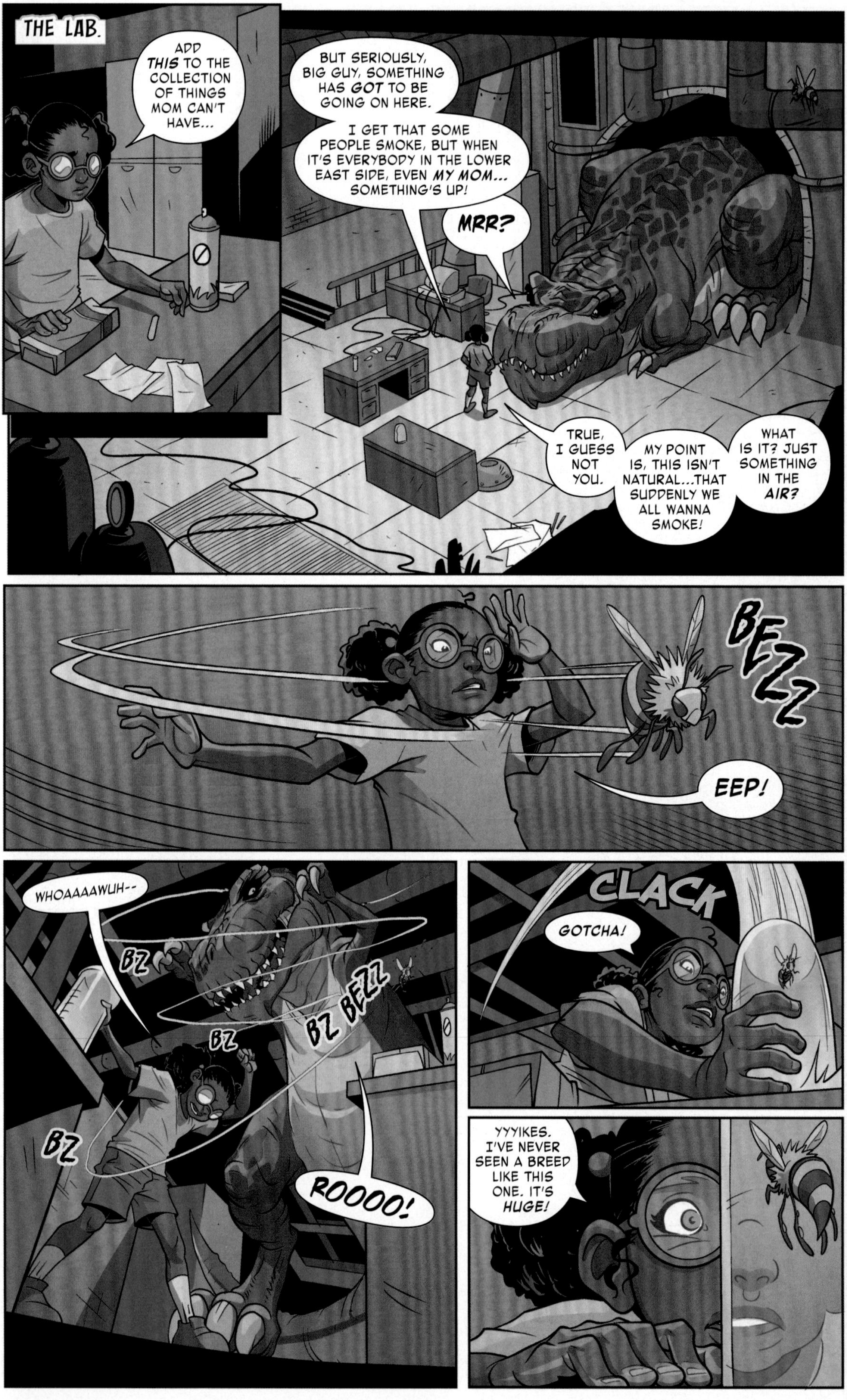
THE LAB.
ADD THIS TO THE COLLECTION OF THINGS MOM CAN'T HAVE...
BUT SERIOUSLY, BIG GUY, SOMETHING HAS GOT TO BE GOING ON HERE.
I GET THAT SOME PEOPLE SMOKE, BUT WHEN IT'S EVERYBODY IN THE LOWER EAST SIDE, EVEN MY MOM... SOMETHING'S UP!
MRR?
TRUE, I GUESS NOT YOU.
MY POINT IS, THIS ISN'T NATURAL...THAT SUDDENLY WE ALL WANNA SMOKE!
WHAT IS IT? JUST SOMETHING IN THE AIR?
BEZZ
EEP!
WHOAAAAWUH--
BZ
BZ BEZZ
BZ
BZ
ROOOO!
CLACK
GOTCHA!
YYYIKES. I'VE NEVER SEEN A BREED LIKE THIS ONE. IT'S HUGE!

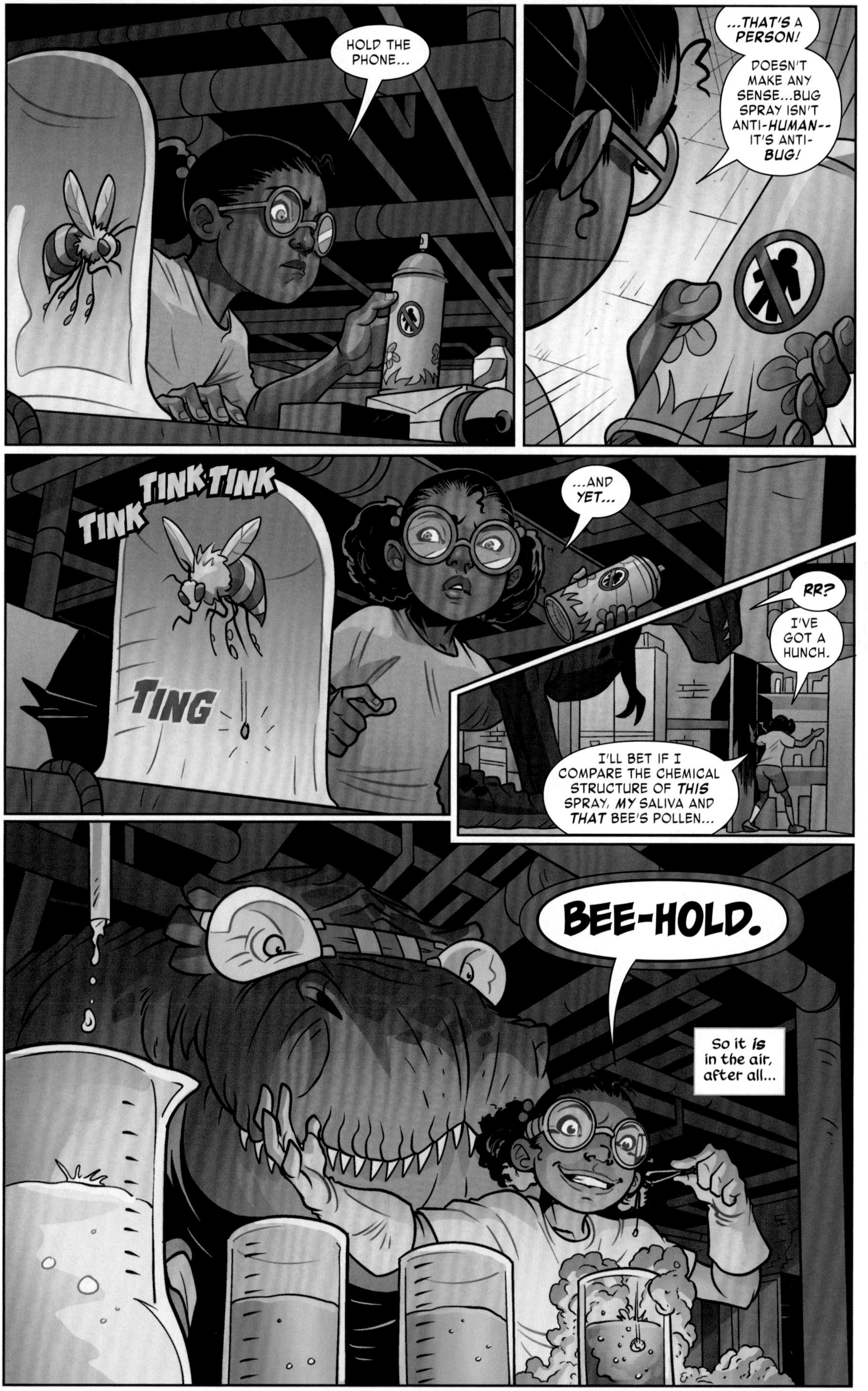
HOLD THE PHONE...
...THAT'S A PERSON!
DOESN'T MAKE ANY SENSE...BUG SPRAY ISN'T ANTI-HUMAN--IT'S ANTI-BUG!
TINK TINK TINK
TING
...AND YET...
RR?
I'VE GOT A HUNCH.
I'LL BET IF I COMPARE THE CHEMICAL STRUCTURE OF THIS SPRAY, MY SALIVA AND THAT BEE'S POLLEN...
BEE-HOLD.
So it is in the air, after all...

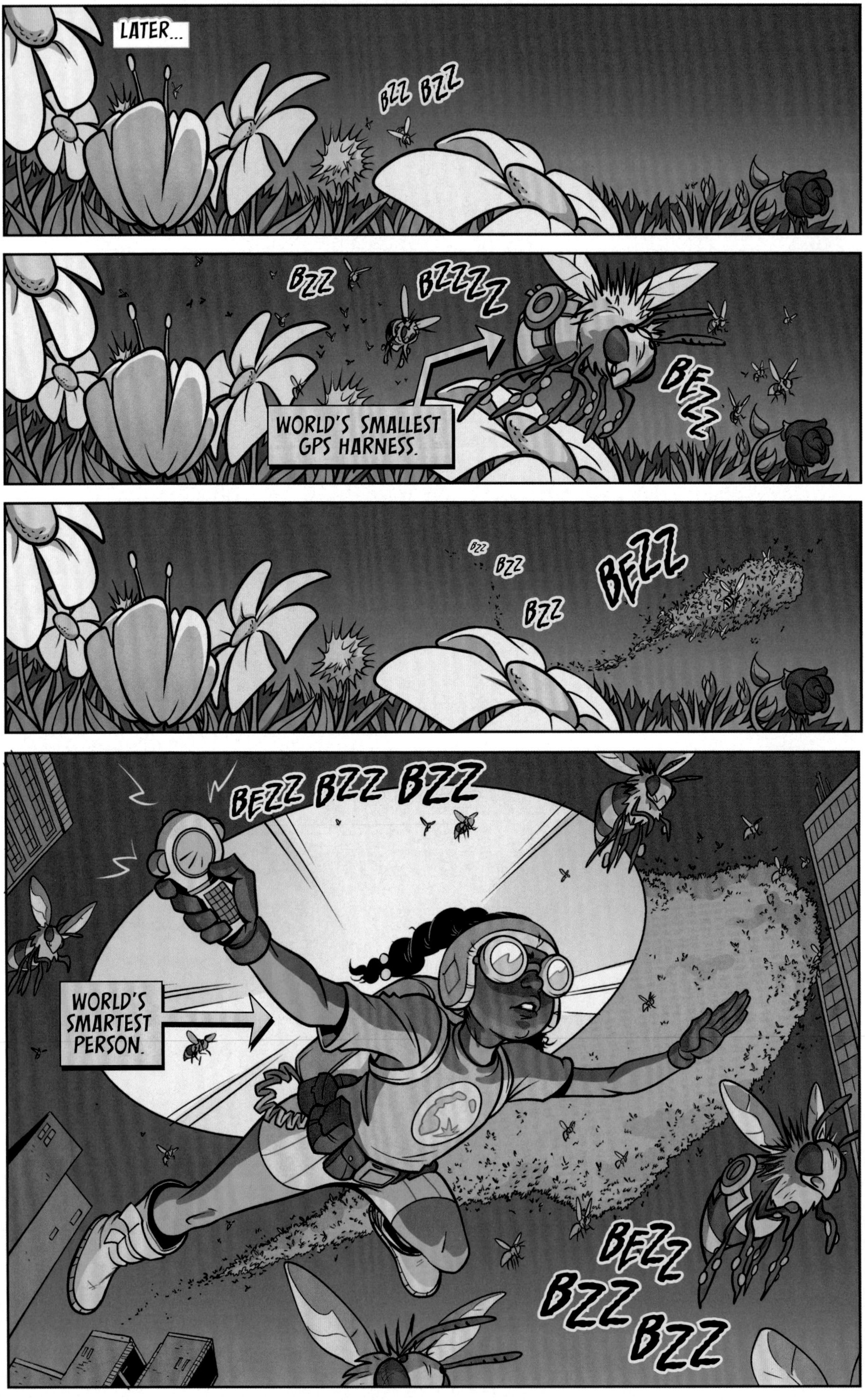
LATER...
BZZ BZZ
BZZ
BZZZZ
BEZZ
WORLD'S SMALLEST GPS HARNESS.
BZZ
BZZ
BZZ
BEZZ
BEZZ BZZ BZZ
WORLD'S SMARTEST PERSON.
BEZZ
BZZ
BZZ

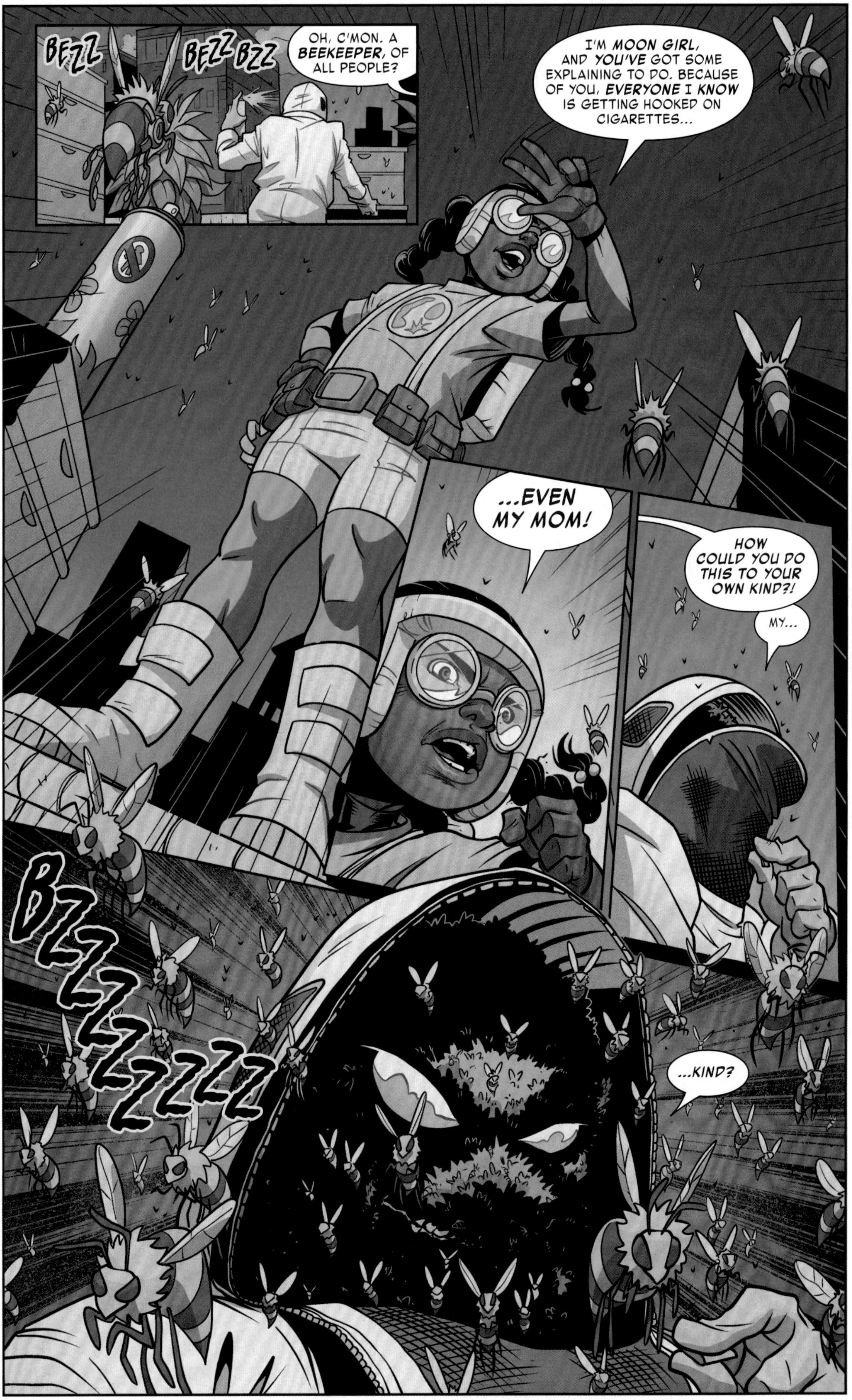
BEZZ
BEZZ BZZ
OH, C'MON. A BEEKEEPER, OF ALL PEOPLE?
I'M MOON GIRL, AND YOU'VE GOT SOME EXPLAINING TO DO. BECAUSE OF YOU, EVERYONE I KNOW IS GETTING HOOKED ON CIGARETTES...
...EVEN MY MOM!
HOW COULD YOU DO THIS TO YOUR OWN KIND?!
MY...
BZZZZZZZZZ
...KIND?

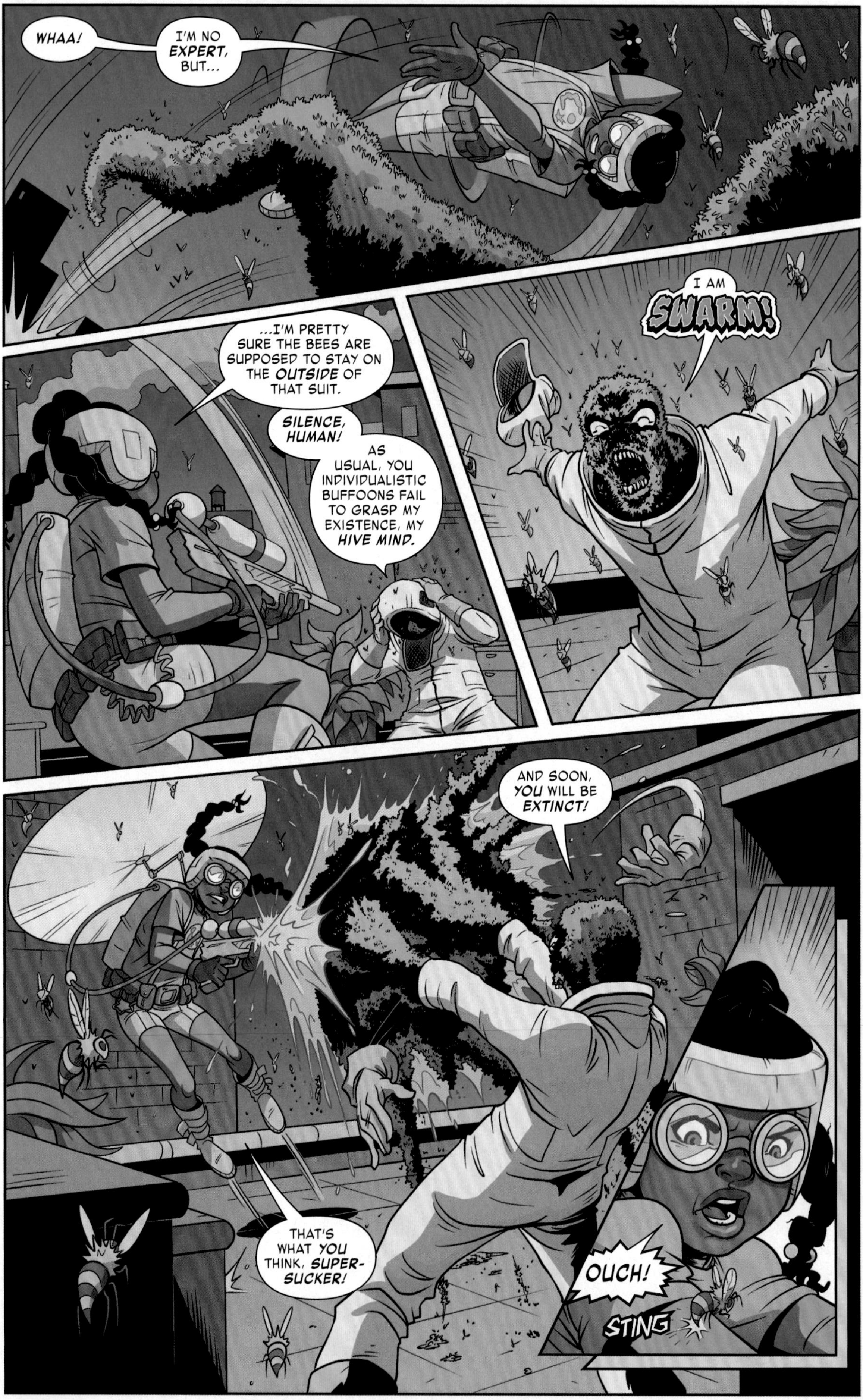

WHAA!
I'M NO EXPERT, BUT...
...I'M PRETTY SURE THE BEES ARE SUPPOSED TO STAY ON THE OUTSIDE OF THAT SUIT.
SILENCE, HUMAN!
AS USUAL, YOU INDIVIDUALISTIC BUFFOONS FAIL TO GRASP MY EXISTENCE, MY HIVE MIND.
I AM SWARM!
AND SOON, YOU WILL BE EXTINCT!
THAT'S WHAT YOU THINK, SUPER-SUCKER!
OUCH!
STING

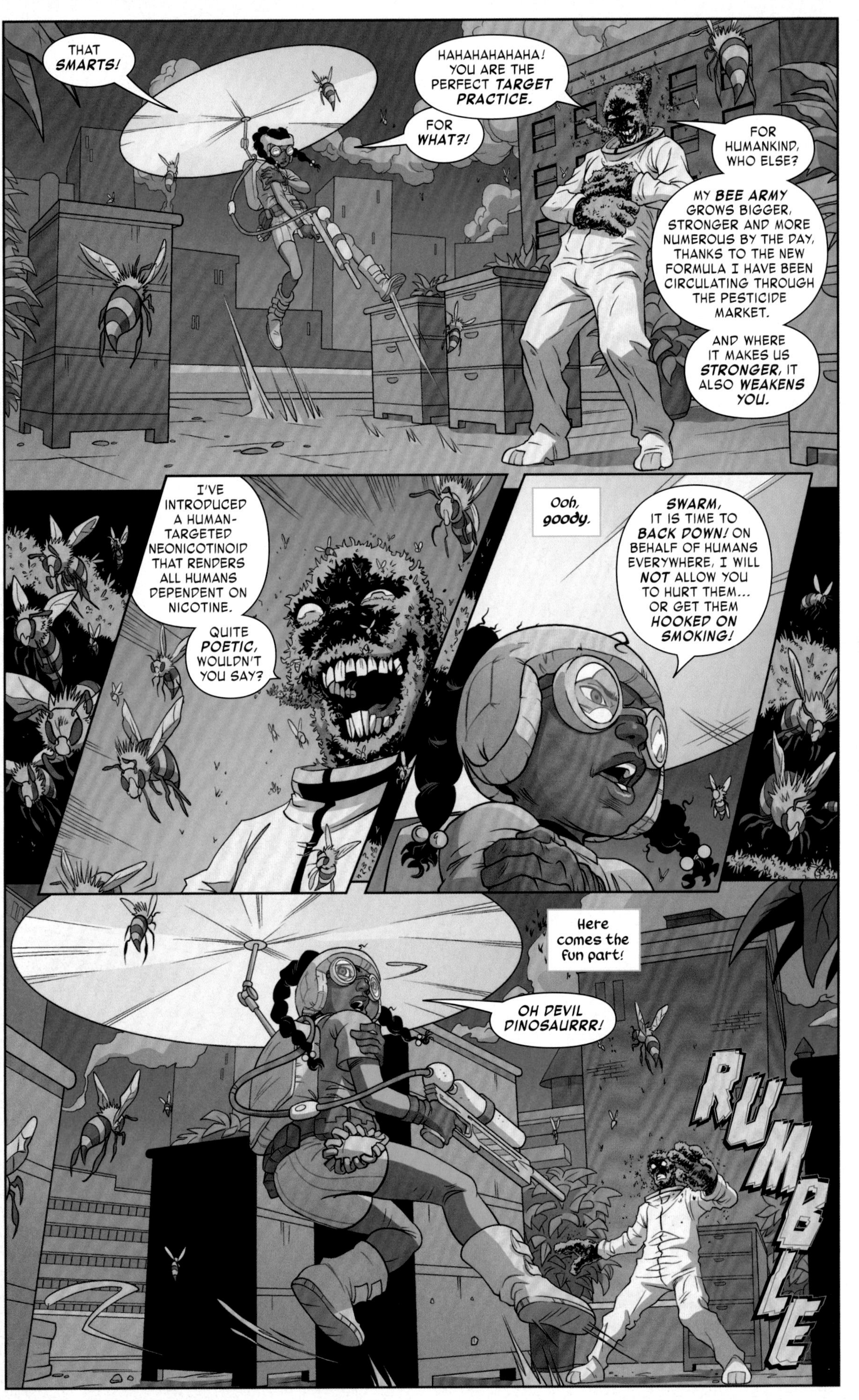

THAT SMARTS!
HAHAHAHAHAHA! YOU ARE THE PERFECT TARGET PRACTICE.
FOR WHAT?!
FOR HUMANKIND, WHO ELSE?
MY BEE ARMY GROWS BIGGER, STRONGER AND MORE NUMEROUS BY THE DAY, THANKS TO THE NEW FORMULA I HAVE BEEN CIRCULATING THROUGH THE PESTICIDE MARKET.
AND WHERE IT MAKES US STRONGER, IT ALSO WEAKENS YOU.
I'VE INTRODUCED A HUMAN-TARGETED NEONICOTINOID THAT RENDERS ALL HUMANS DEPENDENT ON NICOTINE.
QUITE POETIC, WOULDN'T YOU SAY?
Ooh, goody.
SWARM, IT IS TIME TO BACK DOWN! ON BEHALF OF HUMANS EVERYWHERE, I WILL NOT ALLOW YOU TO HURT THEM... OR GET THEM HOOKED ON SMOKING!
Here comes the fun part!
OH DEVIL DINOSAURRR!
RUMBLE

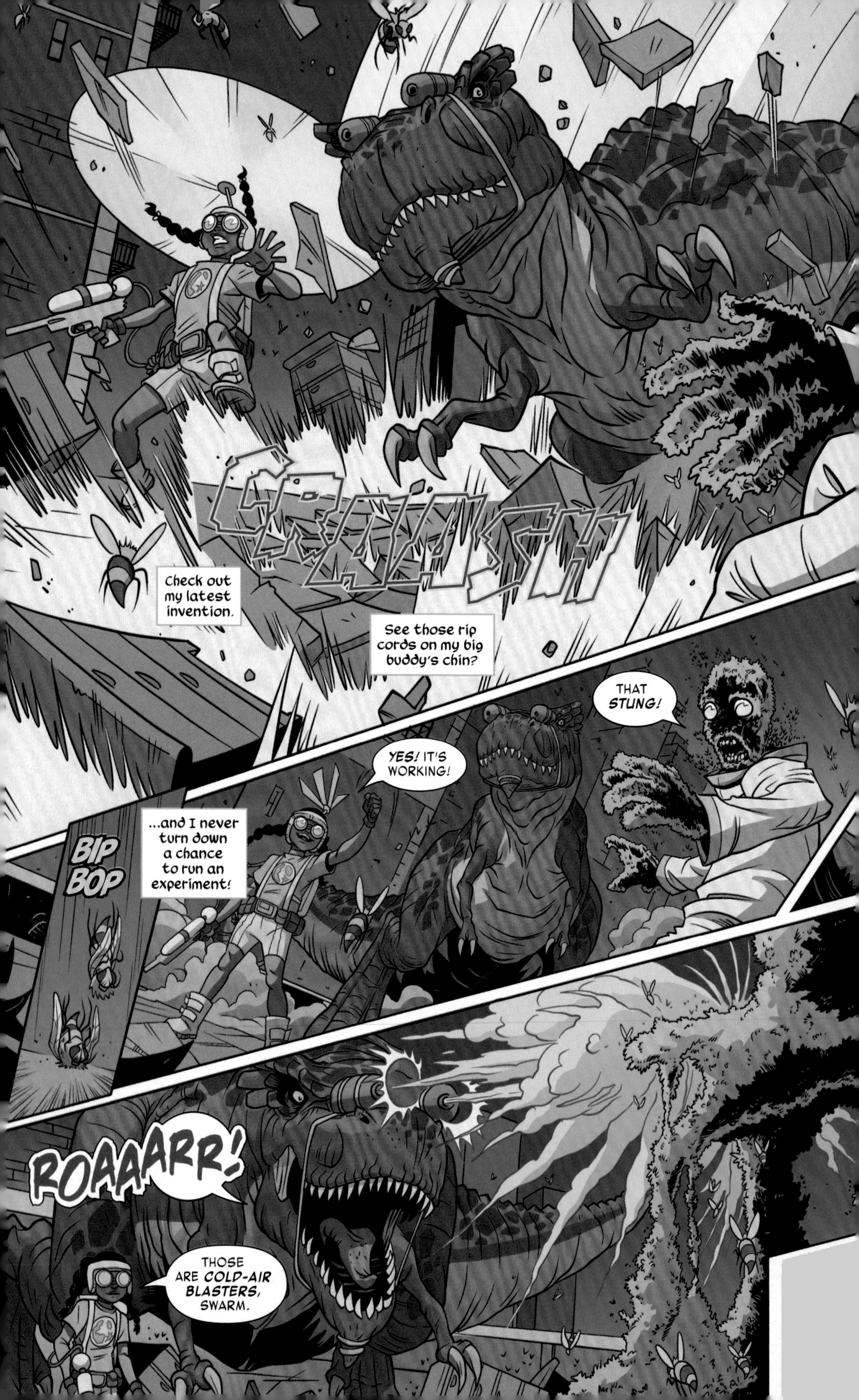
Check out my latest invention.
See those rip cords on my big buddy's chin?
THAT STUNG!
YES! IT'S WORKING!
...and I never turn down a chance to run an experiment!
BIP BOP
ROAAARR!
THOSE ARE COLD-AIR BLASTERS, SWARM.

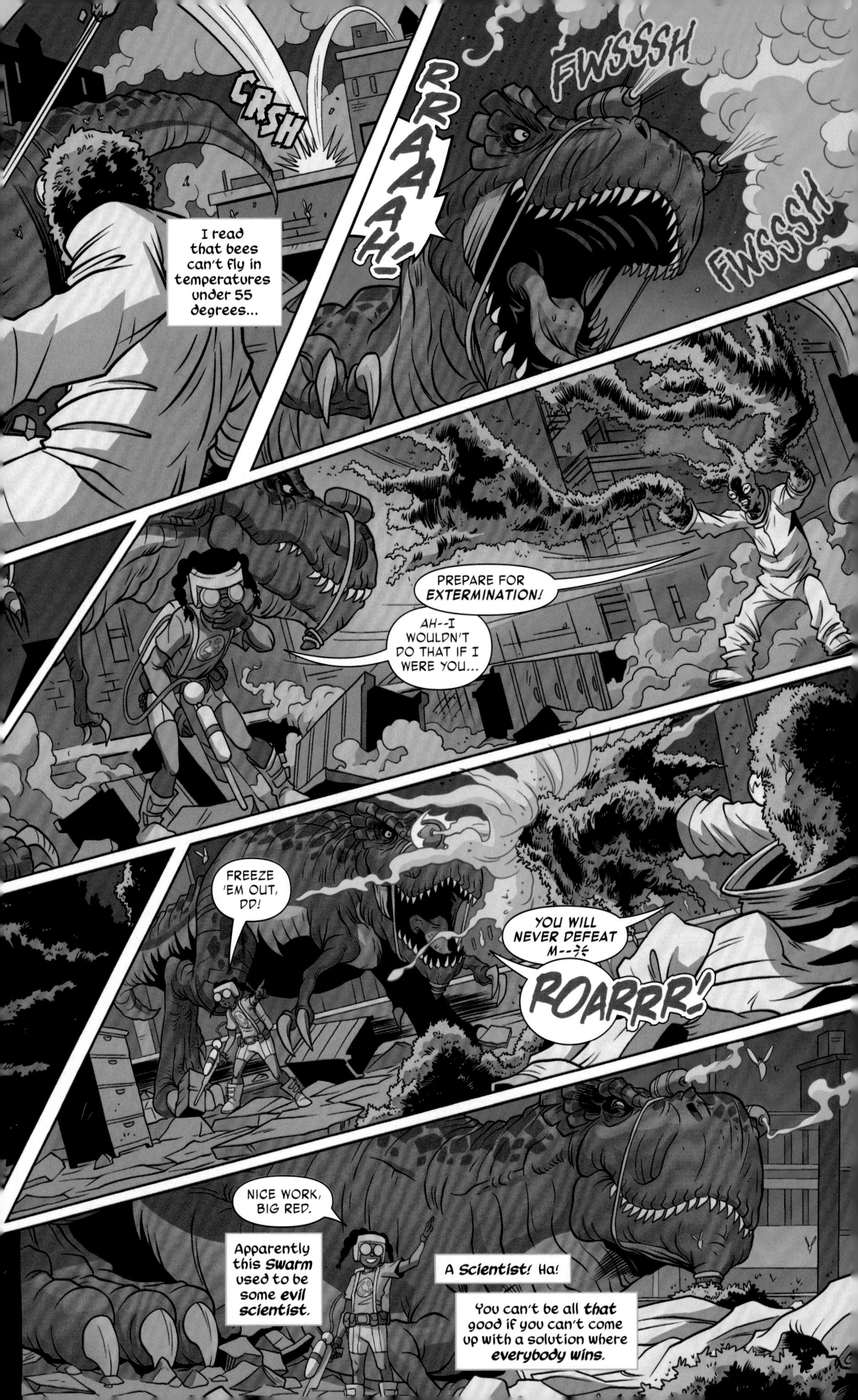
CRSH
I read that bees can't fly in temperatures under 55 degrees...
RRAAAAH!
FWSSSH
FWSSSH
PREPARE FOR EXTERMINATION!
AH--I WOULDN'T DO THAT IF I WERE YOU...
FREEZE 'EM OUT, DD!
YOU WILL NEVER DEFEAT M--
ROARRR!
NICE WORK, BIG RED.
Apparently this Swarm used to be some evil scientist.
A Scientist! Ha!
You can't be all that good if you can't come up with a solution where everybody wins.

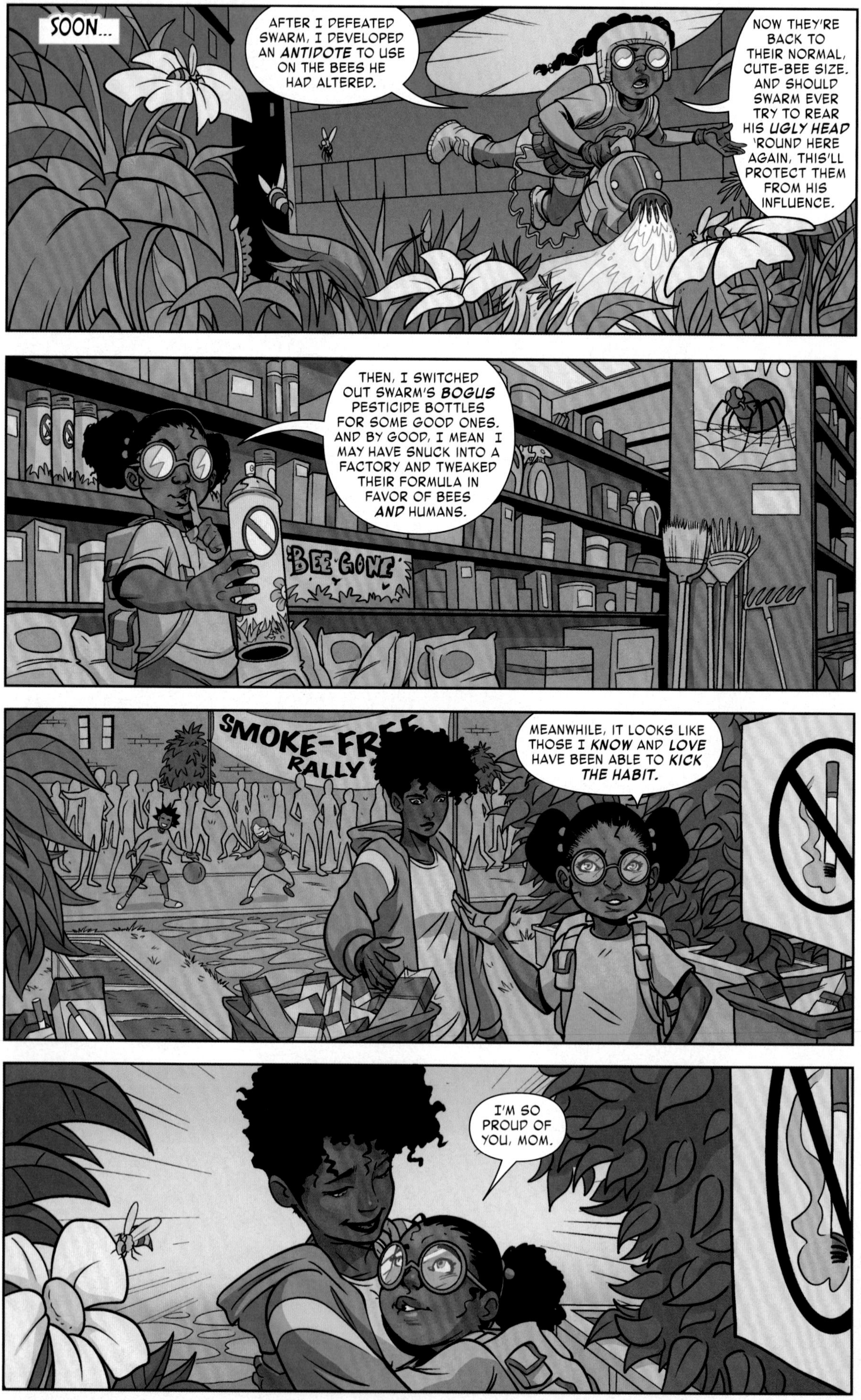
SOON...
AFTER I DEFEATED SWARM, I DEVELOPED AN ANTIDOTE TO USE ON THE BEES HE HAD ALTERED.
NOW THEY'RE BACK TO THEIR NORMAL, CUTE-BEE SIZE. AND SHOULD SWARM EVER TRY TO REAR HIS UGLY HEAD 'ROUND HERE AGAIN, THIS'LL PROTECT THEM FROM HIS INFLUENCE.
THEN, I SWITCHED OUT SWARM'S BOGUS PESTICIDE BOTTLES FOR SOME GOOD ONES. AND BY GOOD, I MEAN I MAY HAVE SNUCK INTO A FACTORY AND TWEAKED THEIR FORMULA IN FAVOR OF BEES AND HUMANS.
BEE GONE
SMOKE-FREE RALLY
MEANWHILE, IT LOOKS LIKE THOSE I KNOW AND LOVE HAVE BEEN ABLE TO KICK THE HABIT.
I'M SO PROUD OF YOU, MOM.

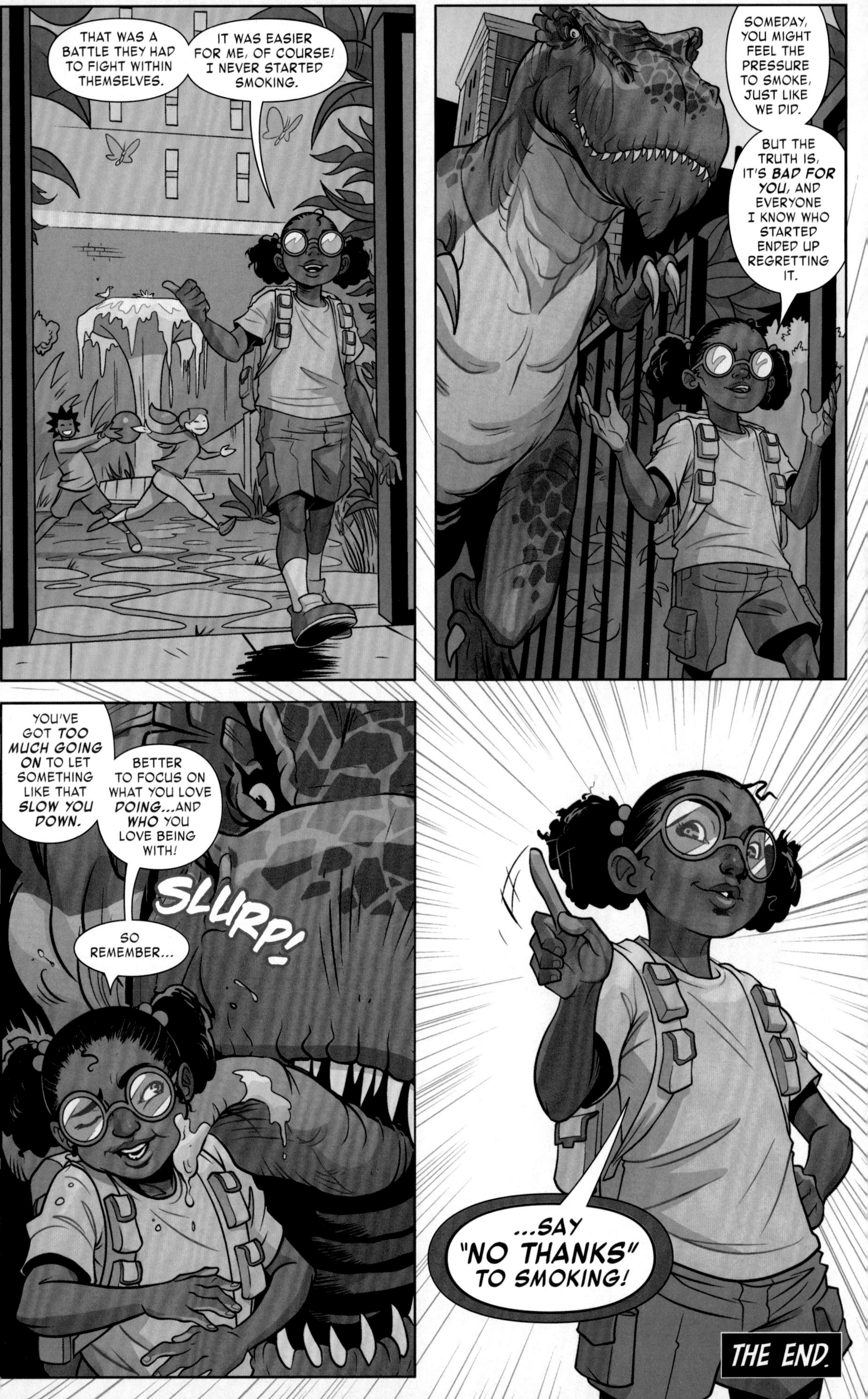
THAT WAS A BATTLE THEY HAD TO FIGHT WITHIN THEMSELVES.
IT WAS EASIER FOR ME, OF COURSE! I NEVER STARTED SMOKING.
SOMEDAY, YOU MIGHT FEEL THE PRESSURE TO SMOKE, JUST LIKE WE DID.
BUT THE TRUTH IS, IT'S *BAD FOR YOU*, AND EVERYONE I KNOW WHO STARTED ENDED UP REGRETTING IT.
YOU'VE GOT *TOO MUCH GOING ON* TO LET SOMETHING LIKE THAT *SLOW YOU DOWN.*
BETTER TO FOCUS ON WHAT YOU LOVE *DOING*...AND *WHO* YOU LOVE BEING WITH!
SLURP!
SO REMEMBER...
...SAY "NO THANKS" TO SMOKING!
THE END.

MAIL BAG AND DEVIL DINOSAUR

SPIDER-MAN
15¢ 96 MAY
the AMAZING SPIDER-MAN
WHAT YOU'VE BEEN WAITING FOR! THIS ONE'S GOT IT ALL!
MARVEL COMICS GROUP
VILLAGE THEATER
SPIDER-MAN'S GETTING AWAY!

SPIDER-MAN
15¢ 97 JUNE
the AMAZING SPIDER-MAN
MARVEL COMICS GROUP
SPIDEY FIGHTS THE GOBLIN-- AND LOTS, LOTS MORE! 'NUFF SAID!

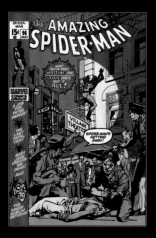

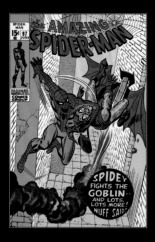

Well that was special, wasn't it?

Whether this is your first issue with us or your thirty-first, thanks for picking up this particular issue of MOON GIRL AND DEVIL DINOSAUR. There's something special about it. Twelve months ago in a diner, I brought series writer Brandon Montclare a request (they call these "editorial mandates on the internet): PSA special. MGDD is a special title in the Marvel U, the kind that reaches and teaches folks. It's uniquely qualified—duty-bound really—to service the public with an announcement. Lunella co-creator Amy Reeder came back to script, play cousin Ray-Anthony Height came back to draw it, and Tamra, Travis and Nat made it a family affair in spirit. Thus, the Anti-Smoking Special you hold in your hands.

But it goes deeper than that. It's only loosely connected to the ongoing adventures of the series and we are breaking a nearly two-decade-long ban on depicting smoking in Marvel Comics. Like I said, this issue is special in a lot of ways.

Except it's not.

Don't forget, Marvel has a long history of PSA comics. In fact, a bunch of them were recently collected in the SPIDER-MAN FIGHTS SUBSTANCE ABUSE trade paperback. And just like our issue is taking place within the monthly MGDD series, who can forget the classic AMAZING SPIDER-MAN #96-98, that defied the Comics Code Authority to spread another substance abuse message? The whole MGDD team salutes that history and is proud to be next in those traditions. Of course, things change ($4.50 movie tickets? Student smoking volunteer???) so don't write a book report with these issues, but the message is the same. Maybe these topics never crossed your mind. Maybe you want to incept them into somebody else's. In any case, we've made the announcement, and now it's up to you to decide what happens next.

CRob

@chrisrobinson

SPIDER-MAN
15¢ 98 JULY
the AMAZING SPIDER-MAN
THE GOBLIN'S POWER!
MARVEL COMICS GROUP
LOSING YOUR GRIP, SPIDER-MAN?
IT HAD TO HAPPEN-- I PLANNED IT THIS WAY!

MARVEL COMICS GROUP
SPIDER-MAN
STORM and
POWER MAN
SMOKESCREEN!

MARVEL
the AMAZING SPIDER-MAN
FIGHTS SUBSTANCE ABUSE

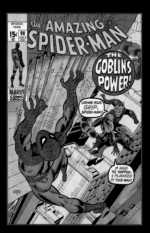

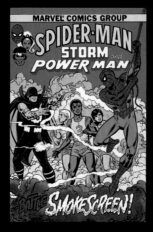

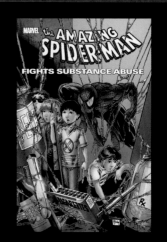

Activity pages from 1982's *Spider-Man, Storm and Power Man Battle Smokescreen.*

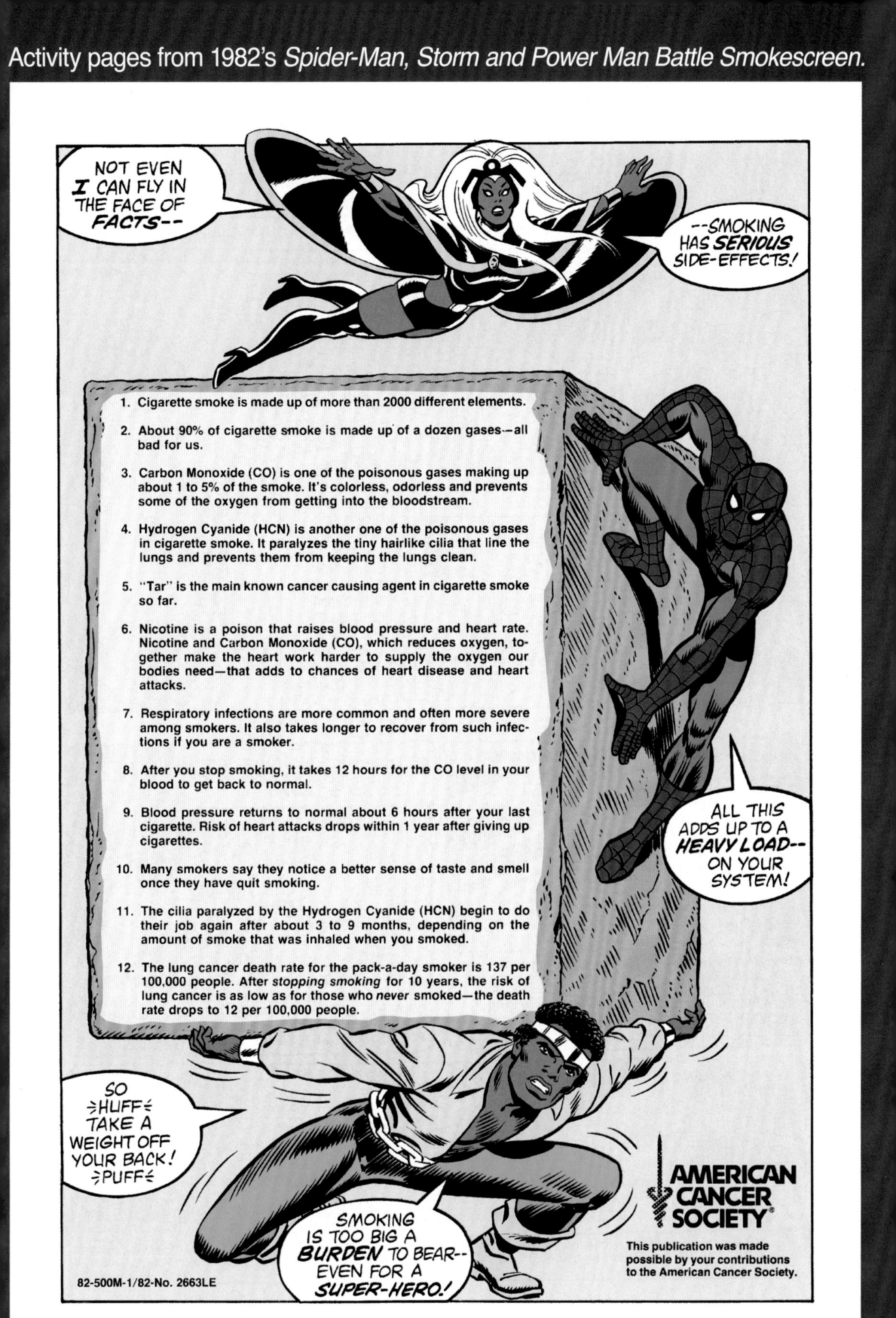

NOT EVEN I CAN FLY IN THE FACE OF FACTS--
--SMOKING HAS SERIOUS SIDE-EFFECTS!
1. Cigarette smoke is made up of more than 2000 different elements.
2. About 90% of cigarette smoke is made up of a dozen gases—all bad for us.
3. Carbon Monoxide (CO) is one of the poisonous gases making up about 1 to 5% of the smoke. It's colorless, odorless and prevents some of the oxygen from getting into the bloodstream.
4. Hydrogen Cyanide (HCN) is another one of the poisonous gases in cigarette smoke. It paralyzes the tiny hairlike cilia that line the lungs and prevents them from keeping the lungs clean.
5. "Tar" is the main known cancer causing agent in cigarette smoke so far.
6. Nicotine is a poison that raises blood pressure and heart rate. Nicotine and Carbon Monoxide (CO), which reduces oxygen, together make the heart work harder to supply the oxygen our bodies need—that adds to chances of heart disease and heart attacks.
7. Respiratory infections are more common and often more severe among smokers. It also takes longer to recover from such infections if you are a smoker.
8. After you stop smoking, it takes 12 hours for the CO level in your blood to get back to normal.
9. Blood pressure returns to normal about 6 hours after your last cigarette. Risk of heart attacks drops within 1 year after giving up cigarettes.
10. Many smokers say they notice a better sense of taste and smell once they have quit smoking.
11. The cilia paralyzed by the Hydrogen Cyanide (HCN) begin to do their job again after about 3 to 9 months, depending on the amount of smoke that was inhaled when you smoked.
12. The lung cancer death rate for the pack-a-day smoker is 137 per 100,000 people. After *stopping smoking* for 10 years, the risk of lung cancer is as low as for those who *never* smoked—the death rate drops to 12 per 100,000 people.
ALL THIS ADDS UP TO A HEAVY LOAD-- ON YOUR SYSTEM!
SO ⇒HUFF⇐ TAKE A WEIGHT OFF YOUR BACK! ⇒PUFF⇐
SMOKING IS TOO BIG A BURDEN TO BEAR-- EVEN FOR A SUPER-HERO!
AMERICAN CANCER SOCIETY®
This publication was made possible by your contributions to the American Cancer Society.
82-500M-1/82-No. 2663LE

Activity pages from 1982's *Spider-Man, Storm and Power Man Battle Smokescreen.*

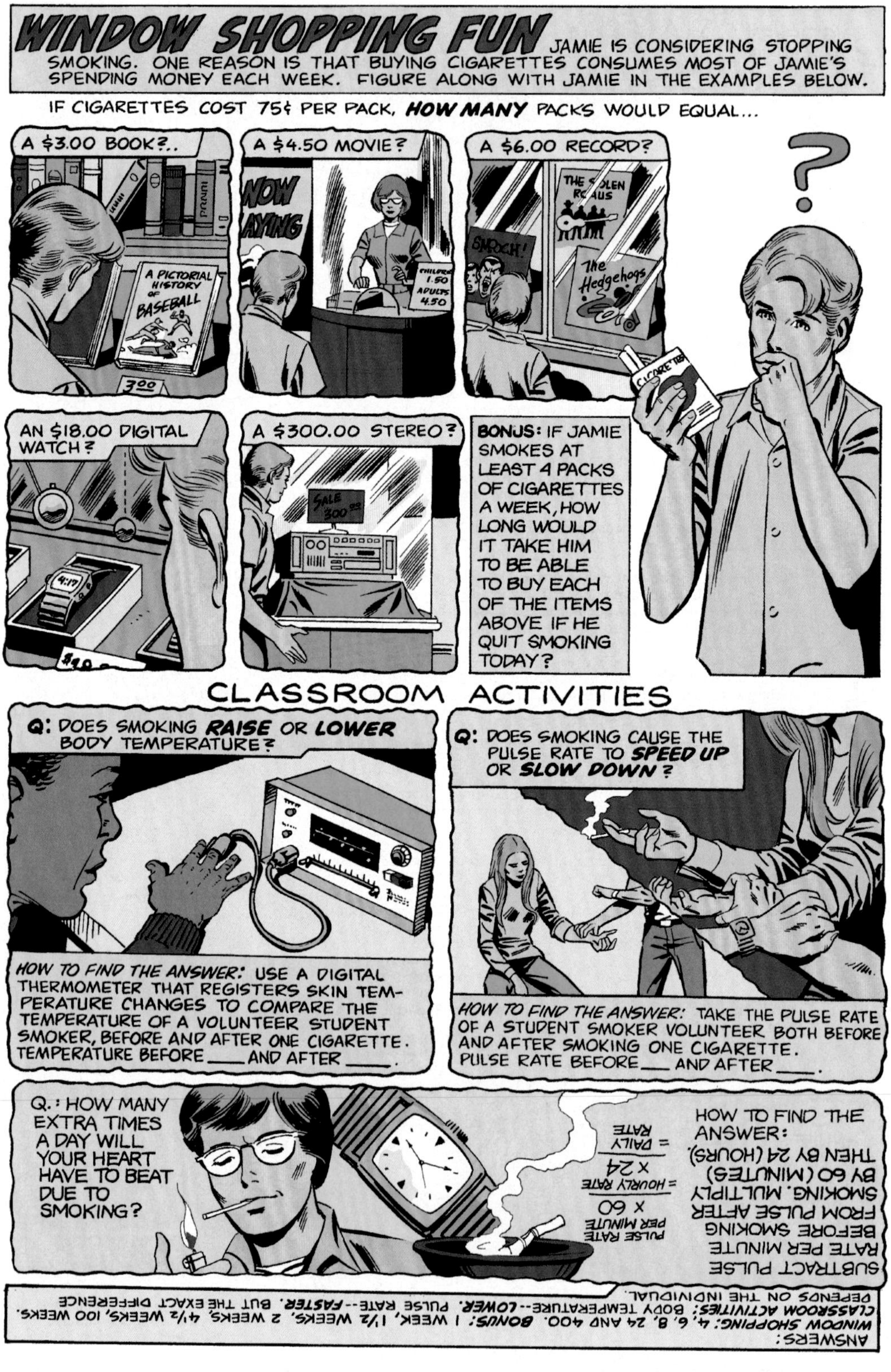
WINDOW SHOPPING FUN
JAMIE IS CONSIDERING STOPPING SMOKING. ONE REASON IS THAT BUYING CIGARETTES CONSUMES MOST OF JAMIE'S SPENDING MONEY EACH WEEK. FIGURE ALONG WITH JAMIE IN THE EXAMPLES BELOW.
IF CIGARETTES COST 75¢ PER PACK, HOW MANY PACKS WOULD EQUAL...
A $3.00 BOOK?..
A PICTORIAL HISTORY OF BASEBALL
3.00
A $4.50 MOVIE?
ADULTS 4.50
A $6.00 RECORD?
The Hedgehogs
?
CIGARETTES
AN $18.00 DIGITAL WATCH?
A $300.00 STEREO?
SALE 300.00
BONUS: IF JAMIE SMOKES AT LEAST 4 PACKS OF CIGARETTES A WEEK, HOW LONG WOULD IT TAKE HIM TO BE ABLE TO BUY EACH OF THE ITEMS ABOVE IF HE QUIT SMOKING TODAY?
CLASSROOM ACTIVITIES
Q: DOES SMOKING RAISE OR LOWER BODY TEMPERATURE?
HOW TO FIND THE ANSWER: USE A DIGITAL THERMOMETER THAT REGISTERS SKIN TEMPERATURE CHANGES TO COMPARE THE TEMPERATURE OF A VOLUNTEER STUDENT SMOKER, BEFORE AND AFTER ONE CIGARETTE. TEMPERATURE BEFORE ___ AND AFTER ___.
Q: DOES SMOKING CAUSE THE PULSE RATE TO SPEED UP OR SLOW DOWN?
HOW TO FIND THE ANSWER: TAKE THE PULSE RATE OF A STUDENT SMOKER VOLUNTEER BOTH BEFORE AND AFTER SMOKING ONE CIGARETTE. PULSE RATE BEFORE ___ AND AFTER ___.
Q.: HOW MANY EXTRA TIMES A DAY WILL YOUR HEART HAVE TO BEAT DUE TO SMOKING?
HOW TO FIND THE ANSWER: SUBTRACT PULSE RATE PER MINUTE BEFORE SMOKING FROM PULSE AFTER SMOKING. MULTIPLY BY 60 (MINUTES) THEN BY 24 (HOURS).
PULSE RATE PER MINUTE x 60 = HOURLY RATE x 24 = DAILY RATE
ANSWERS: WINDOW SHOPPING: 4, 6, 8, 24 AND 400. BONUS: 1 WEEK, 1 1/2 WEEKS, 2 WEEKS, 4 1/2 WEEKS, 100 WEEKS. CLASSROOM ACTIVITIES: BODY TEMPERATURE--LOWER. PULSE RATE--FASTER. BUT THE EXACT DIFFERENCE DEPENDS ON THE INDIVIDUAL.

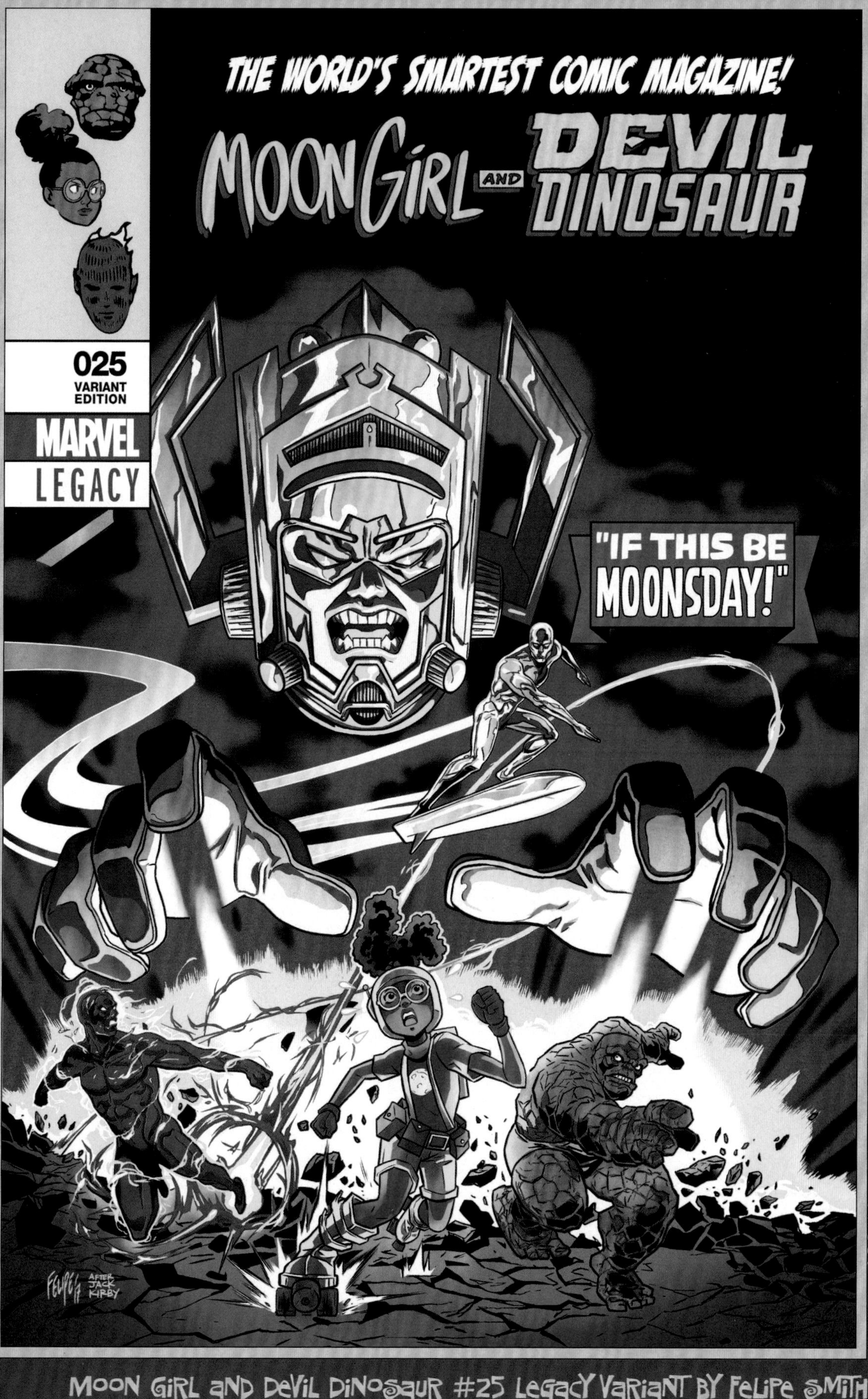
THE WORLD'S SMARTEST COMIC MAGAZINE!
MOON GIRL AND DEVIL DINOSAUR
025
VARIANT EDITION
MARVEL
LEGACY
"IF THIS BE MOONSDAY!"
FELIPE 17 AFTER JACK KIRBY

MOON GIRL AND DEVIL DINOSAUR #25 LEGACY VARIANT BY FELIPE SMITH

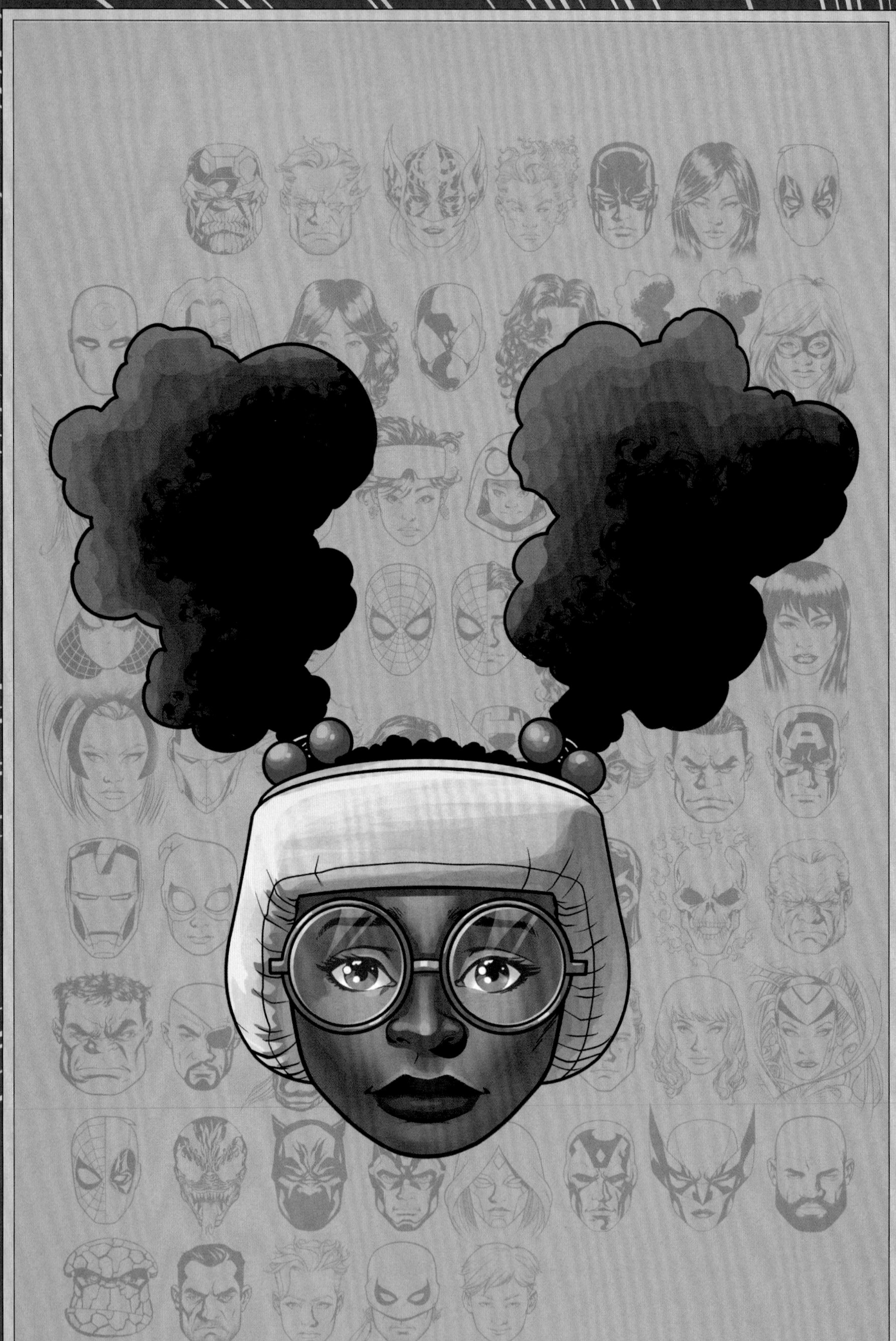

MOON GIRL AND DEVIL DINOSAUR #25 LEGACY HEADSHOT VARIANT
BY MIKE MCKONE & ANDY TROY

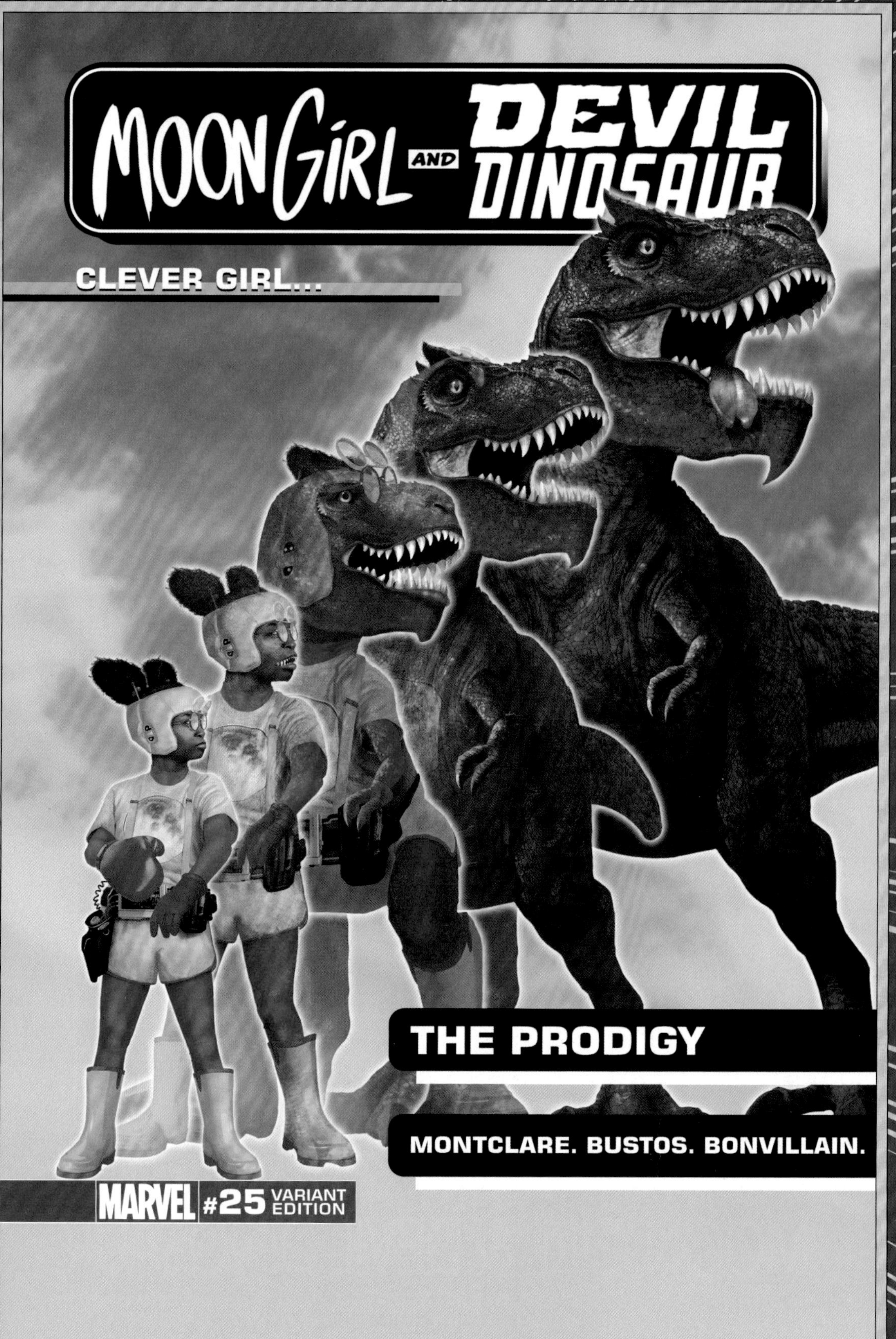
MOON GIRL AND DEVIL DINOSAUR
CLEVER GIRL...
THE PRODIGY
MONTCLARE. BUSTOS. BONVILLAIN.
MARVEL #25 VARIANT EDITION

MOON GIRL AND DEVIL DINOSAUR #25 VARIANT BY RAHZZAH

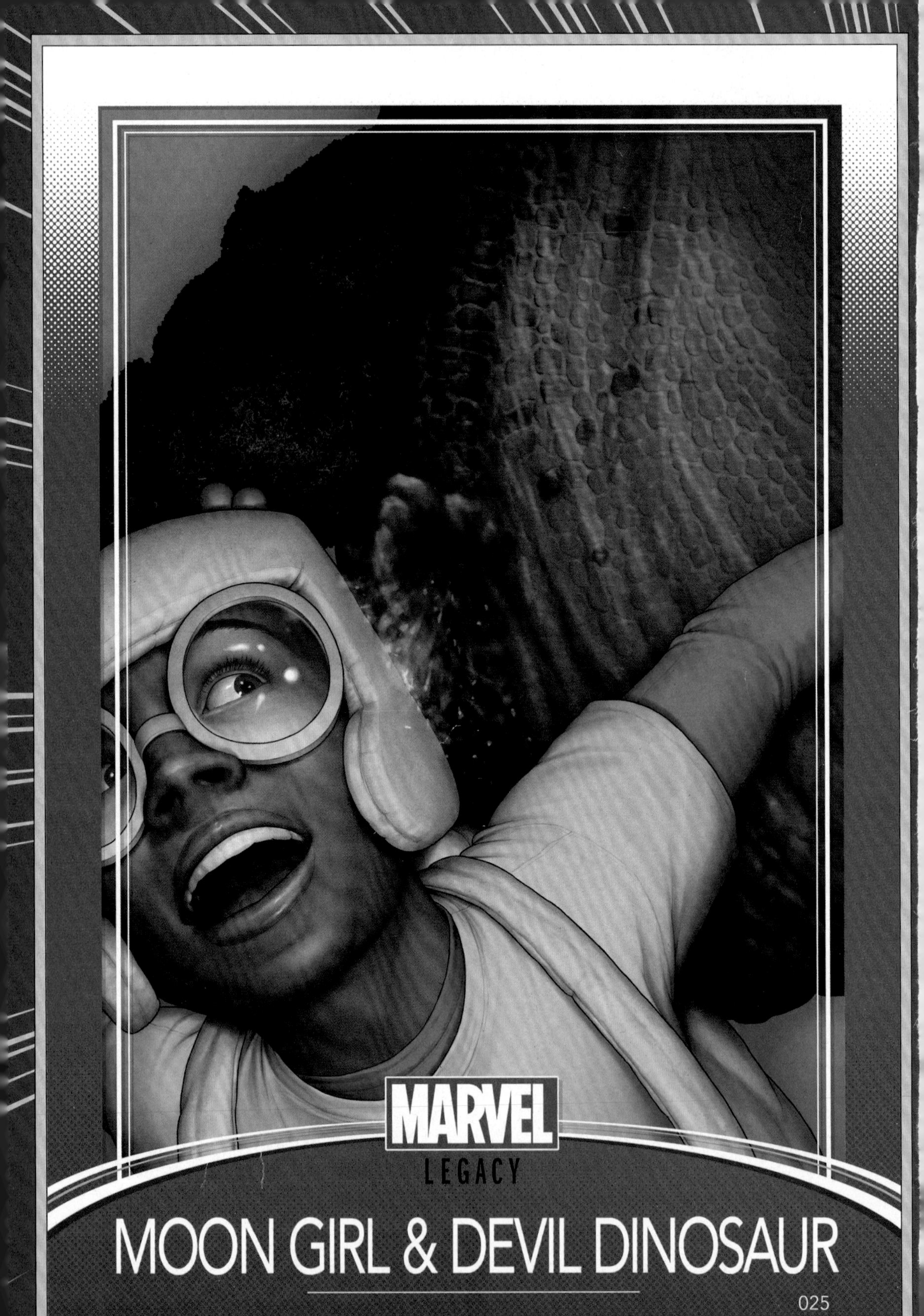
MARVEL
LEGACY
MOON GIRL & DEVIL DINOSAUR
025

MOON GIRL AND DEVIL DINOSAUR #25 TRADING CARD VARIANT
BY JOHN TYLER CHRISTOPHER